9/98

DATE DUE

DEMCO 38-297

No Laughing Matter

Anthony Cronin

No Laughing Matter

The Life and Times of
Flann O'Brien

FROMM INTERNATIONAL PUBLISHING CORPORATION
NEW YORK

First Fromm International Edition, 1998

LIBRARY OF CONGRESS CATALOGING-IN-PUBLICATION DATA
Cronin, Anthony.
   No laughing matter : the life and times of Flann O'Brien / Anthony
Cronin. — 1st Fromm International ed.
      p.   cm.
   Includes bibliographical references (p.   ) and index.
   ISBN 0-88064-183-5
   1. O'Brien, Flann, 1911–1966. 2. Dublin (Ireland)—Intellectual life—
20th century. 3. Authors, Irish—20th century—Biography. 4. Ireland
—In literature. I. Title.
   PR6029.N56Z64   1998
   828'.91209—dc21
   [B]   97-40342
                                                                    CIP

10 9 8 7 6 5 4 3 2 1

Contents

Preface   vii

1 Origins   1
2 The Brilliant Beginning   41
3 The Dubliner   151
4 The Close   209

   Sources   249
   Bibliographical Note   254
   Index   255

Preface

Brian O'Nolan, or Flann O'Brien, or Myles na Gopaleen, was, during his comparatively short lifetime, a writer of mixed and vexing fortunes. He enjoyed some fame within the confines of his native land as the author of one novel in English, one in Irish and a column in the *Irish Times*. Then, as the novel in English remained unavailable and became a sort of intellectual's folk-memory, he was known as the author of the column only, for the novel in Irish was regarded largely as a satirical in-joke for Irish-language enthusiasts which only they could understand.

As Myles na Gopaleen, the author of the column, he gradually came to represent, even for his most fervent admirers, the quintessential Dublin intellectual, combining the wit and brilliance which they liked to think of as characteristic with the acerbic, denigratory outlook which was also common. The type was familiar, perhaps too familiar. If nothing was sacred to Myles, they thought they knew why. He was, as so many of them were themselves, a disappointed man, even, strange paradox, a disappointed writer.

Only a handful of people knew that he was also the author of another remarkable novel in English which had been rejected by at least one London publisher; and most of those who had seen or heard of it believed it to have been lost.

To a large extent what attracted the *Irish Times* readership to his column was what they believed to be its strictly esoteric character. It was meant for the initiated. Only they knew the background to many of its jokes; only they were familiar with the types who were models for its characters; only they could appreciate the subtle accuracies of its dialogue. Indeed for several years, before the view that Myles na Gopaleen too was losing his brilliance began to take hold, the column was almost holy writ to intellectual Dubliners. Its humour became their humour, its mode of response to many sorts of situation, public and private, became their mode of response. Even its dialogue fed back into the world about it, so that it became difficult to know whether some people actually spoke in a particular manner or were only doing so for comic effect and because that was the way 'the Brother' or some other typical Dubliner in 'Cruiskeen Lawn' spoke. The fate of many licensed jesters had overtaken Myles. He had become his admirers and they him, so that it was sometimes difficult to distinguish one from the other.

All of which makes the transformation that has since overtaken the various writers that Brian O'Nolan contained within himself the more remarkable. From being an obscure cult figure for a coterie audience in a city which was then regarded as a backwater through which genius had once passed – and one who, as is often the case with humorists, was patronized by his audience as well as admired by it – he has become a writer who is a shared enthusiasm for a very large and ever-widening circle of ordinary readers, many of whom have never set foot in Dublin or heard a Dubliner speak. All his works are in print, including the posthumously discovered *The Third Policeman* (the novel which was rejected) and the two novels that he wrote towards the end, after the re-publication of *At Swim-Two-Birds*. There have been several collections of pieces from his 'Cruiskeen Lawn' column and there are to be more. Even his juvenilia and the most fugitive pieces that he wrote under other pseudonyms are being published and are being read. If (as I certainly believe) Dr Johnson was right about the soundness of the common reader's judgement of authors, then Brian O'Nolan's place is happily secure. His work has crossed several frontiers and become a necessary solace for many readers in many languages besides English or Irish.

But if the widespread popularity of 'Cruiskeen Lawn' and his other occasional writings of the same ilk is remarkable in many ways, that of the novels he wrote as Flann O'Brien is perhaps even more so. The first and best-known of these, *At Swim-Two-Birds*, has been described by the *Oxford Companion to English Literature* as 'a multi-dimensional exploration of Irish culture and of the nature of fiction'. It is certainly what would have been called at the time of its first publication a 'highbrow' book, a series of severely intellectual jokes depending for their effect on some knowledge of what the phenomenon known as the Irish Literary Revival was all about and even perhaps what part James Joyce played in superseding it or making it ridiculous – matters of concern, one would have thought, only to literary initiates of one kind or another. It is also an anti-novel, deliberately nihilistic in intent as far as the novel-form is concerned, the first (unless one counts Joyce's *Ulysses*) of many anti-novels in various languages and still the most extreme. It is, as I have tried to show, more than these things, but it is these first, and their appeal might be thought to be limited.

O'Nolan's second novel, which was rejected and then, he said, lost in his own lifetime, is *The Third Policeman*, a description, according to its author, of 'the world of the dead – and the damned – where none of the rules and laws (not even the law of gravity) holds good'. It was followed by a book in Irish, *An Béal Bocht*, now translated as *The Poor Mouth*, an assault on official and literary attitudes to the Gaeltachts, the Irish-speaking districts of the west of Ireland; *The Hard Life* and then *The Dalkey Archive*, another work full of in-jokes, this time relating to Catholicism, predestination and James Joyce. As with *At Swim-Two-Birds*, the appeal of such novels might be thought to be limited; but again, one is glad to say, the reality is quite happily otherwise.

In seeking to account for this one ought to advert first perhaps to O'Nolan's position in the general literary scheme of things. He was born almost thirty years after James Joyce into an Ireland which would attain independence while he was still a boy. He had, like Joyce, a Catholic middle-class education, attended the same university, walked the same streets. By the time he and his friends at University College Dublin were growing to some sort of literary maturity the high days of the Irish Literary Revival, Yeats's romantic and backward-looking creation, were long over. Joyce, the great modernist, had, as I have said, in a way superseded it; but in any case the nationalist dreams which informed the Revival and gave it its partly political impetus had been followed by the rather grubby realities of independence. Tradition-loving Ireland was coming up against the harsh realities of the modern world; and though its minor writers still sought for an easy poetry where Yeats and Synge had taught them to look, in the supposedly heroic lives of peasants and fishermen and the heroic myths and legends of the remote past, in reality it was a time for modernism, for satire, for the stripping away of veils.

To an extent it was a misfortune for O'Nolan that Joyce had been there first. When O'Nolan embarked on the writing of his first novel the great modernist was still alive in Paris, occasionally to be visited there by someone he knew, occasionally even allowing a contemporary like Beckett into some sort of intimacy, maintaining his planetary distance from Ireland and its problems, but perpetually visible in its skies all the same, or at least perpetually visible to the sort of young writer Brian O'Nolan was. And there is no denying that Joyce posed a problem for him; indeed there is a sense in which he admitted this in one way or another over and over again. Writers of supreme genius usually do pose problems for their immediate literary successors, but more especially so if they seem to have used up the very life material which one is destined by birth and upbringing to use oneself. Beckett had a similar problem, but since he was a Protestant from a higher stratum of the Irish middle class than either Joyce or Brian O'Nolan his life material had not been used up in the same way; and in any case he solved it by departing from representational, though not from emotional, realism.

The story of how Brian O'Nolan confronted that problem belongs to the main body of this book rather than to its preface; the point to be made here though is that like Joyce and Beckett he was an Irish realist, not an Irish romantic. If he owes any part of his popularity to his Irishness it is not because he presents the place in a rosy or picturesque way. And if he is, right enough, an Irish humorist; he is certainly not an 'Oirish' one.

I think it is proper to describe him as a humorist first and foremost, however; and there is no doubt that this in large part accounts for his relationship with his readers. He is, quite simply, one of the funniest writers to use the English language in this century. I have not laboured that quality in subsequent discussions of his work; but my belief that everything he wrote was intended to be funny and that most of it succeeded can be taken as a rider to anything else that is said.

Yet, having said that, it is necessary to add something else. He was a humorous writer with an unusually strong, indeed very often a nothing less than fierce, sense of propriety. This frequently dictates his attitude to the very grammar and vocabulary of the language he writes: a master of the colloquial and the idiomatic, he sometimes writes English as if it were a dead language which had to be written with the more correctitude because of that and he is immensely scornful of other people's errors and mistakes. But it also accounts for his ire where the behaviour and pronouncements of politicians and other public figures are concerned; his impatience with the slips and mistakes of the bureaucracy of which he was for so long a member, the activities of Dublin Corporation and much else. In these matters he is seldom an idealist or even a reformer. He believes there is a right way and a wrong way of doing things and he castigates the wrong.

I also think, and in discussing *The Third Policeman* I argue, that this fierce sense of propriety of his applied as well to the moral order of the universe, which he felt to be somehow askew. This was a way of perceiving the world which gave a peculiar twist to his Catholicism and resulted in an attitude that can best be described in terms of the ancient Manichaean belief, which has surfaced at least three times in the history of Christendom as a Christian heresy.

But whether or not this is so, I think the fact that he is a humorous writer with such a strong undertow of belief in rightness and order is one of the things that accounts for the widespread appeal of his work. We live in a peculiar world, one in which everybody's sense of propriety is deeply and continually offended. Myles, or Flann O'Brien, as humorist and otherwise, gives expression to that offence.

There is of course much more that one can say about him. A historian of Irish letters might claim that Joyce and Flann O'Brien and Samuel Beckett between them confirmed the existence of a specifically Irish kind of novel, or non-novel. He might observe that in matters such as its joy in speech modes for their own sakes and its abandonment of plot in the old sense it owed something to the Irish novels of the eighteenth and nineteenth centuries, to a tradition that goes back to Maria Edgeworth; and he might note among the important characteristics of the genre, its daring, its humour, its willingness to face ultimates and to go to extremes.

But a historian of the novel or of international letters generally would, I think, also have to regard *At Swim-Two-Birds* as a landmark. In it, for the first time, the merely wilful and autocratic relationship between the creator and his fictions is fully and gleefully exposed. Joyce, in avoiding the question of whether or not an older Stephen Dedalus is the author of *Ulysses*, had spared the novel the final indignity of being revealed as merely the creation of one of its characters. Flann O'Brien was not so forbearing; indeed he reveals that the author of his own book is only a prentice hand, a dependent stripling whose literary activities are part time; and perhaps in answer to Stephen Dedalus's famous statement that the literary artist should be like the god of creation, he invents a book within a book whose author does set up to be god-like and is well and truly punished by his characters for his presumption.

The bold originalities of *At Swim-Two-Birds* were of a kind that Brian O'Nolan subsequently found it difficult either to consolidate or to withdraw from; and this is one of the aspects of his literary career to which I have called attention. Another is his relationship with Ireland. In writing his life I have tried to evoke as fully as possible the background against which he worked, the pietistic, self-isolated, nationalist Ireland of the first decades after independence, of the war years and after: this is a 'life and times' rather than just a life.

My thanks are due to all those who have helped me in one way or another in the writing of this book: to Evelyn O'Nolan and to Brian's brothers and sisters, all of whom were unfailingly kind and courteous; the late Ciarán O'Nualláin who helped me to understand Brian a bit better long before I ever thought of writing it, Kevin who sadly died during its progress, Micheál, who smoothed its path, Niall, Sister Roisín and Sister Maeve. Nuala and her husband Patrick O'Leary; to Brian's lifelong friend Niall Sheridan; Timothy O'Keeffe, Des Roche and T. J. Barrington, my former teacher Michael O'Carroll CSSP and

Sean P. Farragher CSSP of Blackrock College, Jim Bradley and James O'Kane of Strabane, Douglas Gageby, Bruce Williamson and Brian Fallon of the *Irish Times*, Angela and Tommy Conolly, Rosemary Coyle, John Wyse Jackson, Anne Clissmann, Benedict Kiely, Francis Stuart, Anne Haverty, Ulick O'Connor, Terence Brown, Sean J. White, Tony O'Riordan, Harry Boylan, Seán Mac Réammoinn, John Kelly, Pádraig O'hUiginn, Caitriona Crowe of the Public Record Office, Paddy O'Brien, Ted Dolan, Colm Toibin, Denis Hickey, Tess Hurson, Steve Young, the late Justice Thomas Doyle, Hugh Kenner, John Ryan, Patricia Walsh, Catherine Rogan, Cathy Bruton, Kay Rippelmeyer of the Morris Library, Southern Illinois University at Carbondale, the staff of the Special Collections, McFarlin Library, University of Tulsa and the staff of the National Library, Dublin.

I

Origins

Strabane today is a town of some 13,000 inhabitants on the border of County Tyrone and County Donegal, which is also the border between the Republic and the six counties of Northern Ireland. It is a pretty town, bisected by a sizeable, full-flowing river, the Mourne, with views of the Donegal hills on one side and the Sperrin mountains on the other; and in normal times it would be a peaceful place.

The times are not normal however, and in the Bowling Green, where the farmers once brought their flax in carts to Reilly's flax stores, there is an unusually large and strongly fortified police and army barracks, enclosed in wire netting and bristling with the electronic technology which enables the army to maintain surveillance over a considerable area. Beside this is a terrace of pleasant three-storey houses. A plaque on number 15 commemorates the birth of the writer Brian O'Nolan or Brian Ó Nualláin there in 1911. Because nationalists have a majority on Strabane's Urban District Council the plaque is in both English and Irish, but in the Irish version the word *scriobhnóir*, which means writer, is misspelled. The Irish form of the writer's name is also used for a housing development, Ó Nualláin Park, which commemorates him.

Among the working-class housing estates high up on the left bank of the Mourne, the part known locally as 'The Top of the Town', support for the Provisional IRA is strong and there are Provisional slogans daubed on the walls. In recent years most of Strabane's Main Street and many of the familiar buildings of the town centre have been destroyed by bombing, 31 shops, four banks, the town's two hotels and the Town Hall, a classical edifice of considerable architectural merit, being the most recent tally.

The O'Nolans were not natives of Strabane. Brian's father, Michael, came there as a Customs and Excise Officer in 1897. He had been born in nearby Omagh, a somewhat larger town with a greater air of bustle and importance befitting the administrative centre of the county Tyrone. He was not born O'Nolan, but Nolan; and he called himself Nolan for some purposes throughout his life.

Names were always a somewhat provisional matter for Michael O'Nolan, as they also would be later on for his son Brian. Born Michael Victor Nolan in July 1875, he was married as Michael V. O'Nolan, but signed the register as Miceál O Nualáin. His superiors in the Customs and Excise service continued to know him as Michael Nolan; and so, somewhat more remarkably, did the Revenue Commissioners of the Irish Free State when he was appointed a Commissioner later in life, though his colleagues in the office referred to him as Micheál Ó Nualláin. On Brian's birth certificate his father's name is given as Michael Victor O'Nolan, but five years later, in the census return of 1911, he gave his name as Miceál O Nualláin, though someone added Michael O'Nolan in parentheses underneath. When probate was taken out on his estate his name was given as Michael Nolan.

O'Nolan was unusual. Those Nolans who objected to the English form of their name or wished to be known by what they believed to be the Irish version of it called themselves Ó Nualláin, usually with two l's and with a *sine fada*, signifying a long vowel, over the O, in the Irish manner, instead of an apostrophe after it, but on the occasions when law or custom demanded that they should return to the English version they called themselves simply Nolan. To Irish ears O'Nolan has a would-be aristocratic ring, a faint suggestion of chieftainship of the clan.

Michael's father taught music at the Omagh Model School and he was plain Donal Nolan. Although the profession of music teacher at the end of the 19th century may conjure up a vision of an unworldly person in a threadbare coat giving ill-paid lessons to recalcitrant young ladies, the fact is that Donal Nolan was respectably employed within the school system, but he did nevertheless marry a pupil, Jane Mellon, the 18-year-old daughter of a 'strong' farmer from Eiscir Duffey, near Omagh. The couple had eight children, four sons and four daughters.

Michael Victor was the eldest son; and of the others the only ones to play any part in Brian's life were Gerald, Peter and Fergus. Gerald and Peter both became priests, Peter joining the Carmelite Order and Gerald, or Gearóid as he now called himself, becoming in the course of time Professor of Irish at Maynooth College, the principal training centre for the Irish priesthood.

Unlike Michael, and perhaps Peter, Gearóid and Fergus were convivial spirits, talkative, humorous and fond of a drop. Fergus became a teacher and for a while he assisted Patrick Pearse, the poet who led the 1916 rebellion, at Scoil Éanna, the progressive Irish language school for boys which Pearse had founded. Charitable family legend attributed a certain over-fondness for alcohol in later years to the effect on him of Pearse's subsequent execution.

While his family was still young Donal Nolan was transferred from Omagh to Belfast, where the boys grew up and attended the new

Queen's University. They were all classicists and were to be distinguished in later life by a good reading knowledge of Latin and Greek; but their deepest personal enthusiasm was for the Irish language.

Since the Parnell divorce case in 1890 and the split in the Irish party at Westminster which followed it, there had been widespread disillusion with politics in Ireland and a fervent revival of cultural nationalism. All over the country young people began to enrol in Irish language classes. The more enthusiastic went to the Gaeltachts, the Irish-speaking districts, to improve their vocabulary and acquire the authentic *blas* or distinctive pronunciation. Rather constrained late Victorian versions of Irish dancing and singing came back into vogue, the dancing very stiff and rule-bound, the singing much influenced by drawing-room ideas of folk music. Michael, Gearóid, Fergus and Peter all displayed an early enthusiasm for the language. They learned different dialects, Michael's being Donegal and Gearóid's, which Michael thought not very good, Munster.

Michael's attitude to the language was thoroughgoing and systematic, not to say pedantic, as with everything he undertook. On visits to the Donegal Gaeltacht he made notes of pronunciation according to an international system, disagreeing in many cases with the findings of the great Quiggin, a much-respected authority of the time.

With the exception of Peter, the Carmelite, the brothers were also all amateur writers. Michael wrote a detective story later in life which his family believed was accepted for publication by Collins and would have been published were it not for his obstinacy about the terms they offered. Gearóid and Fergus collaborated on a book of short stories which they called *Sean Agus Nua* (Old and New). The stories were written in Irish, but they also made a translation which they called *Intrusions* and they arranged for the private publication of both versions in one book as an assistance to language enthusiasts.

It is an odd sort of book. The stories are heavily plotted, with surprise dénouements, and they have a featureless urban setting which could be anywhere. Running through them is a marked vein of misogynism. The women characters are frequently wicked intriguers who are discomfited in the end. In 1920, when Brian was nine, his uncle Fergus had a play, *A Royal Alliance*, produced at the Abbey Theatre in Dublin, a considerable enough achievement in a city where everybody wrote plays for the same theatre. Gerald also wrote an autobiography in Irish, *Beatha Duine a Thuil*, which has somewhat more literary merit than the stories in *Sean Agus Nua*.

After graduating from Queen's, Michael Victor applied for a job in the Customs and Excise Service. He was posted to Strabane in 1897, which must have pleased him, for the little town on the Mourne was only a few miles from where he had been born. His mother had hoped that he would be a priest – Irish mothers of the time were insatiable in their desire for sons in the priesthood – but there is little doubt that, in becoming a civil servant, he chose a method of earning a living suited to his precise, methodical and pedantic temperament.

Michael Nolan was a nationalist. His job as a civil servant under the crown prevented his giving political expression to his views, but in concentrating on the language and all that went with it, he was, in any case, following the tide of the time. He was not long in Strabane before he began to give night classes in Irish and to organize *feiseanna*, competitions in which the entrants competed for prizes in Irish singing, dancing and recitation.

Like many another young man of the time, he found romance where he had sought merely an expression of his cultural patriotism. Agnes Gormley was the daughter of a newsagent and bookseller who was the principal Catholic shopkeeper in Strabane. She was 18 when they met, 11 years younger than Michael Nolan. Like him, she had been born in Omagh.

The Gormleys had had an extensive business in Omagh, including a bakery, public house and grocery. They lived in some comfort, employing two local girls to look after the children; but in the 1880s, just before Agnes Gormley was born, a failure of the potato crop caused prolonged distress in the area. According to family tradition the Gormleys were ruined by the extended credit John Gormley advanced to local farmers. In any case the business was sold up; John Gormley got a job as foreman in a Derry bakery; and his wife, Agnes's mother, opened a small newsagency and fancy goods business in Strabane, where he later joined her.

This was in Market Street, known as 'the back street' because it runs parallel to the Main Street; but in time John Gormley opened a shop in Main Street as well and was the first Catholic to assert his right to do so. When his daughter Agnes married Michael O'Nolan, John Gormley was one of the best-known and most respected figures in the town, at least as far as the Catholic community was concerned.

Agnes Gormley was one of John Gormley's seven children, five boys and two girls. It was an immensely talented family; and the boys were all characters of the sort who create the quality of Irish small-town life and contribute to its lore and gossip. Eugene, the eldest, inherited the business in Main Street. Succeeding generations were to know him as a courteous, knowledgeable, impeccably dressed, handsome man, acquainted with the contents of the newspapers and books he sold. Naturally enough, these were not as many as a metropolitan bookshop would have carried, but he stocked a surprising number, ranging from penny dreadfuls to the sort of Irish travel books and books about Ireland that were part of the nationalist ferment of the time. He was himself, by long-standing intention anyway, a writer, whose history of Strabane never in fact materialized, though he published fugitive pieces here and there and belonged to the large section of the population of Ireland which had once had a play rejected by the Abbey. As a young man he was a serious-minded and idealistic nationalist and if not a member of the IRA was a close and active sympathizer. Later he became more moderate in his views and disappointed many Strabane Catholics by his lack of militancy about the Council's failure to appoint an Irish teacher in the Technical School. A lifelong bachelor with a paternalistic and Olympian manner, dressed always in grey serge and standing usually at the rear of his shop, he had time for converse with young and old; and he is nowadays rightly regarded as having played a significant part in Strabane's social and cultural history, so much so indeed that, like his nephew, he has been accorded the honour of having a part of one of the new housing estates named after him.

His brother Tom was the inevitable small-town genius who is also a ne'er-do-well. A talented violinist, in later life he would disappear for long periods, frequently returning without even the violin; but, by a paradox not uncommon in Ireland, as his condition worsened his reputation grew, the legend of his wasted talent becoming one of Strabane's topics and surviving even a disastrous appearance at a concert in the Town Hall. Finally reduced to utter dependence on the rest of the Gormleys for support and on strangers for drink, he once sought to punish the upright Eugene for a refusal to give him money by adopting the role of mendicant musician and playing for coppers in Main Street outside the shop. He usually carried a brown paper parcel under his arm, which supposedly contained musical manuscripts, and he was known to have composed operas. In fact one song of which he wrote both words and music, 'Ireland Live On', achieved a certain amount of national popularity and was supposed, in Strabane anyway, to have been considered as a possible national anthem after the Irish Free State came into existence.

If opinion in Strabane was sometimes divided about Tom and his talents, there was more unanimity about his brother Joe. He too was a musician, but whereas Tom wore a tweed cap and looked sometimes in even greater need of a shave than he was of a drink, Joe affected a broad-brimmed black hat and a bow tie and he wore his overcoat slung over his shoulders like a cloak. Like Tom, he also wrote songs and some of them achieved the dignity of performance on the radio and publication in Dublin. He was the impresario and director of many musical productions on the Town Hall stage and coached successive generations of young singers, becoming a very central figure in the town's activities. At one point he also had ambitions to be a photographer and set up his own studio, where he did the inevitable wedding and first communion studies. This was not a success and since Joe's musical activities, however great a figure they enabled him to cut in the town, did not bring in a living either, he was ceded the original shop on Market Street. There he carried on a stationery and newsagency business much as Eugene did round the corner, with the addition of a twopenny lending library which stocked the sort of hardback thrillers and westerns designed for that trade. In later life he too was 'fond of a drop', but his drinking was not as publicly conducted as Tom's.

One other Gormley brother had a notable influence on Brian. This was George, who departed early for Dublin where he became a sports reporter on the daily *Irish Independent* and finally sports editor of the old *Evening Mail*. Talkative, gregarious, a noted anecdotalist even in Dublin journalistic circles and a frequent visitor to his brother-in-law's various houses, George Gormley impressed himself deeply on the imagination of his nephew and cast a certain glamour over the trade of journalism which, in Brian's eyes, it was never quite to lose.

Agnes Gormley was just 20 when she married Michael Victor O'Nolan in 1906. She was an attractive, cheerful girl; and though not as talented as some of the Gormleys – or perhaps, to be more exact, not so accomplished – she had a good singing voice and a more equable disposition. She was not as fond of books as her husband or her brother Eugene were. In later life her favourite reading was hagiographical, though this need not suggest an unusual ambition for sanctity on her part. Like her husband, Agnes Gormley was a devout Catholic, but the lives of the saints, as recorded by Alban Butler, Curtayne and others were favourite reading matter for many Irish mothers in the first half of this century.

In marrying her, Michael Victor married into a family which was certainly warmer, more ebullient and more colourful than the rather serious-minded and ambitious O'Nolans. His son Brian's character would show both sides in fairly equal measure; and almost everything in it can be exemplified among his parents and his uncles. There was a predisposition towards words and music, the modes and the substance of art; and there was equally the methodical, logical, detail-shredding mind of the civil servant. There was a certain harshness and a strong dash of worldly ambition, but there was also a gentle unworldly part of him which shrank from conflict and was quickly despondent. Related to this was a split between a fierce respectability on the one hand and the erraticisms of the easily exacerbated creative temperament, assisted by drink, on the other. Even the urban, urbane and sophisticated humorist can be exemplified in the figure of his journalist uncle, George Gormley.

In marrying Agnes Gormley Michael O'Nolan also married into Strabane, a town with which all his children, including Brian, would have an almost lifelong relationship. Although Brian would very deliberately and consciously decide to be a Dubliner, Strabane always remained home. Among the many terms of abuse which his persona, Myles na Gopaleen, would deploy so magnificently later on, 'corner boy', 'shop boy' and even 'peasant' would betray something of shopkeeping Strabane and its values.

The marriage took place in the parish of Murlogh, the ceremony being performed by the bridegroom's priest brothers, Gearóid and Peter, who conducted it in Irish – 'an interesting departure from the usual custom', remarked the *Derry Journal.*

Shortly after his marriage Michael O'Nolan took a house at 15 The Bowling Green, Strabane, then a quiet residential square in one corner of which was a flax store. As was usual with Irish marriages until very recently, children arrived in quick succession. Brian, born on 5 October 1911, was the third child. He was preceded by two brothers Ciarán and Gearóid (Gerald), and followed by a sister, Roisín. Eventually there were to be 12 children in all: seven boys and five girls. Partly because there was a sister in between and partly because there was then a two year gap before the next brother, Fergus, was born, the three eldest boys formed an exclusive coterie within this large family.

The language of the O'Nolan home was Irish. Agnes O'Nolan's knowledge of the language, though not as extensive as her husband's, was quite sufficient to ensure that there was no necessity to speak anything else; and since even the maids were imported from the Donegal Gaeltacht no English at all was spoken. The size of the family meant that it could be self-contained and as none of the boys was sent to school for a very long time, Irish was Brian O'Nolan's first or cradle language. He heard little English spoken for a number of years except from occasional visitors to the house and passers-by in the street.

Not long after Brian's birth, Michael O'Nolan was transferred to

Glasgow. Not much survives in family lore about this interlude, but they lived in what seems to have been a rented house in Athol Gardens, Uddingston, along with their O'Nolan grandmother and Michael Victor's sister Kathleen, who died of tuberculosis and is buried there.

A transfer to Dublin with its numerous distilleries followed soon after. In order to be near the cluster of distilleries at that end of the city, Michael O'Nolan took a house, by coincidence called St Michael's, in Inchicore. It was a substantial dwelling, one of a terrace of four set back from the road. Inchicore was a mixed district with a preponderance of working-class people, many of them employed in the railway works, but the O'Nolans' standard of living was that of the family of a well-to-do permanent official. They had two uniformed maids who took the boys for walks while pushing their sister Roisín in a pram. These walks often took them as far as Kilmainham, with its gaol where so many Irish heroes, including Charles Stewart Parnell, had been imprisoned, or into the open country towards Ballyfermot, a place of tree-lined roads and pleasant meadows. But the three eldest O'Nolan boys also spent a great deal of time watching life go by over the garden wall. There were tramps to be seen making their way into the city; and one of them, a black-bearded young man known as 'Blackbird Soup', was often a particular target for the jeers of the working-class children who provoked him until he screamed with rage and chased them along the road. One day a detachment of the Fianna, the nationalist paramilitary boy scout movement founded by Countess Markievicz, marched by in their green shirts and wide-brimmed slouch hats, some of them playing stirring martial music on tin whistles. Describing this later, Ciarán recollected a vague but deep impression of heroism and willingness to do brave deeds for Ireland which moved him strongly.

Although Brian was now of school-going age and Ciarán and Gearóid were older, no move was made to send them to school. The main reason for this seems to have been their father's objection to their receiving schooling in the English language. Patrick Pearse's Scoil Éanna was far away on the other side of the city and there was nowhere nearby where the boys could have been educated through what their father regarded as the national language. Concerned about their reading, he decided to teach them to read in Irish, adopting the method of writing the letters of the Irish alphabet on large, cut-out squares of cardboard, which could be arranged in any order.

Thus began the long school-less idyll which was one of the most remarkable features of Brian's childhood. One effect of it was to increase the O'Nolans' isolation. Neither in Glasgow nor in Inchicore were they encouraged to seek playmates or companions outside the family circle. This was partly, of course, on linguistic grounds, though, in Inchicore at least, and in some of their subsequent dwelling places as well, it may have had a class dimension. In any case they were one of those self-contained and inventive large families who seem to need nothing from outside. In later years Brian's shyness was something all his friends were aware of; and they were generally agreed that drink was one of the weapons he used to overcome it. This early isolation within the family circle may have been a cause.

Uncle Peter, the Carmelite, was an occasional visitor to the house in Inchicore. He was blind in one eye and the glass of one lens of his spectacles was opaque. A more frequent visitor was the other priest uncle, Gearóid, who was one of the comparatively small number of people at that time to have a motor car. This was a Ford with a brass radiator, and the boys would immediately climb into it when he parked it outside the house. A breezy character and a chain smoker, he caused a stir in a household where no-one else smoked. He did card and match tricks, which he taught to the eldest boys, and it was from him that Brian, who became quite adept at them, acquired his life-long love of such diversions. Later in life he would often perform simple tricks in pubs and at weddings and other gatherings. This too was a way of overcoming his shyness. In Michael O'Nolan's household Donegal Irish was spoken and so An t-Athair Gearóid's more mellifluous Munster Irish caused the boys much amusement, as did his habit of interpolating English phrases into it. 'Bhfuil sibh all right?' he would ask, coming out to the car where they were pretending to drive.

One night in April 1916, towards the end of their stay in Inchicore, when Brian was four, the night sky over Dublin was seen to be lurid with flames. On the Monday of that week, Easter Monday, Patrick Pearse, the poet schoolmaster, had proclaimed the Irish Republic from the steps of the General Post Office and the conflagration was the result of the shelling of the rebel positions, which had set fire to a large part of the centre of the city. In the days that followed curt announcements from the military authorities told of the execution of the rebel leaders after secret courts martial. They had been unpopular with the people of Dublin to begin with, but now there was a revulsion of feeling. The effect of the executions, James Stephens was to write, 'was like watching blood seeping from under a closed door'. In Inchicore, which is about two miles from the city centre, nothing was seen of the actual fighting, though the crunch of artillery shells had been heard. One day a British airship passed over the house. 'Where is it going?' the boys asked their father. 'To hell, I hope,' was the terse reply.

In 1917, shortly after the Rising, Michael Nolan – to give him the name by which his employers knew him – was promoted, becoming a Surveyor. He now had to travel a great deal and he decided to take a house in Strabane so that his wife could be near her mother and her people while he was away from home.

The house chosen was in Ballycolman Lane, or, as its present-day inhabitants prefer to call it, Ballycolman Avenue. Like the house in Inchicore, the one in Ballycolman Lane was ambiguously situated. It was on the edge of town, near open country, and the nearest neighbours were poor cottagers. While the O'Nolans remained there the isolation from other children continued.

At the back of the pleasant L-shaped house was a steep incline leading through fields and tangled undergrowth to the river. There was a large orchard, but the boys were forbidden to pick the fruit because it belonged to the landlord, a Mr Alexander, a Protestant. Even those apples which grew on a solitary tree in the front garden belonged to him.

Mr Alexander had locked a room in the house, presumably in order to store some things, and, perhaps understandably enough, Mrs O'Nolan and the children soon began to believe that this room was haunted. At night there was a noise as of iron balls rolling across the floor and sometimes a window sash would be heard to crash down, even though no window was open. The window of the locked room was barred, but on one night of great excitement, after the iron balls had been specially mobile, Mrs O'Nolan took out a chair and tried to peer in. Naturally all the children climbed up on it too. Of course they could see nothing likely to cause such a noise inside, but there were other occult phenomena.

Mrs O'Nolan's sister Teresa used to walk over from Main Street to visit and sometimes her steps could be heard tapping on the path half an hour or more before she arrived. And then there was the curious affair of the hens. There was a commodious henhouse, but the hens would not go into it; nor would they allow themselves to be herded in, summer or winter. They would roost in the apple trees at night, even on the coldest nights of the year, rather than slumber in that henhouse.

There was still no attempt to send the three eldest boys to school. Once again, no Irish schooling was available. Tutors were employed spasmodically, but did not last long. There was a Miss Boyle and a retired schoolmaster called Collins, or Ó Coiléain, who read with them a version of the famous story, *The Children of Lir*, written in

Ulster Irish by J. P. Craig. When Mr Collins's visits ceased, their father decided to take charge of their schooling once more. He already had a profitable sideline to his job in the form of a correspondence course he had devised for fellow civil servants who had to sit examinations and now he decided to apply the same method to the boys' education.

He set questions, which he sent by post from wherever he happened to be, graded according to the age and presumed abilities of his three elder sons, of whom Ciarán, the eldest, was now ten and the youngest, Brian, seven. These tests the boys either refused to do at all or did so badly that their well-meaning parent soon gave up. The speed with which he accepted defeat reveals something admirably casual about the otherwise meticulous Michael O'Nolan's attitude to formal education.

But the refusal to subject his sons to schooling through the medium of English no longer prevented them from coming in contact with that language. The rest of Agnes O'Nolan's family had less Irish than she had; and her sister Teresa, who came over nightly and slept in the house because of the ghost, had none at all. In the Gormley shop, where the boys now spent a great deal of their time, the customers spoke only English; and the same was true of most of the adults and such few children as they met.

In fact even among the Catholic population of Strabane, nationalist though it showed itself to be whenever it could, there was a prejudice against Irish. Most of the Catholics had been migrants from the Donegal hills and Irish to them was the badge of an impoverished and unsophisticated rural past which they were quite ready to forget. The Irish that they brought with them usually vanished in a generation.

In any case the boys now had an increasing amount of English and they were educating themselves in ways of which their father might not have approved. For one thing, there were the comics in the Gormley shop. These were picture comics – *Tiger Tim*, *Comic Cuts* and others – with policemen in tall helmets and burglars in hooped jerseys saying rather obvious things. Ciarán had soon learned to read from these, apparently by the method of recognizing whole words, and he was soon reading them aloud to his two brothers as they crouched happily on the floor beneath the counter.

And besides the comics there was the talk, the pithy Tyrone talk that they found the more fascinating precisely because English was unfamiliar to them. They listened to this for hours in the shop. 'Ba sin an comhrá arbh fhiú a bheith ag éisteacht leis.' 'That was talk worth listening to,' Ciarán was to say over half a century later.[1]

One drawback of not going to school, however, was that the three
eldest O'Nolan boys had still virtually no contact with children
outside the family. There was one memorable afternoon when they
joined in a football game at the end of Ballycolman Lane, where some
neighbour boys were kicking a football made of paper and twine
about, but that was almost the only friendly contact in three years.
Usually, such encounters were hostile, consisting of an exchange of
insults, with the O'Nolans safe behind their own front gate and the
other children shouting abuse and even occasionally throwing missiles
from a few yards up the road. Once the occasion of battle was the
defence of Mr Alexander's apples against marauders; and, besides the
defence of property, there was in these skirmishes an element of class
conflict, caused by the difference in social station and the O'Nolans'
presumed standoffishness. If the O'Nolan boys were not positively
forbidden to associate with the children of the lane, they were
certainly discouraged from doing so.

But though it may have contributed to a certain eccentricity for
which they were all, in their various ways, notable later on, the
three elder brothers did not feel the lack of other company as any
sort of deprivation at the time. Nor had they any difficulty whatever
in occupying their school-less days. In the sitting room over the
shop in Main Street there was a gramophone – a comparative rarity
at that time – a piano and lots of records, many of them of operatic
arias and drawing-room ballads sung by John McCormack, the great
Irish tenor, about whose singing Brian was to remain enthusiastic
for the rest of his life. This sitting room had three windows which
looked down on Main Street and here they would perch for long
hours, reading comics and gazing down on the scene below. They
spent much time also wading in the river, their shoes hanging round
their necks. They did not swim or fish – neither then nor later did
the O'Nolan boys have much zest for the sports and pastimes of
their more orthodox contemporaries – and the wading seems to have
been an aimless form of slow walking rather than anything more
purposeful. But they did acquire some knowledge of the life of the
river, enough to find eels under stones and to know where the trout
lurked.

Sometimes they would wade across the river to a place where the
mill stream flowed in, forming a pool where the water was deep and
dark even on the brightest summer day and there were occasional
badgers to be seen. Ciarán was to remember those days by the river
as the happiest of his life, particularly the hours spent lying in the long
grass of the bank while the sun seemed to stand still in the cloudless

summer sky and they could hear the distant clank of mowing machines and the faint hum of the machinery in the linen mill.

These school-free Strabane years were also the first years of 'the troubles'. The rising of 1916 had been followed by a great revival of nationalist feeling and the various shades of more extreme nationalists had come together under the banner of Sinn Féin – 'Ourselves Alone' – to defeat the old Parliamentary Irish Party in successive by-elections.

In 1918, however, Sinn Féiners and parliamentarians formed an alliance to agitate against the conscription measure which the British government was threatening to impose on Ireland. Eugene Gormley was prominent in this anti-conscription drive. He may have been a member of the Irish Volunteers, the paramilitary wing of Sinn Féin which was eventually to be known as the IRA, but in any case he was one of the most identifiable nationalists in Strabane and in 1918 he was arrested and taken under police escort by train to Belfast. From York Street Station he was marched to Victoria military barracks, escorted by a detachment of Northumberland fusiliers with fixed bayonets. He modestly said afterwards that he thought the presence of the fusiliers was an accident – they had simply been on the train and were returning to barracks themselves – but he loved to tell how the people in the streets had stopped to stare and some of them to smile at the man who was important enough to deserve such a large escort.

He was tried by court martial for incitement to sedition. It was the practice among republican prisoners not to recognize the authority or legality of such courts, but when Eugene told the story afterwards, he recounted how before he was taken upstairs a soldier said to him: 'Don't let these fucking bastards send you to gaol Recognize the court.' He didn't; and he got six months, which he spent in Crumlin Road gaol, in company with such subsequently well-known nationalists as Ernest Blythe, who became Minister for Finance in the first Free State government and afterwards Managing Director of the Abbey Theatre, and Austin Stack, an intransigent who took the opposite side to Blythe in the Civil War which followed the Anglo-Irish Treaty of 1922.

All the Gormleys were nationalists, indeed all the Catholics in Strabane were nationalists of one shade or another, and the boys' Aunt Teresa, the elder of the Gormley sisters, was a prominent member of Cumann na mBan, the women's auxiliary section of the Irish Volunteers. Cumann na mBan organized céilidhes, or Irish dances and concerts, in a hall in Barrack Street, which the boys were sometimes allowed to attend for an hour or so. There was also a céilidhe in the town hall at which some young men went through exercises called a drill display. The boys crouching in the balcony were thrilled not only by the general atmosphere of enthusiasm and martial fervour but also by the mere fact of being allowed to be up so late.

Nevertheless the troubles did not touch the boys' lives directly. It was not yet the era of ambuscades and reprisals, the cruel and bloody tit for tat which would often involve the civilian population. The games they played in the two storerooms of the Gormley shop, among the chinaware, the delf and the fancy goods which were part of the Gormleys' stock in trade, were not about nationalist derring-do or British villainy.

Besides the room which Mr Alexander had locked, there was another virtually empty room in the house in Ballycolman Lane known as the washroom. Here there were brown paper parcels containing dozens of copies of such improving works as *Tá Na Francaigh Ar An Mir*, Drama le Cu Uladh, or *The French Are on the Sea*, a Play by the Hound of Ulster, *Prátai Mhichil Thaidhg, The Potatoes of Michael Ted, Tadg Gabha, Ted the Blacksmith*, etc. These had been intended as readers for Gaelic League classes, but had somehow never been distributed. The boys soon discovered that the paper in which they were wrapped made excellent play cigarettes. The paper burned slowly and the smoke had a nice taste and an aroma resembling that of the Turkish cigarettes that Father Gearóid smoked, so they smoked these tobaccoless cigarettes for several months, until the brown paper had all been used up.

Their father came home every two weeks and took them for long walks. He was always a fierce walker; and wherever they were, these silent tramps remained one of his primary methods of communication with his three eldest sons. Brian was six when they settled in Ballycolman Lane. He had learned under his father's tuition to read Irish and under Ciarán's, English; and he may also have learned something about the art of story-telling from Ciarán, who told long stories in bed at night; but that was all the schooling he had. One afternoon he went into the cobbler's shop by the bridge and asked for work. Juveniles of 11 or 12 offering themselves for hire to prosperous farmers was a common sight at the hiring fairs in Abercorn Square, but it is doubtful if the cobbler took the eight-year-old seriously, though he did tell him he could start next day. Naturally his mother put a stop to this proposed employment when she was told of it.

Strabane was to be a second home to all the O'Nolans for many years to come, but in July 1920 Michael O'Nolan was transferred to

Tullamore, a town situated in the flat, rather featureless central plain of Ireland. Brian was to use this landscape many years later as the background to *The Third Policeman* and to give its very emptiness and lack of individuality a curiously threatening and disturbing quality.

It was Michael O'Nolan's job to oversee the payment of excise duties by the distilleries in his area. The principal ones were D. E. Williams of Tullamore, who made a brand called Tullamore Dew, and Locke's of Kilbeggan. Both of these were often mentioned later in Brian's *Irish Times* column; and in later years also he was to affect more than a drinker's knowledge of the law governing the proof strength or otherwise of whiskey, sometimes to the annoyance of publicans.

The family's new home was a house called The Copper Beeches, about two miles outside Tullamore. Leased from the Odlums, a local flour-milling family, by Irish standards it was a small mansion, its size reflecting Michael O'Nolan's status as a senior excise official. It had a lawn in front, a garden and a yard with outbuildings at the back. There was still no attempt to send the boys to school and the apparent idyll continued. As in Strabane they would wander off together and were seen only at mealtimes. Each of them was allotted a patch of garden and Brian made surprisingly good use of his, growing vegetables which were eaten at table.

There was a donkey which had its own stable in the yard at the back, though it stubbornly refused to be ridden, making straight for a wall when mounted and threatening to crush its would-be rider's knee. There were also fowl in which the boys took a great interest, observing with glee the consequences of putting duck eggs under a brooding hen. When they hatched out the tiny ducklings made straight for the water of the stream, to the bewilderment of their foster mother.

Michael O'Nolan, always a great book-buyer, now had his books about him again; and for the first time the boys were making full use of them. According to Ciarán, Brian soon had 'every book in the house read'. These included works by most of the great writers of the English language, from Defoe to Stevenson, as well as more contemporary authors, such as Conan Doyle, Wells and Bennett. The boys especially enjoyed *The Pickwick Papers* and, for some reason, Trollope's *Autobiography*. James Stephens seems to have been the only representative of the so-called Irish Literary Revival, then in full swing, though the poems of the two most important Irish poets of the 19th century, James Clarence Mangan and Samuel Ferguson, were in the house, as well as Douglas Hyde's eccentric but richly rewarding history of Gaelic literature, *A Literary History of Ireland*.

If Brian read all of these, or even a good proportion of them, between the ages of nine and 12, he was, though still free from what Ciarán called 'the foolish demands of school', a very well-educated youngster indeed.[2] But besides the books in the house, the boys also soon had access to a library run by the nuns in Tullamore. Here they found many of the best-selling authors of the time, including Rafael Sabatini, who wrote swashbuckling historical romances, and H. de Vere Stacpoole, an Irish romanticist who wrote about imaginary South Sea islands. Conan Doyle's Sherlock Holmes stories were well represented in this library; and it is not difficult to discern their influence on the future creator of De Selby, Count O'Blather and even Myles na Gopaleen. Another book Brian read which made an impression on him was George A. Birmingham's comic novel *Spanish Gold*. This is a stage Irish but genuinely comic tale and one of the few books the boys read which was set in the Ireland of the time. They would visit the nuns' eclectic library every Sunday morning after Mass and take away a couple of books each, to be read and returned by the following Sunday.

The vast majority of the books in the house were in English, though there was some Irish poetry, and there is an element of comedy in the fact that Michael O'Nolan was undermining his own efforts to bring the boys up to speak and think in Irish by providing them with so much engrossing reading matter in the tongue of the foreigner.

He became aware that Brian's reading in that language was now fairly extensive on a day when they were laying linoleum in an upper room, the window of which was open. A car pulled up some yards away along the road to discharge a couple of passengers and as they said their farewells to the remaining occupants Brian began to mimic their flat Offaly accents. 'Bí do thosc. Clainfhidh siad thu' – 'Be silent. They will hear you,' his father said to him sternly. 'And as for you, sir,' Brian replied in English, 'if you do not conduct yourself I will do you a mischief.'[3]

They are his first recorded words in the English language and it is evident that he was already a pasticheur of promise. It was also the first time that one of the boys addressed his father in that language. Fortunately Michael O'Nolan seems to have seen the joke. He certainly put no obstacles in the way of his sons' continuing to read his books or make use of the library, though, like most parents of the time, he locked away some reading matter that he considered unsuitable.

The O'Nolan children were now seeing a great deal more of their father than they had in Strabane. On summer evenings they would all play croquet on the big lawn in front of the house, using a second-hand set of mallets and hoops that Michael O'Nolan had bought. The game was generally quite decorous, but on one occasion, when his father's ball was poised to go through a hoop, Brian drove his own at it with such vicious force as to send it across the lawn and behind some rose bushes. This was an instance of *lèse-majesté* so unusual as to be long remembered by the younger children.

Michael O'Nolan now owned a car, an Overland, and he often took the three eldest boys with him on his business trips. It was a time when the rough, potholed roads were sometimes blocked by trees felled across them by the local IRA. Each of the numerous bridges spanning the Grand and Royal Canals was a checkpoint guarded by parties of soldiers; and they were often forced to the side of the road by speeding Crossley tenders, the military sitting back-to-back with their rifles across their knees.

Although Michael O'Nolan was a servant of the crown and not an active nationalist, his attitude to these soldiers was clear. They were foreigners, 'the enemy', and they should be sent back to their own country forthwith. Shortly after moving into The Copper Beeches he received a visit from a party of them. The house was not searched, nor the occupants seriously questioned, but the intruders did a little casual looting, removing a sword belonging to the Odlum family which was hanging in the hallway. Michael's children were disappointed that their father had not sent the soldiers packing or at least given them a piece of his mind. He was not there when another party came to the house looking for helpers to clear away some trees which had been felled nearby. Such temporary press ganging was a common practice, but since there were only women and children in the house there was no corvée this time.

On another occasion when some soldiers came, there was nobody at home except the three eldest boys. Brian and Ciarán had both built 'houses' made of sacking against the wall in their patches of garden. Finding no-one in the house the soldiers went into the garden, guns in hand, and looked about. Seeing them through the gaps in their sacking, the boys decided with one instinct to keep quiet and crouch where they were. Luckily, the soldiers soon left. Given the general state of nervousness of the military a cough or an involuntary movement might have had serious consequences.

But Offaly was not one of the more disturbed counties and apart from such incidents life at The Copper Beeches was peaceful. There were visits to the cinema in Tullamore where the usual programme of silent feature plus one-reel comedy was to be seen. Brian had first been to the cinema on a memorable occasion during the Inchicore period, probably in 1916, when his father had taken him and his brothers to a newly opened cinema in O'Connell Street and they had seen a western full of galloping horses in which someone was shot dead every 30 seconds. Now as often as they were given permission they would walk into town to see much the same sort of fare, varied sometimes by a feature-length Chaplin comedy and even an occasional epic. As in most Irish county towns the cinema was an ordinary hall, used as well for concerts and whist drives.

Ciarán, Gearóid and Brian now decided that they would make their own films. They constructed a projector by placing an oil lamp inside a cardboard box with an aperture cut out of one side. The images for the picture show were drawn on squares of brown paper which were held up one by one, interspersed with sub-titles, in front of the aperture. The highly inflammable nature of the whole contraption was aggravated by the discovery that letting a drop of paraffin fall on each square would render it more translucent.

All three boys had a talent for drawing, or at least for quickly executed heads and faces, somewhat in the style of *Comic Cuts*, and Brian was to remain a great embellisher of margins and odd scraps of paper all his life. And each of them had an inventive faculty. The mad inventor in Brian was exhibited to the full in 'Cruiskeen Lawn' and in later years Gearóid had many ideas for the improvement of such well-known inventions as the internal combustion engine. While they were growing up Ciarán was supposed to be the writer of the family and during the Tullamore years he filled many copy-books with a novel he was writing. He and Brian took the largest share of responsibility for the story-line of the films and these vanished film scripts were Brian's first creative efforts.

As we have seen, these years in Tullamore were the climactic years of the conflict the Irish people had decided to call 'the troubles'. Regular troops had been poured into Ireland in large numbers and the Royal Irish Constabulary had been rendered at once more formidable, more ferocious and less effective by the introduction of new British recruits and the addition of a brigade of ex-army officers known as Auxiliary Police. The former soon became known to the Irish people as the 'Black and Tans' and the latter as 'the Auxies'. They were opposed by comparatively small numbers of guerrillas who began by attacking individual policemen and then isolated police barracks, often manned by no more than a sergeant and two or three constables. Emboldened by their successes in these forays, they soon began to attack military convoys, ambushing them by blocking the roads with trees and carts.

The authorities reacted to what they called terror by counter-terror, raiding the homes of known nationalists, burning creameries, shops and farmhouses, or, in some cases, whole villages and towns. Martial law was proclaimed in many counties and in Strabane Uncle Eugene was arrested and taken without trial of any kind to the prison ship the *Argenta*, moored in Belfast Lough.

Except in a few counties of the Protestant Unionist north-east and the Trinity College constituency in Dublin, Sinn Féin candidates had been elected everywhere in 1918. They had refused to go to Westminster and had constituted themselves Dáil Éireann, or The Parliament of Ireland. Although many of them were in gaol the rest proceeded to set up a governmental infrastructure which, in accordance with the Sinn Féin doctrine of self-sufficiency, was supposed to replace British institutions and make independence an accomplished fact even while the military versus guerrilla conflict dragged on.

There is little doubt that the guerrillas, now known as the IRA, enjoyed the passive support at least of most of the civilian population outside the north-east, particularly as the authorities abandoned restraint and brought the law they were supposed to uphold into contempt through a policy of reprisal and official or semi-official terrorism. Many civilians sheltered guerrillas, carried messages and spied for them. But the ambiguity of the situation in which others found themselves is illustrated by the fact that Michael Nolan could be a nationalist in principle while continuing to perform his duties and of course draw his salary as an exciseman.

By the summer of 1922, when Brian was nearly 11, the suppression of armed revolt and the overcoming of passive resistance was becoming impossible for Britain, given such restraints as had still to be exercised in their conduct of the struggle in face of world, and particularly American, opinion. A truce between the combatants was agreed and in December of that year a form of settlement was made between the Irish representatives and those of the British government in London. This recognized the independence of about four-fifths, or 26 counties, of Ireland along the lines of the status already accorded to the Dominions of Canada and Australia; and under the terms of this settlement the British now proceeded to withdraw from what was to be known as the Irish Free State.

Unfortunately, this was not to be the end of armed conflict. One of the first acts of the Dáil Assembly in 1918 had been to affirm the existence of the Republic which had been proclaimed in 1916 amid the flames which the O'Nolans had seen reflected from the sky over Dublin. Before very long those loyal to the abstract republic and those loyal to the new Free State were at loggerheads, so that the cessation of the conflict against Britain was accompanied by the beginning of a new conflict between Irishmen. Once again there were ambushes, raids, reprisals and rather more executions in a shorter space of time by the new government than there had been in four years under the British. As the firing died away with some thousands of republican intransigents in gaols or internment camps there remained a sense of disillusion which would last throughout Brian Nolan's formative years. Independent Ireland, such as it was, had got off to a bad start. The waking, and the realization, were extraordinarily different from the dream.

In years to come it would be fashionable to speak of the 'bitterness' resulting from the Civil War. Of course there was bitterness and a sense of betrayal too, but it was more acutely felt by those who had been active participants, as combatants, propagandists or political functionaries, than it was by the majority of the Irish people. What they felt was something else. It was a let-down; and it took the form of a relapse into a basic irreverence and cynicism which are never far from the surface in Ireland. There had been a cleansing suspension of politics during the years of struggle. Now politics were back and, with many of the nobler or more glamorous figures killed off, they were a glum and rather shabby business. There had been idealism, heroism, even a willingness to embrace martyrdom on the part of many. Now the hunt for jobs was on again, and a sordid if realistic acceptance of everyday necessities.

Instead of elevated patriotic sentiment, cynicism and disillusion would soon become the fashionable modes among writers and intellectuals. These would in any case have been inclined to react against the rhetoric of their immediate predecessors, the nationalist poets and dramatists of the Irish literary revival, but the Civil War and the sort of independence that followed provided a watershed and speeded up the process. Brian O'Nolan's generation came to awareness during the first wave of this reaction against the poetic idealism of the revivalists – Sean O'Casey's *The Plough and the Stars* was produced at the Abbey in 1926 and Denis Johnston's *The Old Lady Says No*, a satire on the new Ireland, at the Gate in 1928. That the politicians continued to employ an increasingly outmoded rhetoric of love of country, sacrifice and struggle would add to their disgust and amusement.

*

The ink was scarcely dry on the treaty before the Free State government decided to set up a Board of Revenue Commissioners, which would amalgamate the functions in Ireland of the old United Kingdom Commissioners of Customs and Excise and Commissioners of Inland Revenue. Since Michael O'Nolan's area of jurisdiction was in the new Free State, he became an employee of the new Commissioners. If it had been in the north, he would have remained an employee of the crown and his son Brian would have been brought up in Northern Ireland, becoming a 'northerner' instead of a 'southerner', going to Queen's University, Belfast instead of to University College Dublin (UCD) and perhaps having, in the end, an entirely different life-story and literary history.

As it was, the changeover to Irish rule created vacancies throughout the Civil Service, for generous retirement terms were offered to those who did not wish to serve the new state. Michael O'Nolan received a transfer to Dublin, entering the employment of the Commissioners with the rank of Inspector, second-class. According to the official history of the Commissioners, his subsequent rise was 'meteoric'. He became a Superintending Inspector (headquarters) in April 1924; a Collector (Dublin collection) – a higher grade – in August 1924; and finally a Commissioner on 1 April 1925.

The fact that he was a northerner who had fluent Irish may have helped. The new state was anxious to show that it was not partitionist in outlook and by 1925 it had begun to favour Irish speakers for promotion in the Civil Service. Michael O'Nolan always spoke Irish to those of his colleagues who could converse in that language and he preferred to be known to them as M. V. Ó Nualláin, though oddly enough he remained M. V. Nolan on all official documents relating to his employment.

On his transfer to Dublin M. V. Ó Nualláin, or Michael Nolan or Michael O'Nolan took a house in Herbert Place, one of a terrace of tall Georgian houses in a quiet backwater overlooking the Grand Canal. This was what house agents would call a highly desirable residence on the fashionable south side; and the fact that he could afford it reflects the family's status in the new scheme of things. W. B. Yeats, now a Free State Senator, had just taken a house in nearby Merrion Square and his brother Jack, the painter, lived in Fitzwilliam Square in the same vicinity.

One most important effect of the move was to make Brian a Dubliner, something he was proudly to remain for the rest of his life. He had of course resided in the environs of the city as a very small boy during the Inchicore period, but its full impact was delayed until now when he was 11. It is doubtful if the kind of glee that Dublin afforded him would have been quite the same if he had been born in the capital or had come to Dublin later in life, as did many of his literary contemporaries.

Shortly after settling in Dublin Michael O'Nolan at last decided to send his three eldest sons to school. As Ciarán was to remark wryly, he did not ask them if they wanted to go, 'nor if that would be against our principles. He simply said that a decision had been made.'[4] The educational institution he chose for them was the Christian Brothers School at Synge Street, off the South Circular Road, about ten minutes' walk away down Adelaide Road. There could hardly have been a worse choice for such a sudden and long-delayed immersion.

The Christian Brothers were notorious crammers, adept at forcing recalcitrant pupils through the various levels of the examination system and not averse to using violence in the process. Their ethos was strongly nationalist and Catholic and since the majority of boys' schools in the Free State were in their hands, they had a considerable influence on the mentality of the country in which Brian was now growing up. Members of the order were not very well educated, usually having no more than a Christian Brothers' second-level education followed by a spell in one of the Brothers' training colleges. Since they were sworn to poverty and celibacy, they had all the disadvantages of the priesthood, and none of its presumed advantages, in terms of social prestige, public deference or sacerdotal powers. In Flann O'Brien's novel, *The Hard Life*, the hero enters 'the sinister portals of Synge Street School' with a foreboding soon to be confirmed and makes the acquaintance of 'the leather':

> It is not, as one would imagine, a strap of the kind used on bags. It is a number of such straps sewn together to form a thing of great thickness that is nearly as rigid as a club but just sufficiently flexible to prevent the breaking of the bones of the hand. Blows of it, particularly if directed (as often they deliberately were) to the top of the thumb or wrist, conferred immediate paralysis followed by agony as the blood tried to get back to the afflicted part.[5]

And while not everything that his later persona, Myles na Gopaleen, described can be taken as true of Brian O'Nolan's experience, the searing account of Synge Street given in 'Cruiskeen Lawn' 40 years later is an accurate one:

> The secondary schools are the true scenes of brutality and degradation and it is with sardonic glee that I give readers the toast of Synge Street ...

at least as that diabolical academy was over thirty years ago. I was there! No matter how assiduous and even intelligent a student was he was bound to get a hiding every day of his school life. It was normal routine for a class to have four teachers in the course of the day, each of the teachers regarded the class as his personal and private concern and distributed punishment and homework as if in watertight seclusion.

A youngster getting home to his dinner about 4 P.M. having had a slice of bread for lunch, found himself faced with at least seven hours' written homework, to say nothing of having been ordered (how well I remember this!) to learn 'Lucy Gray' by heart overnight. With school starting at 9 A.M. the desks were crowded well before 8 with students engaged in frenzied cogging from each other. If your sums were wrong you would get a thorough bashing with 'the leather', but if the answers were correct and you could not explain why, then you would get what was known as a murdering.

Teachers were both Christian Brothers and laymen and, though they were not by any means uniformly savage, the worst of them were scarcely human at all. To a coarseness of personality they added abnormal intellectual ignorance and uncouthness. No matter how bright a lad was with his Latin, God help him if his translation did not accord literally with what was in the *Bell's Keys to the Classics* as concealed in the teacher's copy of the text.

I remember a loutish teacher announcing that since it was only six weeks to the Inter Cert exam he was about to start a reign of terror. 'I'll make ye dence,' he said, with unintended pronunciational ambiguity. I would not be bothered today to denounce such people as sadists, brutes, psychotics, I would simply dub them criminal and would expect to see them jailed.[6]

Gearóid was to describe this first experience of school as a 'disaster' and there is no doubt that it must have been a psychological shock of the most extreme order. Synge Street was decidedly no place for oddities, and the O'Nolans, with their Strabane accents and their lack of familiarity with the rough give-and-take of adolescent life, were certainly that. They were not at home, either in the tyrannically ruled classroom or the crowded concrete recreation yard.

Their fellow pupils realized quickly that the newcomers were fair game and that some sport was to be had. At the first recreation break they gathered round and began to torment them. The ones in front would distract their attention while others ran up behind and punched or kicked them. The O'Nolans retreated to the wall, followed by a mob, but this gave little security as a number of their tormentors climbed on top of it and began to kick them on the head or reach down to pull their hair while the others danced around, jeering and putting out their tongues. Only the harsh clanging of the bell for the end of the lunch period brought their agonies to an end for the time being.

This went on for three days, until finally Ciarán lashed out in rage at one individual, to such effect that some of the bigger boys decided there was a good fight in prospect and matched him with the aggressor. Usually the O'Nolans were followed part of the way home by a jeering group, but now the two combatants were led to the lane off Harrington Street and the arranged fight began. At a fairly early stage Ciarán landed a lucky blow to his opponent's nose, which began to bleed to such an extent that Ciarán was adjudged the victor. This eased things for the brothers, though sporadic bullying still continued and Gearóid and Ciarán often had to assert themselves with their fists when driven into a corner.

Reflecting on their first school experiences in his book, *Óige An Dearthár* (The Youth of the Brethren) afterwards, Ciarán was to say:

> From being able to do exactly as we wanted from our birth until this time, without having any companionship or contact with other boys, no duties to fulfil, with no stranger having a right to get in on us or give us tasks to do, to be unburdened with lessons to prepare or do correctly – there is no imagining the great anxiety all this caused us, it was like a terrible test, putting people into a fire or into icy water. Indeed it was so hard on us and it took so long for us to get used to it, that I would nearly say that the freedom of our young days was not worth the high price we paid for it.[7]

As the first awful weeks passed, however, Ciarán began to notice something about Brian. Some personality trait, or something baleful beyond the ordinary in his eye, would seem to deter aggressors and keep them at a distance, so that whatever insults were traded he never had to engage in physical violence.

Fortunately all three boys were placed in the same class, so that at least the very close companionship of the preceding years was not broken and none of them was alone in his misery. They were all put into Fourth Year, which was supposed to be the preparatory year for the Intermediate Certificate. According to Gearóid, however ill-prepared for school they were psychologically, academically they turned out to be better at certain subjects than their classmates, or even than their chief tormentor among the teachers, a certain Brother Brick. Yet Brian was to stay in this class for the whole of his three years in Synge Street and was not allowed to sit the Intermediate Certificate – which he eventually passed with honours – until the end of that period, while Ciarán and Gearóid were kept in the class for two years.

The reason for this was probably that their ignorance of such subjects as Latin, science, algebra and Euclidean geometry was complete. They knew some history, they were as good at arithmetic as anybody else and they were better at English and Irish, though some of what was in the English reader caused them great amusement. A particular example was Edmund Burke's famous passage about the Age of Chivalry being dead and Marie Antoinette scarcely touching the orb she walked on. This was still to give Brian a laugh whenever he thought of it later on and it features several times in 'Cruiskeen Lawn'.

Coming fresh to the school system Brian was particularly struck by the injustice of having to face a considerable amount of homework after a long day in the classroom; and of course they felt the loss of leisure and the free inventiveness of a long day's play more acutely than others.

Michael O'Nolan would occasionally assist them with those parts of the homework which they found especially difficult, but these occasions were rare. In general there was little communication between him and his eldest sons. He did not discuss current affairs with them, or history, or ideas of any sort. At mealtimes in the O'Nolan family an extraordinary silence reigned, which was accepted as part of the natural order of things. Later, when the boys began to make other friends – which did not happen until after they had left Synge Street – and to visit their houses, they were amazed by the number of topics raised around the table at mealtimes and at the vivacity, eagerness and sometimes even anger with which all the members of the family would make their contributions, sometimes forgetting to eat while they tried to make a point.

'There are different kinds of father, I suppose,' Ciarán was to say later, 'and they are as different from each other as people are. There are fathers who explain things, who illustrate the ways of the world to children as soon as they reach the use of reason. I hear them often at it. It's a good thing I suppose.' At the same time he was at pains to draw a distinction between Michael O'Nolan's habitual reticence and that of the 'Victorian father'. The fact of the matter, he insisted, was simply that 'he would not be, nor would we be, great communicators together, talking about ideas for instance. It was no great pity. It was not our way, nor our nature.'[8]

On Sundays Michael O'Nolan would take the three eldest boys for long silent walks along the leafy, almost deserted sideroads that ran between stone walls and past small demesnes into the foothills of the Dublin mountains. A typical Sunday excursion might take them up Appian Way and along Ranelagh to Dundrum, then on to Goatstown or Kilmacud before the return along the Bray Road to Herbert Place. The roads were so free of traffic that it was even possible to walk on the Bray Road itself, now a six-lane arterial highway, instead of on the

footpath. Since the boys played no organized games, these walks were
virtually their only form of exercise and they seem to have enjoyed
mooning along, each with his own thoughts. Every Sunday on their
return they would sit down to a joint of beef which had been sent up
by a Tullamore butcher. The boys came to hate the unchanging
monotony of this Sunday dinner. 'One man's meat,' as Ciarán sagely
remarked, 'is another man's poison.'

In his dealings with his children Michael O'Nolan seems to have
been a just, if distant, parent. It was not easy to make him angry and
there is no record of any occasion on which he had to invoke severe
sanctions or punish anybody physically in order to maintain discipline. Yet maintain it he did and his authority was never challenged.

He was a devout Catholic and a regular Sunday communicant all his
life. Towards the end of it he went to Mass every day and attended two
Masses on the Sabbath. This was not an unusual degree of piety for the
Ireland of that time; but the atmosphere of unquestioning Catholicism
in the O'Nolan household, as in most other Irish households at the
time, was strong. There was a holy water font in the hallway and
religious pictures on the walls. None of Michael's children, including
Brian, ever questioned the basic tenets of the Catholic belief, though
naturally Brian's Catholicism was coloured and modified by his own
temperament and rather nihilistic outlook.

Michael O'Nolan was now a person of some consequence in the
world and he was enjoying the cultural life of Dublin, in which
theatre-going bulked inordinately large, to the full. He took his wife
and sometimes his three eldest sons to every new production in the
Abbey and even to see the visiting English companies who brought
plays to the Olympia or the Gaiety. They also attended the celebrity
concerts at the Theatre Royal, where Heifetz, Paderewski and others
performed. Mr and Mrs O'Nolan were particularly fond of the
Glasgow Orpheus Choir, which made several visits to Dublin in those
years; and by the time he left school, Brian had heard John McCormack, then past his best but still a world renowned celebrity, sing in
Dublin on at least three occasions. In the 1920s Dublin had still, as in
Joyce's day, a thriving amateur musical culture. In *At Swim-Two-
Birds* the hero's uncle and his friend Mr Corcoran are members of the
city's principal amateur group, the Rathmines and Rathgar Musical
Society, 'an indifferent voice in the baritone range' having won for the
uncle a 'station in the chorus'. When they bring home a gramophone,
the hero views their enjoyment of 'the *Patience* opera' with a
malevolence and distaste which he finds it difficult to conceal. He
retreats to his bedroom, where he can still hear the music, 'thinner and

hollower through the intervening doors but perceptibly reinforced at the incidence of a chorus'. Finally he leaves the house.

From as far back as the boys could remember, there had always been a gramophone in the O'Nolan house and their father had always bought records, mostly of popular concert and drawing-room pieces or operatic arias. There is no warranty whatever for the assumption that the portrait of the hero's uncle in *At Swim-Two-Birds* was in any way modelled on Michael Victor O'Nolan, who was a far more cultured and sophisticated man in every way, as well as being a somewhat kindlier and certainly less garrulous one. But the scene does suggest that Brian O'Nolan viewed the musical enthusiasms of his father's contemporaries satirically, in retrospect at least. Curiously also, though the O'Nolan boys were encouraged to play one or other musical instrument from an early age and Brian was to become quite an accomplished violinist, having begun to take lessons before they left Strabane, none of them was ever known to sing. And what is perhaps stranger still, other people's efforts to sing in any sort of informal domestic context caused the three eldest boys unfailing amusement. Whenever they sat in on any of Uncle Joe's rehearsals of musical productions in Strabane they were quickly convulsed with laughter and had to leave, while any effort to perform for grown-ups by any of the younger children also aroused their derision.

Michael O'Nolan's level of cultural discernment is in part indicated by the fact that he was a regular reader of the English publication, *John O'London's Weekly*, while the ambiguities of his cultural situation are reflected in the fact that the other two journals he 'took' on a regular basis were the Irish-language *Fáinne An Lae* and *The Irish Statesman*, edited by the poet George William Russell, 'AE'. *John O'London's* consisted almost entirely of book reviews, written in a talkative popular manner and, in the case of biographies or books of memoirs, rehashing the life-story of the subject or author. It was deliberately and sometimes aggressively middle-brow where poetry and fiction were concerned and the weekly short story it published was of the trick-ending variety. Since it was Brian's first introduction to the literary scene some part of his later impatience with highbrow pretentiousness may possibly be traceable to its influence.

Another of Michael O'Nolan's enthusiasms was chess, which the boys also learned to play. In later life Brian was quite boastful about his own abilities as a chess player, but it is doubtful whether he ever achieved his father's level of skill. At this time one of his own enthusiasms was photography. He had acquired a camera and had rigged up a darkroom at the top of the house where he could develop and print his own pictures. Those that have survived show him to have been competent enough, but oddly conventional in his choice of subject, seldom looking beyond the members of his family.

Apart from the fact that he liked to attend first nights and concerts, Michael O'Nolan was not a particularly gregarious man and certainly not a habitué of public houses. Visitors to the house, however, included George Gormley, now well on his way to becoming a well-known character in Dublin journalistic circles. George was one of those newspapermen for whom journalism never loses its glamour. He had many anecdotes about the trade and its personalities and was not averse to suggesting that it could be the road to easy riches. Sometimes he arrived a little tipsy and on these occasions Michael O'Nolan would not pass any comment but would leave it to his wife to entertain her brother as best she could. He did not drink or smoke himself, though at major festivals like Christmas he might take one or two bottles of stout or even accept a cigarette. When he did so his way of putting it in the middle of his mouth and gripping it firmly but primly with his lips caused his three eldest sons much amusement. They were developing between them a sort of half secret comic view of the world generally and finding things that struck others as solemn, portentous or even tragic a source of laughter.

In 1927 the O'Nolans moved again, this time to number 4 Avoca Terrace, a large house in a quiet side road near Blackrock. Originally a separate township, Blackrock had been absorbed by Dublin's expansion along the pleasant southern littoral of its bay during the 19th century, but its origins were still revealed by its narrow, winding main street through which the trams clanged and groaned. Avoca Terrace was about a mile away, uphill towards the fashionable district of Foxrock on the Bray Road.

The O'Nolans lived here in considerable middle-class state, with two maids who wore blue or pink uniforms in the morning and black in the evening. The house was a substantial one, but the dining room was only used as such on special occasions like Christmas Day; and most of the living was done in the large breakfast room, where there was a gas fire at which the children made toast with a long fork. The whole house was gas-lit when they moved in and the range in the kitchen was fuelled with paraffin oil. The room Brian would eventually share with his youngest brother Micheál was at the back on the left side of the house with a small window overlooking a lane where there were carriage houses. Like the other bedrooms it was lit by gas, but the gas jet here was without a mantle and the naked flame went pop pop in the evenings. Here he would eventually write a large part of his first book, *At Swim-Two-Birds*.

Blackrock is about six miles from the centre of Dublin and so, to their great relief, it was now impossible for the boys to continue at Synge Street and Michael O'Nolan had to look around for a new school. He made the obvious choice in deciding on Blackrock College, the Holy Ghost Fathers' nearby establishment at Williamstown, on the main road from Blackrock to Dublin.

French in origin, the Holy Ghost Fathers had become very much a part of Irish life since establishing themselves at Blackrock in the late 19th century. They were primarily a missionary order, sending priests to Africa and elsewhere to convert the heathen peoples to their own Irish brand of Christianity; but like other religious orders they had found a rewarding sideline in the education of the newly emergent Catholic middle classes.

At Blackrock they had begun by purchasing Williamstown Castle, a fittingly ecclesiastical-seeming product of the Gothic revival and proceeded to build extensively in its spacious grounds. The day pupils came from the prosperous southern suburbs of Dublin and the boarders were mostly the offspring of provincial shopkeepers and professional people. These both paid what was for the time a considerable fee; but there was a third category, known as scholastics, who were boarded and educated free on the understanding that they were on their way to the priesthood and service in the mission fields.

The ethos of the school was strongly Catholic, with overtones of honour, uprightness and fair play adapted from the British public school system. There was a heavy emphasis on unspectacular middle-class success and the duller virtues which might be supposed to ensure it in afterlife. The ideal past pupil was one who had risen high in politics, the Civil Service, business or the professions by obeying the rules of the game; and the possibility of rising high by other means was not adverted to. Eminent past pupils in Brian's time included the politician, Eamon de Valera, who was much talked of, and the writer Liam O'Flaherty who was never mentioned.

Catholic dogma was taught as containing all the truths that mattered about the world. In Catholic apologetics there was an emphasis on the Aristotelian prime mover or first cause, St Thomas Aquinas's principal proof of God's existence; but a devotion to the Blessed Virgin amounting almost to Mariolatry played a large part in the theology of the Irish Holy Ghost Fathers. Her statue surmounted the school's clock tower and her blue and white colours were the colours of its famous football team.

Photographs of those who had successfully attained places in the British and Indian Civil Services adorned the corridor outside the refectory, for the Holy Ghost Fathers, who were used to co-operating with the Imperial apparatus in Africa, were only very mildly nationalist; but though these successes were esteemed the school was not an all-out cramming establishment. There was some degree of latitude and respect for the acquirement of knowledge for its own sake as well as some talk of literature in the classrooms; but science was a very hole-and-corner affair in the curriculum and scientific discoverers were not among the role models offered for admiration. Physical punishment was administered by the Deans, who used a cane which raised welts on the outstretched palm of the delinquent pupil; but it was much more selective in its application than it had been in Synge Street.

There was also a heavy emphasis on rugby, at which the school excelled and which was supposed to produce what was called manliness. All in all, the 'verray parfit gentil knight' that the Holy Ghost Fathers sought to produce would have been manly in the physical sense but also very pure and virginal; devoted to the virgin mother and unremitting in religious observance; charitable towards his less fortunate fellow mortals but successful enough to be a desirable member of the past pupils' union.

The three O'Nolan boys fitted in here as well as they were likely to fit in anywhere. There was a certain degree of tolerance for eccentricity among both the pupils and the staff; and although bullying was common enough among the boarders it was almost non-existent where day pupils were concerned. Years later Ciarán was to remark on the softer regimen and the more expansive atmosphere at Blackrock. He also declared that the Brothers had dinned so much knowledge into their heads at Synge Street that there was no necessity for them to learn anything at the new school; and although the boys' code was barbarous enough, oddities who were known to be clever were treated with rather more respect than those who were thought to be not very bright.

To begin with, the O'Nolans were friendless. They would be seen walking together at recreation time, their hands in their pockets, sometimes in absolute silence; but gradually they began to make acquaintances among those boys who lived near them, or walked home the same way; and finally they even had friends, which was a new and exciting development for them. There were the Kennys who lived near them at Blackrock, the Quigleys and, above all in Brian's case, Richard McManus, to whom the *Irish Times* paperback edition of *Cruiskeen Lawn* was to be dedicated in 1941. Richard was a laughter-loving boy with an interest in literature and public affairs and he spoke fluent Irish. Photographs show him to have been good-looking and although he was an extrovert he was also an intellectual. He was Brian O'Nolan's first and for a long time his firmest friend.

When these and other friends visited the O'Nolan household, however, one of the first things that struck them was the silence that pervaded the whole house except when the gramophone was on or somebody was playing the piano. There was no shouting; indeed the O'Nolans never seemed to address one another at all, each being occupied with his own game, book or business. Nor, on the odd occasion when one of their friends met their father, would he prove very communicative either. He might come into the front room when one was visiting, say a word or two in Irish in his almost inaudible voice, and go off again. If the visitor had no Irish he was unlikely to be addressed a second time.

But of course the O'Nolan boys were now speaking English more and more outside the family circle and in fact their new-found friends, the Kennys, did not speak any Irish at all, or only so much Irish as the average reluctant schoolboy of the time might be expected to speak, which was certainly not a lot. Although the assumption was that it was still the O'Nolans' main language of converse, from now on it was increasingly less so. Towards the end of his life, Brian was reluctant to speak Irish at all and would not do so when addressed in it by anybody apart from Ciarán. Their father's lack of fanaticism is shown by the fact that, unlike some parents who were zealous for '*an teanga*', or 'the tongue' as the Irish language was called among enthusiasts, he did not attempt to impose any rule about English-speaking acquaintances. If he heard his children speaking English to their friends, he made no comment. In Blackrock, Irish was kept pretty firmly in its place, being taught as a subject in the classroom along with French, Latin and Greek but no more; and you could not opt, as you could in the Christian Brothers, to study certain other subjects through the medium of the Irish language.

One of their teachers in Blackrock was the redoubtable John Charles McQuaid, afterwards to be Archbishop of Dublin and to impose, for most of Brian O'Nolan's lifetime, an iron discipline on the Catholics of the diocese in all the wide range of matters over which he had influence. At this time he was Dean of Studies and a teacher of English, Latin and Greek. He was subsequently, before becoming

Archbishop, President of the School and an important influence on its past pupil Eamon de Valera when he came to draw up the Irish Constitution of 1937.

McQuaid was a slight narrow-featured man whose generally ascetic air and bearing were somehow emphasized by the fact that he carried one shoulder higher than the other. He had a piercing eye, a mouth that betrayed a certain humorous expectancy and an undoubted presence. A theocrat whose theocracy was complicated by a devout Mariolatry, he was something of a prose stylist in a rag-bag, Edwardian, mandarin way, and he told his English classes that the greatest living writer of prose was Hilaire Belloc.

Belloc and Chesterton were popular in Ireland at this time as upholders of the faith against the mockers and freethinkers of godless England. Their debates with the agnostic Wells and Shaw were much referred to by the more literate type of English teacher, particularly clerics, and their ripostes and sallies much admired. This admiration was naturally transferred into the sphere of literary criticism so that in many schools, and perhaps in Blackrock especially, they were recommended reading for the brighter students and their books were readily available.

McQuaid's clerical colleagues held him in something approaching awe and would inform their pupils in hushed tones of the evidences of his intellectual prowess, including the fact that he could discuss the theory of relativity with Eamon de Valera and that he had learned French overnight from a book. His mannerisms were much copied by the boys but the imitations were on the whole respectful and usually stopped short of outright irreverence. He made rather a pet of Ciarán, who was in his sixth-year English class during his year in Blackrock, discussing literature with him and recommending books for him to read. His comments on his pupil's exercises were succinct, and though generally kindly, could sometimes be devastating. They were written in his extraordinarily neat and noncursive handwriting with wide spaces between the letters. Brian became a notable copyist, not only of the handwriting but of the succinct manner of expression, and he spent long hours developing a very passable imitation of McQuaid's handwriting. One example which survives has the title of Thomas à Kempis's ineffably boring work, the *Imitatio Christi*, a famous medieval work of piety which was recommended reading for every Blackrock boy, copied out several times in its Irish, Latin and English forms, together with McQuaid's favourite dictum that the object of writing was 'to interest, to amuse, to elevate'.

All in all the move to Blackrock had been a liberation for Brian and during his two years there his personality began to develop. At the beginning of his time there, when he and his brothers had been accounted oddities, his contemporaries remarked something formidable and perhaps dangerous in his character which might come to the fore in the event of any kind of interference or aggression, just as the boys of Synge Street had done. Now, in his second year at Blackrock, he achieved a measure of fame, becoming a frequent attender at debates, more especially those conducted in Irish. This was noteworthy in itself for it was not usual for day boys to attend debates or to have anything to do with the College after school hours. When he discovered that the blazers which it was compulsory to wear on formal occasions were not manufactured in Ireland but in Leeds Brian hammered home this fact apropos of any subject that could be made to have a remote connection with it, rather in the manner in which subjects were to be returned to in his 'Cruiskeen Lawn' column in later years.

And he did not stop there. A little later he and a friend Oscar Quigley (who was not a Blackrock boy) made their way up the avenue with a bucket of whitewash to the recreation yard, the most prominent feature of which was a concrete handball alley. Across the wall of this they wrote: 'Don't buy British Blazers' in large letters, an inscription which created a sensation the next day. It was quickly washed off by the College authorities, but, as Ciarán was to remark, it was the first prose sentence in any language that Brian O'Nolan published.

Shortly afterwards though, he and Ciarán and the Kennys cooked up a correspondence in a new weekly, the *Catholic Standard*, on the subject of schoolboys' homework. There were letters from 'Concerned Parent', 'Father of Four', even from supposed teachers who declared that they would prefer not to write under their own names. All these letters were manufactured on the dining-room table in Avoca Terrace, where Brian was later to write so many thousands of words. It was Brian's first foray into the field of the manufactured correspondence which was later to become a speciality of his; and when the *Standard* advertised the exchange of letters on a poster he considered it a great success.

At this time the O'Nolan boys were strongly nationalist, whether through parental influence or otherwise. And since many of the inhabitants of Dún Laoghaire, a sizeable township which adjoins Blackrock, were of the contrary persuasion and strongly west British, the brothers and their friends could indulge in some schoolboy fun at their expense. Dún Laoghaire had been called Kingstown up to the advent of the Free State five years before and some of its residents still chose to refer to it as such. These people would ask for tickets to Kingstown in loud aristocratic voices on the trams. If the King or Queen appeared on newsreels in the cinema they would applaud loudly. They would hang out Union Jacks and red, white and blue bunting for royal birthdays and the like. These the O'Nolan boys and their friends would take down whenever they could. On one occasion they went so far as to remove the large Union Jack which the Dún Laoghaire Royal Yacht Club, a very loyal institution, had hoisted on the flagpole in front of its premises, took it home to Avoca Terrace and burned it in the Kennys' garden.

The Blackrock years seem on the whole to have been happy ones for Brian, though two school photographs show a somewhat withdrawn and aggressive adolescent burning with some intensity or resolve of his own. He was good-looking, with level brows, deepset eyes and a rather small mouth which when he spoke or laughed displayed slightly protruding but small rather rodent-like teeth. He sat the Leaving Certificate Examination in June 1929, obtaining honours in Irish, English, Latin and History with a pass in Physics. This was an honours certificate but it seems to have been obtained without much swotting, or 'stewing' as it was known in Blackrock.

Brian O'Nolan was in fact, for good or ill, a natural exam passer. He had small neat handwriting, a surprisingly orderly mind and the capacity for mastering the essentials of a subject and giving the impression of a deeper familiarity with it than was the case. His honours certificate sufficed for Matriculation at University College, Dublin where Ciarán had preceded him and where it had already been decided that he should go.

Apart from correspondence in the *Catholic Standard*, there is no evidence that he had done any extra-curricular writing while at Blackrock. Although many aspirant writers sought to have pieces included in the school annual, the 1928 volume contains nothing by him. In 1929, however, he had written a little poem which was published in the annual that year. It is called 'Ad Astra'.

> Ah! when the skies at night
>   Are damascened with gold,
> Methinks the endless sight
>   Eternity unrolled.

His mentors at Blackrock were pleased with this and their successors still are because it is supposed to show some religious feeling, even some depth of meaning. Perhaps what it exhibits is a well-known adolescent yearning for the infinite. But the use of the word *damascened* has a certain distinction and the encompassment of the short but still three-stressed last line shows considerable accomplishment.

Although known in Blackrock as Brian O'Nolan he signed this contribution to the annual 'Brian Ua Nualláin', a somewhat pedantic Irish version of his name which he was now to use for a while.

Among those of his classmates who were also going to UCD were Vivion de Valera, the son of Eamon de Valera, Blackrock's most eminent past pupil, who had now formed a political party, Fianna Fáil, out of the defeated Republican movement, led it into the Free State Dáil and was leader of the opposition.

While in Blackrock the three eldest O'Nolan boys had acquired bicycles, and Brian, Richard McManus and a schoolmate, Tom Kenny, had already spent a couple of weeks camping in the wild picturesque Glen of Imaal in County Wicklow. Now they planned a more ambitious expedition. They would cycle to the Irish-speaking district or Gaeltacht of Donegal, taking camping equipment with them. The party consisted of Ciarán, Brian, Joseph and Desmond Kenny, who were their neighbours in Avoca Terrace, and the other Kenny, Tom, who was not related.

The O'Nolans had been making annual trips to the Gaeltacht since 1927 and these had usually been combined with a long stay with their Gormley relations in the house over the shop in Strabane's Main Street. On these visits they were witnessing the last of the life portrayed by Seamus O'Grianna in the Donegal novels that Brian was later to parody in his own novel, *An Béal Bocht*. There were women in red petticoats and even old men wearing trousers and waistcoats as well as jackets made of sheepskin. Once when Ciarán was alone in the kitchen of a house with an old woman, she had taken something out of her skirt pocket and pushed it down the front of his jersey, making signs to indicate that she was giving him a gift of some significance. When he got to the door and was able to retrieve it, he found that it was a small morsel of meat.

One day when out walking they had come upon a small thatched mud cabin in the middle of the bog. It was in such ruinous condition as to appear unfit even for animals, but there was smoke coming from a hole in the thatch. Peering into the smoke-filled darkness at first they could see nothing but heard the voice of an old woman singing five words of a dirge over and over. Frightened, they ran away. Next day however they did see her and the sight was unforgettable. She had only one leg which was bared to the thigh. With no crutch or any other kind of support, she was executing giant hops along the road, a form of progress broken by occasional periods of rest on a bank or in a ditch. 'Cow jumps' was how Ciarán later described these leaps. On enquiry they were told that it was in this manner that she accomplished the two-mile journey to Mass every Sunday. Some people who lived by the roadside told them that they had often seen her pass thus in the snow. In wet or dirty weather when she could not sit down by the roadside she would rest by standing and holding on to a wall or gatepost every 50 yards or so. It appeared that she lived with her brother in the darkness of the little cabin in the middle of the bog and had never possessed or learned to use a crutch.

During their trips to the Gaeltacht the brothers often went to the local dances or céilidhes. Many students and visitors from Dublin attended these but according to Ciarán the O'Nolans preferred to go around with the local girls with whom they could converse in Irish and who were nicer and prettier than the visitors. They could, he said, meet with the visiting girls any old time in Dublin or wherever else they came out of. To Ciarán, everything in the Gaeltacht areas seemed more beautiful than elsewhere, even the very sunlight being more golden.

On this 1929 trip they were unable to go through Strabane because the Kennys, who were interested in shooting, were carrying a .22 rifle and a shotgun on their bicycles and these were licensed only in the Free State. It was raining when they set out and they spent a lot of time sheltering under trees by the roadside, smoking. They all smoked but did not drink, which, as Ciarán sagely remarked later, was just as well for otherwise they would never have got beyond Lucan.

On the second night they reached Belturbet and, finding an empty house on the outskirts of the town, broke into it. The night after, on the advice of a Guard, they pitched their tent in a field beside the River Shannon in County Leitrim but were disturbed by a crowd of people brandishing sticks who threatened them and told them to move on. It seemed they had been mistaken for itinerant members of a religious sect who had visited the locality on bicycles the week before and were also camping out; when the mistake was explained they were allowed to remain where they were.

Their little tent, or bivvy as they called it, was inadequate for five and it seemed to be raining all the time. So the following night, in Clonee, they again broke into an empty house, this time one in the middle of the town, with big trees around it. It was clear that it had not been lived in for a long time. There were thick drifts of dust everywhere, four inches deep in places. The most tolerable room was in front at the top of the stairs and here they all decided to settle down together. Its window, however, was half open and stuck; and at twilight there was an invasion of bats, many of which they killed by chasing them around the room and striking them with whatever was handy. It was the first time that Brian or Ciarán had ever seen bats and they noted the mouselike heads and the extraordinary lightness of the tiny furred bodies.

But when Brian was shaving next morning, he put his razor down for a moment on a board that had a thick layer of dust on it and when he resumed, nicked himself slightly. The result was an infected sore on the lower lip which refused to heal and plagued him throughout his first year in UCD, necessitating frequent visits to specialists and the use of various inefficacious creams. The bats had taken their revenge.

They stayed for three nights in the house before they discovered that the owner lived beside it and had been aware of their presence. He had seen the glimmering of the candles they lit at night but was afraid to make any inspection. Whether his fear was of ghosts or intruders they did not know. After the first night, the bats had sensibly not returned.

When they moved on they sought shelter from the rain wherever they could. One small farmer who welcomed them into his kitchen and gave them a pot of jam to take away with them was extremely proud of his wife's cooking. She could cook for any member of the Dáil, he said, which was not a judgement of the sophistication or discrimination of Dáil members that Brian would have echoed later on.

Ciarán's account of their arrival in the Gaeltacht tells us something of his almost mystical attitude to the Irish language: 'At that time when I would be approaching the Gaeltacht,' he says, 'my heart would rise and I would be looking around me, grinning foolishly and trying to guess was I in the Gaeltacht yet, where the women would be more comely, the men more manly, the houses more beautiful, the apples redder and the countryside nicer than the countryside in any other place.'[9]

2

The Brilliant Beginning

University College Dublin was a constituent College of the still fairly new National University of Ireland, a successor to the Catholic University, which Cardinal Newman had come to Ireland to found, and the Royal, which Joyce and his generation had attended.

It occupied a large, supposedly Greek classical building in Earlsfort Terrace, off St Stephen's Green, as well as the premises of its predecessors in the Green itself. Brian O'Nolan was to describe the impression the Earlsfort Terrace building made on the newcomer more than once, notably in *At Swim-Two-Birds* and in *A Centenary History of the Literary and Historical Society, University College, Dublin*, a book of reminiscences by various hands published in 1957 to which he contributed. In *At Swim-Two-Birds* the premises of the College were described as follows:

> Outwardly a rectangular plain building with a fine porch where the mid-day sun pours down in the summer from the Donnybrook direction, heating the steps for the comfort of the students. The hallway inside is composed of large black and white squares arranged in the orthodox chessboard pattern, and the surrounding walls done in an unpretentious cream wash bear three rough smudges caused by the heels, buttocks and shoulders of the students.

In the *Centenary History* description the sordidity is marginally increased:

> The hall was quite empty. The plain white walls bore three dark parallel smudgy lines at elevations of about three, five and five-and-a-half feet from the tiled chessboard floor. Later I was to know that this triptych had been achieved by the buttocks, shoulders, and hair-oil of lounging students.[1]

Some of his friends were later to describe his arrival as if it was immediately noteworthy – Niall Montgomery, for example, was to say that he descended on UCD 'like a shower of paratroopers'[2] – but this was not quite the case. To begin with at least he kept, like many another first-year student, a low profile, attending lectures and seeing mostly the friends of his last years at school, the high-spirited, knowledgeable Dickie McManus, who lived at the other side of Blackrock Village on Rock Road, and Oscar Quigley who lived in Williamstown. They had now begun to drink and when not meeting in the Quigley or the McManus house, would go to Keegan's Public House which was opposite Blackrock College in Williamstown. It was only very rarely that any of Brian's or Ciarán's friends gathered in the O'Nolan house.

Towards the end of his first year in College, however, Brian began to achieve a certain amount of fame. This was mostly through the figure he cut at meetings of the Literary and Historical Society. These took place at 86 St Stephen's Green, one of a pair of chastely beautiful Georgian mansions which the University had inherited from its Catholic and Royal predecessors. Writing a quarter of a century later in the *Centenary History*, he was to describe the venue and the scene:

> The students' many societies, of which the L. & H. was the principal one and the oldest, held their meetings in a large building at 86 St Stephen's Green. In my day it was a very dirty place and in bad repair . . . If I am not mistaken, lighting was by gas, and it was in this 86, in an upstairs semi-circular lecture theatre that the L. & H. met every Saturday night. It was large as such theatres go but its seating capacity could not exceed two hundred, whereas most meetings attracted not fewer than six hundred people. The congestion, disorder and noise may be imagined. A seething mass gathered and swayed in a very large lobby outside the theatre . . . This most heterogeneous congregation, reeling about, shouting and singing in the hogarthian pallor of a single gas-jet (when somebody had not thought fit to extinguish the same) came to be known as the mob . . . A visitor would probably conclude that it was merely a gang of rowdies, dedicated to making a deafening uproar [as] the *obbligato* to some unfortunate member's attempts to make a speech within. It was certainly a disorderly gang but its disorders were not aimless and stupid, but often necessary and salutary . . .[3]

He had already described the mob and its activities as seen through the eyes of the narrator of *At Swim-Two-Birds* who, unlike O'Nolan himself, takes no part in the proceedings and affects to regard it as an almost meaningless spectacle of disorder:

> Outside the theatre there was a spacious lobby or ante-room and it was here that the rough boys would gather and make their noises. One gas-jet was the means of affording light in the lobby and when a paroxysm of fighting and roaring would be at its height, the light would be extinguished as if by a supernatural or diabolical agency and the effect of the darkness in such circumstances afforded me many moments of physical and spiritual anxiety, for it seemed to me that the majority of the persons present were possessed by unclean spirits. The lighted rectangle of the doorway to the debate-hall was regarded by many persons not only as a receptacle for the foul and discordant speeches which they addressed to it, but also for many objects of a worthless

nature – for example, spent cigarette ends, old shoes, the hats of friends, parcels of damp horse dung, wads of soiled sacking and discarded articles of ladies' clothing not infrequently the worse for wear.

This mob was the particular terror of the politicians and notabilities who were visiting chairmen at meetings of the L. & H.; but it was not unresponsive to wit and even to oratory. By stationing himself near the door of the lecture theatre a dominating and ready speaker could command both assemblies at once, and this Brian O'Nolan now discovered he had the nerve and the talent to do.

Positioned by the door, so that he was dimly visible from within, but making sure that he was seen to be more a part of the mob than of the assembly proper, he would engage in contests of readiness and repartee with speakers, visiting chairmen and the auditor of the society, sometimes embarking on a flight of oratory himself by way of interjection or intervention in debate. He was the first who proved able to fuse the two parts of the proceedings, those of the unruly mass outside and those of the more orderly gathering within. He began by single quick interjections, to which only his more immediate neighbours in the mob paid attention, and then gradually extended his range. Having scored some successes on his first night, and having experienced the heady delight which a successful interjection in debate can bring, he returned on the following Saturday and soon became a talked-of performer at meetings of the L. & H.

He now had a new friend, an engineering student, Jack Nevin, with whom he would repair to the Winter Garden Palace, a public house at the corner of Cuffe Street and St Stephen's Green, to have a few pints before meetings, for there was some dependence on alcohol for the panache and effrontery needed to be a successful leader of the mob. Nevin was an ingenious fellow and he began to apply the talents which later enabled him to design the first refrigeration systems in the palaces of the Saudi Arabian royal family to the control of the lights both inside and outside the assembly. In this way he could plunge one or other or both into darkness at will, often as a backdrop for one of Brian's better interjections, sometimes merely for the devil of it. Nevin was variously referred to as O'Nolan's manager, his technical adviser and his effects man.

Then one Saturday night, towards the middle of his second year in College, O'Nolan went into the theatre and began to speak from the benches, with such success that he continued to do this thereafter. The new departure was not well received by some of his former adherents, and even Ciarán was inclined to think that it was something of a concession to respectability or to authority. Soon, however, a portion of the mob followed him in, while the majority of those outside the door continued to regard him as someone who was speaking on their behalf and who would not put up with the pretentiousness and phoney legalism that frequently reigned within.

The Literary and Historical Society was the only society in UCD with any sort of real tradition. It was to the L. & H. that James Joyce had delivered his famous Ibsenite Address, 'Drama and Life', and it was to the same gathering, of course, that Stephen Hero had somewhat disdainfully consented to impart his aesthetic doctrine in the first version of *A Portrait of the Artist as a Young Man*.

Thirty years later, the society had become much more political. Literature was never debated and history only in the Irish way – as an embittering dimension of politics. In Brian O'Nolan's time, political tensions were especially acute. Although De Valera had led his party into the Dáil, and was already poised to take office, the issues over which the Civil War had been fought and the merits and demerits of the Anglo-Irish Treaty or, as some would have it, sell-out, of 1922 were still inflammable topics.

Whatever his views, O'Nolan did not take part in these wranglings. His stance was already that of the satirical observer who regards the pretensions, hypocrisies and falsehoods of all parties as more worthy of comment than their actual views, and whose shafts are designed to puncture rather than to persuade. He was not a mob orator in the demagogic sense; nor, even if the society in his time had been prepared to listen to it, is it possible to imagine him revealing his philosophy of aesthetics to any of its meetings as James Joyce and his hero had done. He was a licensed satirist and jester whose aim was to deflate and to amuse.

There was nevertheless some social content in his contributions. One of the best remembered was his impromptu speech on the motion 'Sweet are the Uses of Advertisment'. He began by standing in silence while he elaborately searched the pockets of the overcoat he was still wearing. Finally he produced from the breast pocket a crumpled copy of the *Evening Herald*, which he slowly unrolled, opened and searched for the advertisement he wanted. It was for Lux washing powder and its headline read 'I wonder does he see that faded slip?'

At this point he proceeded to deal with the ludicrous aspects of the advertisement with frequent references to the text while the house rocked with laughter. Gradually his line of argument turned until in the end it became a savage onslaught on the deceits of advertisement generally and the cruel manner in which it raised people's expectations. This was the speech for which he won the impromptu medal for oratory in that session.

By now O'Nolan was a well-known figure in College and he was making new friends. Like many who had lived fairly sheltered lives and been the victims of bullying, he wanted to be liked by the tough guys, the 'hard men' or 'hard chaws' as they were known in UCD. Nevin was among these and so were other prominent members of the mob; but most of his new friends were to some degree his intellectual equals and most of them had literary ambitions.

His was an exceptionally talented generation in UCD and it was also the first generation to be educated and to become possible critics of the society they confronted in an independent Ireland. There was much to criticize. Although De Valera's Republican Party still had radical elements and he himself was even characterized as the red menace incarnate by some of his opponents, the politics and public life of the Free State were governed by the values of the peasant and bourgeois elements who had been the principal beneficiaries of the struggle against Britain. In Dublin there was widespread poverty. Quite close to Earlsfort Terrace, around Cuffe Street and York Street, were some of the worst slums in Europe, where whole families still lived in single rooms in crumbling and insanitary Georgian tenements.

After ten years of independence, emigration was still the only recourse of landless people from the poor rural areas. There had been little attempt at industrialization and except for some division of the remaining estates of the ascendancy none at all at establishing any sort of social equality in the new order.

The outlook of the Government was legalistic and fanatically Catholic although it had a certain reverence for the book-keeping virtues of the Protestant business community which had continued to thrive after independence. Its greatest fear, other than the spread of godless, atheistic communism to Ireland, was deficit financing. The Free State scrupulously paid its debts and expected everybody else to pay theirs.

During the struggle for independence which had been in large part a struggle against the Anglo-Irish landlord class for ownership of the land, there had been concealed class divisions. The interests of the farming class, which had benefited most from the various land acts extorted from the British, and now expected to benefit further from independence, were not the same as those of the landless labouring class or those who scratched a living from a few barren and rocky acres in the west. Nor were those of the emergent Catholic bourgeoisie the same as the interests of the many who lived in the poorer streets around the edges of Irish small towns; still less the same as the interests of the Dublin working class who were employed by old-fashioned Protestant or newly prosperous Catholic masters. Throughout O'Nolan's lifetime acquiescence in emigration and the passive or active encouragement of it would be the main weapon against social disorder of those who had done fairly well out of the struggle, as well as being the only recourse of those who had gained nothing. The division between pro- and anti-treaty elements in the Civil War was in part a reflection of these divisions of interest, and for a while the programmes of the political parties had seemed to reflect them too with De Valera's party appearing the more radical.

But although the confusions of Irish politics and the nationalist ethos which was common to all parties disguised this, the real division was between those who had some sort of a stake in independent Ireland and those who had not; and the students of UCD were one and all among the former. The medical and engineering students among them, who expected to emigrate when they had obtained their degrees, knew that they would do so with the important asset of a professional qualification and looked forward to the prospect with some cheerfulness. Lawyers knew that they belonged by profession to the political governing class of the new state. Even the arts students could expect to become teachers – with luck university teachers – or administrators.

Only the intellectuals felt uncomfortable, for it was they who were most irked by the Catholic triumphalism, the pious philistinism, the Puritan morality and the peasant or *petit bourgeois* outlook of the new state. But they were in an ambiguous position, though one which had its compensations, for in the first place they were themselves inheritors of whatever privileges were going, and in the second they found it almost impossible to break with formal Catholicism, either in belief or practice.

The hold of Catholicism in Ireland in those years was partly parental. To disavow the faith, whether in public or in private, was a gesture so extreme that most people who had doubts or reservations suppressed them on the grounds that it would cause their parents too much suffering, might indeed even 'break their hearts'. True, Joyce had managed the business a quarter of a century or so before, but the extreme song and dance he had made of it showed how difficult he found it; and he had, after all, to refuse to kneel at his mother's bedside, to go into exile and to render himself both *déraciné* and *déclassé* to do it.

For the hold was also partly ideological. A break with Catholicism would involve questions of your very identity, racial, social and historical. It would also involve questions of your future and your position in the scheme of things: even your ability to earn a living might be in jeopardy. Social pressures might not always be overt, but they were not to be forgotten.

The result of these two discomforts – being a beneficiary of a nationalist revolution which you had largely come to despise: though however much you despised it, it was also unthinkable that you could regret the passing of British rule; and being a passive or active upholder of a faith which you often found abhorrent either in its beliefs or, at the very least, its public attitudes – was for some of O'Nolan's contemporaries a curious kind of latter-day aestheticism.

You were in an ambiguous, not to say dishonest position, morally, socially and intellectually. You were a conformist among other conformists in terms of the most important social or philosophical questions you could face. But yet you knew about modern art and literature. You had read most of the great moderns and, above all, you had read James Joyce. That was what marked you out as different, the joke you shared against the rabblement of which you were otherwise a part.

Joyce's work had not been banned in Ireland under the newly enacted Censorship of Publications Act when O'Nolan and his friends were in UCD, though the work of many lesser and less outspoken authors quickly was. But the English Customs authorities, who had seized copies of the Shakespeare Press edition of *Ulysses* at Dover, and the pusillanimous Dublin booksellers had done the censors' work for them, and copies of the book were almost impossible to obtain. This increased the snobbery attaching to an acquaintance with *Ulysses* and the feeling of being part of a select circle when eventually you got hold of the book and read it. Donagh MacDonagh, one of O'Nolan's friends, had a copy of an attractive Swiss edition in two volumes, which was passed eagerly from hand to hand until eventually Brian appropriated it. MacDonagh was afterwards to say: 'He stole the first volume and as the second was of no use to me I gave it to him. He never forgave me.'[4]

It is impossible to exaggerate the importance of Joyce in their view of things. Naturally enough, given the time, they were self-conscious modernists; and Joyce was the great, native Irish, Catholic – or, at least, Catholic-minded – modern, not only an Irishman but a Dubliner, the local boy who had made good where it mattered, among the giants of the modern movement. His hero, Stephen Dedalus, had

attended the same educational institutions as they had and received the
same sort of grounding in the Catholic faith. Like them he had gone in
and out of 86 St Stephen's Green every day and discussed literature on
the steps of the National Library in Kildare Street. Like them he had
been burdened by the claims of 'nationality, language, religion', those
nets which in Ireland, he said, were flung over the soul to hold it back
from flight. Like O'Nolan and most of his immediate circle he was a
Dubliner who had attended one of Dublin's better and more sophisticated Catholic schools and who viewed the predominantly rural ethos
of Ireland with suspicion and fear.

The difference was that Stephen had, in fact, flown by those nets.
He had rebelled and escaped; and through transforming himself into
Leopold Bloom he had, as it were, become a member of the human
rather than just the Irish race. They, however, were, in varying degree,
stuck. They walked in and out of the same portals. They confronted
the same pastors and teachers, the same vulgarities, half-truths and
nationalist distortions, rendered even more objectionable by the
victory of nationalism and the Sinn Féin philosophy, such as that
victory was. And again in varying degree, they found it spiritually
impossible or circumstantially undesirable to make the clean break so
epically made by Joyce.

Yet they were an immensely talented generation. Donagh Mac-
Donagh, who had lent or given Brian the precious copy of *Ulysses*,
began as a poet, whose somewhat Audenesque verses fitted admirably
into Faber and Faber's list. A son of the martyred 1916 leader Thomas
MacDonagh, also a poet, he was a law student who, later in life, found
it temptingly easy to claim an inheritance in the new order as a District
Justice. Niall Montgomery was a quick-eyed and quick-witted architectural student who was to play an important role in Brian O'Nolan's
life, not only as a collaborator in some of his journalistic enterprises,
but as a sort of intellectual mentor. His attitude to Joyce was obsessive
but ambiguous. According to another friend, Niall Sheridan, Montgomery's conversation was 'sometimes so elliptical and recondite that
he seemed to be telling jokes to himself'. A wit and the son of a noted
Dublin wit, the Free State's film censor, Jimmy Montgomery, Niall
Montgomery regarded Joyce's works as an intellectual's playground:
esoteric, cabbalistic, logomachic. He left out, in so far as it can be left
out, the human content and the compassionate purpose, and he
encouraged Brian to do the same. He wrote plays and poetry, both
deliberately modernist, neither very widely performed nor published.
However in the Dublin of his heyday, a place which preferred promise
to performance and where it was in some ways a mistake to publish, he

would retain a reputation for brilliance and sustain it by an occasional much talked about essay in such periodicals as the *Texas Quarterly*.

Like Montgomery, the poets Denis Devlin and Brian Coffey, who were somewhat older, were both rather deliberate modernists. Much influenced by French models, Devlin entered the Department of External Affairs and wound up as Irish ambassador to Italy. Coffey, the more considerable poet of the two and the son of the President of the College, was less ambitious socially, being content to teach school for a living. Of all this brilliant circle he was the only one who may fairly be said to have had a wholehearted dedication to his art, but, partly because of the age gap between them, he was less close to Brian than the others. Also less close, and the only one to have a commitment to fundamental social change, was Charles Donnelly, who within a year or two of leaving the College joined the International Brigade and gave his life for the Spanish Republic. The handful of poems he left behind him testify to an extraordinary talent and make him the missing figure of Brian O'Nolan's generation. While at College, Donnelly, who was on bad terms with his family because of his communist beliefs, was sometimes temporarily homeless and his circumstances were reflected in his appearance. One day when he came into the main hall Brian was moved to remark, 'Poets should be dipped every so often, like sheep.'[5]

Other than Niall Montgomery, the friend who was closest to Brian O'Nolan, however, was Niall Sheridan. He too wrote poetry and shortly after leaving UCD published a small collection jointly with Donagh MacDonagh. He shared with the others a consuming interest in Joyce and was even to become acquainted with the master in Paris later on; but his sense of humour was less dependent on literary allusions than Montgomery's and he provided, besides literary converse, that interest in ordinary humanity which one side of Brian O'Nolan's character preferred. Besides being a college intellectual, he was a bit of a 'hard chaw', who was at home in the poker schools or in the bookmakers in the lane beside Hartigan's pub, and he had a streak of humorous realism which appealed to O'Nolan. He was subsequently to become, as 'Birdcatcher' of the *Irish Times*, the winner of the annual *Sporting Life* tipster's award; and he wound up as public relations officer for the television service when television finally arrived in Ireland.

Finding the break which Joyce had made and Joyce's dedication to his art (here Coffey is an exception) beyond them, most of this circle had to find some sort of accommodation with Ireland and its creeds – as well as some sort of a stance in relation to them – while yet retaining and justifying their admiration for Joyce and his ethic of revolt and severance. The result was that literature tended to become an in-joke, a badge of superiority and a freemason's clasp among them rather than something whose impulse would feed back into life. Lacking the sort of final dedication to art that Joyce and the other great masters of the modern movement had given, they yet embraced a sort of 'art for art's sake' doctrine.

True, O'Nolan's position was different from that of some of the others. He did not have a problem in relation to Catholicism inasmuch as he was a believer all his life; and he did not have a problem in relation to nationalism because basically and instinctually as well as by heredity he was a nationalist, at least of sorts. He was not a Francophile or an Anglophile and his elaborate critique of Ireland in later years was based on the rough premise that, with all its shortcomings, it was as good a place as anywhere else: both as Myles na Gopaleen and otherwise he was always very quick to resent insults to his country or implications that other countries were inherently superior.

His conformism was therefore of a less ambiguous nature than that of some of his friends; but, even so, he too had to acknowledge that his path was a different one from Joyce's; and he too had to find a stance in relation to Ireland which would enable him to make a career in it – to some extent even of it. The resulting synthesis was largely Montgomery's solution. Joyce and his challenge would be defused by making him a mere logomachic wordsmith, a great but demented genius who finally went mad in his ivory tower. Admittedly he was a great low-life humorist as well, but he was one whose insensate dedication to something called art would finally unhinge him. On the other hand, Joyce and a view of modernism as a predominantly aesthetic philosophy could still provide a sort of absolution and a sort of charm against infection for those who despised the new Ireland while yet conforming to parental and other expectations within it. It was a circular solution, but it had the advantage of neatness.

About mid-way through their University College careers, O'Nolan and Sheridan paid a visit to Joyce's father. John Joyce was then a partially bed-ridden old man, who lived in digs at 5 Claud Road in the lower-middle-class district of Drumcondra, on the city's inner north side. They found him sitting up in bed in his room and cheerful enough, but he refused to touch any of the half dozen bottles of stout they had brought with them, saying stout was 'a jarvey's drink'.

He said he thought his son Jim had had a great future as a singer and should have pursued that career. 'But,' he added, 'I suppose he has done well enough.' Told that James's new book, which was then being serialized in the Paris magazine *transition*, was an account of the night thoughts of the principal character, he said he hoped they were better than his (meaning the author's) day thoughts.[6] To his sympathetic audience John Joyce then reminisced a little about days gone by, particularly his career as a supporter of Charles Stewart Parnell and his part in unseating the sitting member for a Dublin constituency, Sir Arthur E. Guinness, in the election of 1885. As we shall see, Dublin gossip and rumour subsequently made much of this visit and attributed to Brian and his friends the authorship of an account of a visit to the old man which appeared in the *James Joyce Yearbook* almost twenty years later.

The sort of academic fare on offer in UCD did not lessen the intellectuals' sense of superiority. There were scarcely any tutorials and most of the teaching consisted of lectures to large numbers of apathetic students. In the English Department these lectures were simply readings aloud of the set text by lecturers who seemed unable to add any comment of their own. Modern literature played no part in the curriculum; nor had the new criticism yet arrived to impose any sort of a methodology on teachers of English.

O'Nolan attended English lectures only in his first year. After that his subjects were Irish and German. The Irish lectures he did not find much of an improvement. The Professor of Irish was Douglas Hyde, the revered founder of the Gaelic League, and through it the principal organizer of the attempt to revive the Irish language. This had spread like wildfire through the country when Michael Victor O'Nolan was a young man but was now, like much else, regarded with a considerable degree of cynicism by O'Nolan and his friends.

To Brian's surprise – or so he was later to claim – Hyde spoke Irish 'inaccurately and badly'. Ten years after the great man died (having attained the office of first President of Ireland under De Valera's new constitution of 1937) 'Myles na Gopaleen' wrote an obituary of him which was in part a description of Brian O'Nolan's academic career:

> After some experience of his lectures ... I decided to abstain from his tuition ... but one morning I found myself accidentally present and answered to my name at roll call. He blanched as if struck by lightning and swivelled those extraordinary eyes. 'Ní féidir, ní féidir,' [it is not possible, it is not possible] he groaned. Apparently he had assumed I was a myth.[7]

In his contribution to the *Centenary History of the Literary and Historical Society* he was to speak again of his shock when he found

that Douglas Hyde 'spoke atrocious Irish', as also, he claimed, did
Agnes O'Farrelly, another luminary of the Irish Department. He
added that they both had hearts of gold, presumably on the strength of
their indulgence towards him during the presentation of his Master's
degree.

O'Nolan and his friends now constituted, in Sheridan's words, 'a
sort of intellectual mafia, which strongly influenced the cultural and
social life of the University College, and controlled – through rather
dubious electoral ruses – most of the College clubs and societies
concerned with the arts'.[8] They were all regular contributors to the
alternative student magazine *Comhthrom Féinne* which was published
by the Students Representative Council as a rival to the longer
established and less adventurous *National Student*. The editorship of
this magazine 'usually passed from one member of the group to
another' and in it Brian O'Nolan began to deploy, as Montgomery
was to put it, 'a myriad of pseudonymous personalities in the interests
of pure destruction'.[9]

Sheridan was to claim that when he was editor he asked O'Nolan to
write a series of short fictional pieces describing contemporary Dublin
life, a sort of Dublin *Decameron*. O'Nolan agreed to do this but only
on condition that he be allowed to write them in Old Irish, in which
language he said he would be free from any sort of censorship by the
College authorities since none of them could read it.

No sooner had the first piece been published, however, than
Sheridan was summoned before the President of the College, Dr
Denis Coffey, the father of the poet, to answer a charge of having
published obscene matter in a College magazine which was supported
by the College authorities. Coffey was a noted eccentric who arrived
every morning at the College in one of Dublin's few remaining
horse-drawn cabs.

Sheridan, who had taken advice from some law student acquaintance, pleaded culpable negligence rather than criminal intent, saying
that since he could not read the matter himself, his crime was not a
grave one. He soon discovered that Coffey suffered from the same
inability, having no knowledge of Old Irish either.

> Mutual regret over our cultural shortcomings generated a more con-
> genial atmosphere, and we moved on to general topics including a
> consideration of the ethical and metaphysical aspects of the hippocratic
> oath and a lengthy (if somewhat one-sided) discussion of the icon-
> ography of St Patrick in Scandinavia – topics not frequently canvassed
> among my student cronies.[10]

Seizing the opportunity, Sheridan reminded Dr Coffey that the College Chess Club had had practically to be disbanded because of lack of official support and departed with a grant of £25 towards re-establishing it. Since he and Brian O'Nolan were among the few regular chess players in the College, there was no difficulty about the one being President and the other Treasurer of the reconstituted Chess Club. This meant that they were £25 to the good, a considerable sum of money at that time when reckoned in pints and fags.

It is a good story and it is rather a pity that a search of *Comhthrom Féinne* reveals no such contribution; it may of course have been drawn to Coffey's attention while in proof.

Probably this episode from the supposed *Decameron* was in fact an extract from Brian O'Nolan's very first, finally abandoned novel. This was a work in Irish which he described in a letter to the art critic Ned Sheehy some years later as 'uproariously funny and ... intelligible to anyone with a competent knowledge of Irish, as the Civil Service Commissioners say.'[11] In this letter he admits that the uncompleted book has been lying by him for some time, but claims he is still engaged on it. (This was in 1938 or when his first work in English, *At Swim-Two-Birds*, was in its closing stages.) He goes on to say that 'when published' it 'will be the absolute works as far as the Irish language is concerned – a lengthy document comprising every known & unknown dialect of Irish, including middle-Irish, altirisch, bog-Irish, Bearlachas, civil service Irish, future Irish, my own Irish and every Irish. Accordingly it is labelled "Extractum Ó Bhark i bPrágrais".'

'Work in Progress' was a fashionable term in 1938, and one well-known to O'Nolan and his friends, for it was under that banner that *Finnegans Wake* was appearing in *transition* and Samuel Beckett (whom O'Nolan knew) and others had just published their *Exagmination Round His Factification of Work in Progress*. The letter to Sheehy was an attempt to persuade him to publish some of the Bhark i bPrágrais in *Ireland Today*, of which the art critic was one of the editors. Finally they did publish a very short extract, about a page and a half, which they consigned to a smaller typeface than that used in the rest of the magazine. It is a quirky piece, full of puns and written in a language which owes more to Joyce than it does to Old or Middle Irish and is set in Grogan's public house in Lower Leeson Street, where a group of people are drinking. Although O'Nolan claimed in the letter to Sheehy that 'A copy of the article is – genuinely – deposited in the Arciv fur Celtische Philolojia or whatever it is called in Stockholm' this appears to have been one of his fibs and the only section that survives now is the short bit in *Ireland Today*. The letter to Sheehy is, however, noteworthy as being the only place in which he ever admitted that any work of his had been influenced by James Joyce. 'It is idle to deny its affinity with the work of another eminent Irish author now resident in the French capital.' This admission was made before the publication of *At Swim-Two-Birds* and the widespread application of the Joycean tag to O'Nolan and his works. It is impossible to imagine him making it afterwards.

Brian now began to contribute voluminously to *Comhthrom Féinne*, publishing under a number of pseudonyms. Sheridan's claim that 'he burst on the scene fully equipped as a writer'[12] is not far from the truth, for what is really extraordinary about the UCD writings is how early he found his line. 'Brother Barnabas', the principal pseudonym he deployed, was a proto Myles na Gopaleen. He had the same extraordinary history which had brought him into contact with the great and famous, the same weary prescience, the same amused tolerance of the foibles of human nature and the shortcomings of his Irish audience. Biographies of Brother Barnabas are as oblivious of the laws of time and space as biographies of Sir Myles were to be, and human history, seen through his eyes, is the same sort of surrealist and somewhat pointless romp. He has been a Russian nobleman who escaped across the steppe in a sled pursued by wolves; he has horsewhipped the Kaiser in Vienna in 1912; he has known Bernard Shaw as well as Harry Wharton, Billy Bunter and the boys of the Remove. He has discovered 'and hastily recovered'[13] James Joyce.

But the most remarkable piece in many ways – certainly from the point of view of the literary historian – was written towards the end of O'Nolan's student career. It was headed 'Scenes in a Novel (probably posthumous) by Brother Barnabas' and it told how one night when he had 'swallowed nine stouts and felt vaguely blasphemous', Brother Barnabas created a character called Carruthers McDaid. He 'gave him a good but worn-out mother and an industrious father, and coolly negativing fifty years of eugenics, made him a worthless scoundrel, a betrayer of women and a secret drinker.'

Some writers, Brother Barnabas went on, 'have started with a good and noble hero and traced his weakening, his degradation and his eventual downfall; others have introduced a degenerate villain to be ennobled and uplifted to the tune of twenty-two chapters, usually at the hands of a woman – "She was not beautiful, but a shortened nose, a slightly crooked mouth and eyes that seemed brimful of a simple complexity seemed to spell a curious attraction and an inexplicable charm." In my own case, McDaid, starting off as a rank waster and a rotter, was meant to sink slowly to absolutely the last extremities of human degradation. Nothing, absolutely nothing, was to be too low for him, the wheaten headed hound ...'

One night, 'fortified with a pony of porter and two threepenny cigars' Brother Barnabas retires to his room and addresses himself to Chapter Five. At this point, McDaid, who has been living precariously by selling kittens to foolish old ladies, in other words, existing on the immoral earnings of his cat, is to be required to rob a poor-box in a church. He refuses point blank to do it.

> 'Sorry old chap,' he said, 'but I absolutely can't do it.'
> 'What's this, Mac,' said I, 'getting squeamish in your old age?'
> 'Not squeamish exactly,' he replied, 'but I bar poor-boxes. Dammit, you can't call me squeamish. Think of that bedroom business in Chapter Two, you old dog.'
> 'Not another word,' said I sternly. 'You remember that new shaving brush you bought?'
> 'Yes.'
> 'Very well. You burst the poor-box or it's anthrax in two days.'

It turns out that this supposedly depraved character has undergone a religious conversion. When the author sent him to 'a revivalist prayer meeting purely for the purpose of scoffing and showing the reader the blackness of his soul', he remained to pray; and two days later he is caught sneaking out to Gardiner Street Church at seven in the morning.

Worse still, the other characters had begun to revolt. Shaun Svoolish, the hero, the composition of whose heroics have cost the author 'many a sleepless day', has fallen in love with a slavey in Griffith Avenue, and Shiela, his steady, an exquisite creature who has been produced for the sole purpose of loving him and becoming his wife 'is apparently to be given the air'. The author remonstrates with him.

'What about Shiela, you shameless rotter? I gave her dimples, blue eyes, blond hair and a beautiful soul. The last time she met you, I rigged her out in a blue swagger outfit, brand new. You now throw the whole lot back in my face ...'

But Shaun stands firm.

> 'I may be a prig,' he replied, 'but I know what I like. Why can't I marry Bridie and have a shot at the Civil Service?'
> 'Railway accidents are fortunately rare,' I said finally, 'but when they happen they are horrible. Think it over.'

Gradually all the characters revolt until the book seethes with conspiracy. McDaid gets hold of a paper knife which was given to another character, Father Hennessy, simply to give him something to fiddle with on a parochial call. It strikes Brother Barnabas that posterity is 'taking a hand in the destiny of its ancestors'. We leave him sitting at his window 'thinking, remembering, dreaming'. He considers calling in the Guards, but 'We authors have our foolish pride.' As the piece ends the clear implication is that he is about to be murdered by the characters he has created.[14] The origin of the revolt of the characters in the novel within a novel, *At Swim-Two-Birds*, is clearly here.

By the beginning of the 1930s, when Brian O'Nolan and his friends were contributing to *Comhthrom Féinne* and discussing literature in Grogan's of Lower Leeson Street, the great days of the Irish Literary Revival were over. Neither then nor later did he display much interest in Celtic twilightery. He was positively hostile to Synge and even, it seems, somewhat indifferent to Yeats, who had published a volume called *The Tower*, which included 'Sailing to Byzantium' and 'Meditations in a Time of Civil War', in 1928, the year before O'Nolan entered UCD.

Although his own verse translations from the Irish have great freshness and sensitivity, O'Nolan had what almost amounted to a blind spot for most poetry, but in any case Yeats had been effectively typecast in Dublin as a mixture of the fairy lover, the spiritualist and the pompous 'great man'. Much of this would have got through to O'Nolan and his friends through Jimmy Montgomery, Niall Montgomery's father, a typical Dublin insider who knew all the great figures and all the gossip about them.

But if the poets of the Irish Literary Revival held little interest for him, neither did the school of rather whimsical poetic realists such as Frank O'Connor and Sean O'Faoláin who were looked on as the new movement; still less the sort of dramatists who were now writing kitchen comedies for the Abbey that gave emancipated bourgeois audiences a comfortable feeling of having risen above their peasant origins. His gods and the gods of his friends were the gods of the time, big and little: Eliot, Joyce, Aldous Huxley and Hemingway; as well as odd and perhaps confined enthusiasms such as the Americans Joseph Hergesheimer and James Branch Cabell. According to Sheridan, they also read the 19th-century Russians as well as Proust, Kafka and Kierkegaard, which last three Brian greatly admired, though his admiration did not prevent him from striking an attitude which was to become familiar in later years in speaking of 'layabouts from the slums of Europe poking around in their sickly little psyches'.[15]

But it would be a mistake to imagine the delights of reading, of literary converse and of shared enthusiasm as taking up an inordinate amount of his time. There was a billiard room downstairs beside the men's lavatory in UCD where Brian was often to be found. Here there were four tables, two standard size and two smaller, and visitors were struck by the unusual fact that all the players wore hard black hats pulled down over their eyes, or perhaps pushed back when the player was leaning across the table to make a stroke. The hard hats had originally been the property of the Jesuit students from Clonliffe College who wore them when they walked in decorous pairs across the city to the University. Each clerical student had a wooden locker in the cloakroom beside the billiard room and in these they deposited their hats while they attended lectures and read in the library.

One day a joker put one of those toy bombs which were known as slap bangs in the keyhole of the locker of a Jesuit student. It blew the door open and exposed a hard hat sitting inside on a pile of books, which he appropriated and wore when he went next door to play billiards.

The other students were immediately envious and since slap bangs only cost a couple of pence, a fashion was set. A series of minor explosions took place in the keyholes of the Jesuit students' lockers and soon every regular player had a hard hat of his own. Since the Jesuits did not play billiards, they never knew what had become of their hats.

Besides the billiard room, the amenities for male students included a supposed reading-room, with armchairs and tables on which the morning papers were set out. These were soon disposed of and it was usual to see them lying around on the floor after the first hour or so. Then the room was given over almost entirely to poker schools.

Hardened players, arriving in College in the morning, would go straight to this room where they remained for the rest of the day, hunched over their cards in an atmosphere that was soon thick with smoke. Stakes were high and cheating was common. Ciarán, who sometimes played, once discovered five aces in the pack. The cards were thrown in the air, a fight broke out and, for some reason, a corner of the room was set on fire.

In these unlikely surroundings, chess was also played. Sheridan has described Brian's highly theatrical and intimidating way of playing: 'He would sit glaring at the board, lips drawn back from his rabbit-like teeth, making odd hissing sounds as he drew in his breath in concentration. Suddenly, he would seize a piece and plonk it down in a new position, making every move with an air of delivering the *coup-de-grâce*.' He invented a new opening combination called the Nolan Phalanx and boasted about the victories over the great Russian champion, Alekhine, and others this had brought him – he was still boasting about Alekhine 20 years later. But Sheridan recalled him 'spitting with fury when a red-haired student from the wilds of Co. Cavan unhorsed him with a home-made variation of the Ruy Lopez gambit which he had elaborated during the long nights after Samhain'.[16]

Another amenity of the college was what Brian was to call 'a small restaurant of the tea and buns variety'.[17] This, in his words, 'provided the sole feasible place in the college for the de-segregation of the sexes', since men were naturally not allowed into the women's equivalent of the reading-room, called the 'rest room' and innocent alike of morning papers and of poker schools.

The place to which he and his friends repaired most often, however, was Grogan's public house (now O'Dwyers) at the corner of Leeson Street, a hundred yards or so away from the College entrance. A pint of stout was sevenpence at the time, a pint of plain, or plain porter, a sourer-tasting and less potent liquid, fourpence ha'penny.

He was now earning 30 shillings every Saturday night by scrutinizing those who claimed to be students at the turnstiles of the dog track at Shelbourne Park. Students could claim a special concessionary entrance charge, though a scrutineer was necessary to identify them as such, since in those days they carried no identity cards. By what means he was supposed to tell the real from the pretenders is unclear and the probability is that he let almost everyone in. This job had been fixed for him by George Gormley who had many contacts in the dog and horse-racing world and it made him comparatively prosperous.

One way or another, he and his friends spent a lot of time in Grogan's and he was becoming, even by UCD standards, quite a heavy drinker, although his drinking must have been modified by his having to return for the evening meal, known as tea, at Avoca Terrace, and by the necessity of concealing evidence of it from his parents.

Even by the modest standards of the time, he does not seem to have had much of a sex life. Nor, significantly, did his contemporaries expect him to have, though, as students will, they took note of one another's richness or poverty of experience. 'He was always fizzing so much intellectually that it didn't occur to you to think of it,' says Niall Sheridan.[18]

On a few occasions, he walked home an Arts student, Rosemary

Coyle, after the L. & H. She lived in Haddington Road, by the canal, and they walked there under the trees. On the first night, her mother, for some reason, was waiting at the door. This was an unusual occurrence, but it became a joke between them that her mother was accustomed to keep a sharp eye out for her and that he would put that in *Comhthrom Féinne*. On a few occasions, he took her to the little room under the stairs at 86 St Stephen's Green where courting couples sometimes went after meetings, bringing a few bottles of stout with him. His advances were not over-ardent, but then girls at that time did not expect that any fellow student's would be. As such attractions do, theirs withered away quite naturally. He did retain some affection for Rosemary however; and when she came back to Ireland in the late 1950s, after her marriage to an oil executive had taken her abroad for many years to the Middle East and Japan, he was happy to resume the acquaintance. They met a few times for a drink, in the course of which he would sometimes discuss his literary projects and circumstantial difficulties.

This brief association passed almost unnoticed by O'Nolan's UCD contemporaries, most of whom assumed that his feelings about the opposite sex were a mixture of indifference and hostility. It was an impression that others were to share in the years ahead; but it did not lead to the sort of speculation about his sex life that it might have aroused in the post-Freudian era in another time and place. Ireland was a country where apparent celibacy was not only accepted as a normal state, but was even encouraged as a way of life. The marrying age for males was the highest in Europe, almost certainly in the world. In rural parts, since the Famine, there had been economic reasons for this. Elder sons could not marry until they 'came into the farm'. Younger sons and daughters were destined for the emigrant boat. There was a horror of sub-division of the family holding among small farmers because uncontrolled sub-division had led to the Famine, and to divide the holding would mean that everybody fell below the poverty line. Only one son could marry; and then only when parents decided that they were ready to relinquish control. Unwanted pregnancies were a disaster for everybody.

Aided by English Victorian prudery and perhaps the monkish asceticism inherent in Irish Christian tradition, what began as an economic imperative for smallholders became an ethos for the country as a whole. The church taught that virginity was itself a form of sanctity. Words like 'pure' and 'immaculate' were among the most powerful in its vocabulary. Next to the incarnate Christ, the Blessed Virgin was the most perfect of beings. Thousands of official, clerical celibates thronged the land, living proof that the state was not unnatural and that its difficulties were exaggerated elsewhere. Unofficial celibates were common in all walks of life, among both men and women, and not all of them found it necessary to sublimate the urgings of the libido through drink, though many did; or through prayer, though many did that too.

So common was lifelong celibacy and so little accepted were Freudian theories about the dominance of the sexual impulse that nobody questioned these celibates or looked at them askance. It was not axiomatic in Ireland that those who were apparently uninterested in heterosexual relationships were interested in something else. A lack of interest in the opposite sex could be accounted for by religious zeal, circumstance, natural indifference or a combination of all three; but it was so common that most did not feel it necessary to account for it at all. Most of Brian O'Nolan's friends regarded him as a natural celibate, even a kind of anchorite, fierce and formidable rather than effete or emasculated, the cells of whose hermitage were the pubs, from which women were for the most part debarred.

Besides his own contributions, *Comhthrom Féinne* made various references to Brian of a facetious or gossipy nature. Some of them reflected the aversion to College women which he often expressed. In May 1932, when he was in the final year of his B.A. course, the editors of the magazine wrote, 'Mr Ua Nualláin's opinion of college women, coming under the Amendments (Censorship of Publications) Act and in deference to the already tender feelings of female members of the Pro-fide society, was very reluctantly blue-pencilled but may be seen on application at our office'.[19] Pro-fide was a Catholic action group with which his name was sometimes associated in these gossip columns. Probably the joke is that he had given expression at various times to the antipathy he felt for the ludicrous aspects of its programme. Thus, he is named as director of Pro-fide's newly established information bureau; and, under the heading 'Believe It Or Not', someone wrote: 'Mr B. Ua Nualláin goes for a three-mile walk on Sundays. Pro-fide or Bona-fide?' – the latter a reference to the fact that public houses at a certain distance from the city were entitled to serve drinkers outside the normal licensing hours. These pubs were known as bona-fides because their patrons were deemed to be bona-fide travellers.

The magazine declared on another occasion that it could tell its readers about Brian O'Nolan 'but our censor won't pass it'.[20] Only once does his name appear to be linked with that of a female student. This was in the summer of 1931.

The alluring and coy M-lly W-r
As she swam in the Mull of Cantyre
Remarked to the fishes
I've got all my wishes
It's BRINE OH NO LAND I desire.[21]

The joke was probably the association of the name of a noticeably shy and blushing girl student, Molly Wyer, with a college notoriety of declaredly misogynistic views.

In the summer of 1932, Brian sat his final B.A. examination in the subjects German, English and Irish. He passed with second-class honours, a reasonable enough degree considering his well-established reputation for not doing any work. In his College Notes for 1932, Brother Barnabas had forecast that O'Nolan would gain a first-class honours degree and a travelling studentship in the end-of-year exams: and the legend of idle brilliance which it pleased him to create was furthered at the New Year by a 'Believe It Or Not' item which said 'Mr B. Ó Nualláin is reading for his degree.'[22]

In fact he worked quite hard for the six months or so preceding the examination, frequenting the College library in the evenings, setting himself a minimum of one and a half hours' intensive reading, and even going so far as to write a letter under his own name to the magazine protesting against the closure of the library one evening to allow a dance to be held there.

From the autumn of 1932 onwards, O'Nolan was a graduate student and a senior figure in UCD, famous not only for his L. & H. exploits and his contributions to *Comhthrom Féinne* but also for the short stories in Irish he had begun to contribute to the *Irish Press*, the new daily newspaper of the Fianna Fáil party, and to the *Evening Telegraph*. Like most of his stories, these are anecdotes, with a basic idea rather mechanically worked out; but in a milieu where publication in a daily newspaper would have increased the prestige of a professor, they added greatly to the standing he enjoyed.

And enjoy it he did. Fame in a closed circle such as that provided by UCD can be sweeter and more intense than the more diffused fame the larger world may provide later on; indeed so heady can it be that some people, even those who enjoy a measure of later fame, look back on it with nostalgia; and some lives have been ruined by it.

All the evidence suggests that Brian O'Nolan enjoyed his UCD fame immensely; and the curiously sentimental tone of his contributions to such publications as the *Centenary History of the L. & H.* show clearly that he did look back on it with nostalgia. In the

Centenary History, he was to refer, in a disturbingly uncharacteristic phrase, to 'the magic those years held'.[23] Indeed, UCD had become his world to such an extent that his leaving of it was rather ragged and inconclusive: he was one of those students who are reluctant to leave the scene of their triumphs.

In 1932–33, Brian and his friends were still deeply involved with *Comhthrom Féinne* and it was in January 1933 that he took over the editorship. Not only was he still attending the L. & H. but it was actually in the year 1932/33 that he made the decision to stand for the Auditorship of the Society which somewhat clouded his final exit from College.

His opponent in the election was Vivion de Valera who had been his classmate in Blackrock and whose father's party had won the elections of 1932 five years after its entry into Dáil Éireann. De Valera's candidature was, as might have been expected, frankly political and, in the prevailing atmosphere, the anti-political or apolitical Ó Nualláin had little chance of election. Even his occasionally serious political contributions to debate had always been couched in ironical terms and were never other than humorous.

Thus the true import of a speech in which he guyed and ridiculed the blue-shirts, a fascist organization which seemed to be making great headway at the time, was lost and it was easy for his opponents to characterize him as a mere jester. According to R. N. Cooke, writing in the *Centenary History*,

> Unfortunately his fame as a funny man was such that he was typed. The society expected it from him and he seldom disappointed it, but it meant that his real standing as a first-class serious speaker was never acknowledged and it gave the sun-bursters, of whom we had plenty, an opportunity of running him down as a potential auditor of which they availed to the full during our campaign.
>
> Vivion de Valera on the other hand was in those days the most serious-minded man in Ireland. It is only right to say that he was probably the most fair-minded also. That proved our and Ó Nualláin's undoing. At the last meeting of the year, speaker after speaker poured out the most nauseating tripe adulatory of the national aspirations which Vivion was alleged, vicariously of course, to personify until it seemed that a vote for Ó Nualláin was a nail in the coffin of the Republic. Ó Nualláin was present. He spoke quietly and with restraint in reply to the egregious nonsense of his opponents. But some of his remarks were rather personal to the President's Vicar in College and the four of us drank our Saturday night coffee in the Savoy in solid gloom.[24]

Brian himself came to much the same conclusion:

The session 1932–3 was of some importance, for it was then I decided it was time for myself to become Auditor. My opponent was Vivion de Valera. The Fianna Fáil party was by then firmly established, heaven on earth was at hand, and de Valera gained by this situation. I believed and said publicly that these politicians were unsuitable; so I lost the election.

... The affairs of the L. & H. were cluttered with too many politicisms, objectionable not because politics should have no place in student deliberations, but simply because they bored. Perhaps I am biassed for it was to be my later destiny to sit for many hours everyday in Dáil Éireann, though not as an elected statesman, and the agonies entailed are still too fresh in my memory to be recalled without emotion.[25]

It is not necessary to search out special reasons to account for a distaste for Irish party politics in the decades after independence, more especially on the part of someone who had to sit long hours in the Dáil, but it is possible that O'Nolan may have been confirmed in a lifelong attitude to party bickerings and to those who engaged in them by the result of this election. De Valera won by the fairly hefty margin of 42 votes to 12. When James Joyce contested the same election in 1900, he had lost to a law student, Hugh Kennedy, subsequently a High Court Judge, by 15 votes to 9. (The present writer did rather better than either of them. He lost the same election – also to a law student who would become a Judge – by a margin of one vote and the validity of that was disputed.)

The defeat, however, was not the end of O'Nolan's connection with the society. The novelist Patrick Purcell remembered a 'magnificent satirical oration made during the session 1933 to 1934 in which Ó Nualláin equably ridiculed all those who took part in Irish politics under whatever party name';[26] and according to R. N. Cooke 'it was in this year, after he lost the Auditorship, that some of his best speeches were made'.[27]

Whether or not he had hopes of an academic career, he had now decided to enrol for an M.A., choosing as the subject of his thesis 'Nature in Irish Poetry'. This was arrived at after discussions with the great Douglas Hyde, a man whom Brian now came to know rather better and respect more than he had done as an undergraduate, and also with Agnes O'Farrelly, his thesis adviser. The subject seems, as is often the case, to have been lazily agreed to in accordance with an adviser's suggestion, but it was a surprising choice all the same.

Nature plays some part in his novel *The Third Policeman* and is essential to the pervading wretchedness of *An Béal Bocht*; but the actual observation of it in both books is limited and generalized, as is the language used to describe it. Of course, as the thesis makes clear, the same could be said of Irish poetry, where the descriptions of nature are standardized and Homeric rather than particular and minutely exact as the English tradition demands. His younger brother Kevin, who became a lecturer at UCD and knew the academic ropes, was critical of both his attitude to his thesis and his choice of adviser: 'He was finished with his degree and he wanted to do something and he picked what I think was an easy supervisor, Agnes O'Farrelly who was in charge of poetic studies and that sort of thing, to do the degree under, rather than somebody like Bergin.'[28]

Osborn Bergin was one of the three great authorities on early Irish whom Myles na Gopaleen was to ally together in a rhyme: 'Binchy and Bergin and Best'. There is justice in the criticism, as an ambitious scholar of O'Nolan's abilities would certainly have opted for Bergin. But O'Nolan was not an ambitious scholar; he was an ambitious writer.

According to Kevin, Agnes O'Farrelly was 'an easy-going person':

A really serious man would have been Osborn Bergin. If he wanted to do a degree in Irish studies of some kind, and got him, it would really be a whole-time job to satisfy him. And he picked this thing and was given 'Nature in Irish Poetry'. He really liked it, I think, and got a lot out of doing it, but the actual thesis was a very straightforward sort of thing, you know, cataloguing different poems and all that sort of thing, and talking about them in a critical way.[29]

The thesis consisted merely of an anthology of Irish poems with a somewhat obvious critical commentary. He did no original or textual research, taking everything from printed sources; and both then and later he referred to it as a joke. Castigating Professor Alfred O'Rahilly, who had signed himself M.A. in the course of an attack on Myles na Gopaleen, Myles was to say: 'An M.A., by Gob? I, too, am an M.A. of the same wretched university and can prove documentarily (by producing the preposterous "thesis") that the degree, like the university, is a fake.'[30]

He submitted his thesis in August 1934 and got a considerable shock when the easy-going Agnes O'Farrelly promptly rejected it. His story to his friends was that he was simply going to type it out again on pink paper and re-submit it; and after the event, this is what he claimed to have done, so that the unrevised thesis which he had conned Agnes O'Farrelly into accepting became part of his legend. In fact he did revise it, expanding the essay, though not rendering it any the less pedestrian; and making some alterations in the anthology that went with it. Conned or not, Agnes O'Farrelly accepted the thesis in the following year, 1935, and he was awarded an M.A.

His reference in the *Centenary History of the L. & H.* to Douglas Hyde and Agnes O'Farrelly having 'hearts of gold' suggests that he felt they had been lenient, perhaps because by then he had begun to earn his living, and that he was grateful.

Those who have so far attempted biographical summaries of O'Nolan's career usually assign the early months of 1934 as the date of a foray to Germany which he made about this time and which he himself subsequently elevated into legend. December 1933 to June 1934 are the dates generally put forward. The facts are as follows. In 1943, *Time* magazine published a feature about O'Nolan, who was then writing his 'Cruiskeen Lawn' column in the *Irish Times* under the pseudonym Myles na Gopaleen. It describes his entry into the Civil Service as 'a pale-faced, buck-toothed youngster of 23' and says that he 'had lived until then without noticeable incident, save a visit to Germany in 1933.'

It goes on: 'There he went to study the language, managed to get himself beaten up and bounced out of a beer hall for uncomplimentary references to Adolf Hitler: "They got me all wrong in that pub." He also met and married 18-year-old Clara Ungerland, blonde, violin-playing daughter of a Cologne basketweaver. She died a month later. O'Nolan returned to Eire and never mentions her.'[31]

From the day it was published, O'Nolan's friends regarded this account of his German trip as a joke. None of them had heard of Clara Ungerland before; and they had no doubt at all that he had simply spoofed Stanford Lee Cooper, the *Time* writer responsible for the story. And there is a considerable amount of evidence which casts doubt on the idea of any sort of prolonged stay in Germany; and even more against a sojourn between the dates usually accepted.

First, UCD has no record of his having gained a travelling studentship; and neither has Cologne of his ever having pursued any sort of studies there. He had no money of his own to finance a prolonged stay and certainly none on which he could contemplate marriage.

He had stood for the Auditorship of the L. & H. for the session 1933–34 in May 1933. He failed in his bid but, as R. N. Cooke records in the *Centenary History*, he remained active in the society until the autumn term of 1933 and only faded out gradually during the spring and summer terms of 1934. He made a number of contributions to *Comhthrom Féinne* in the early part of 1934, including the brilliant

'Scenes in a Novel' by Brother Barnabas previously referred to. Anyone with a knowledge of student magazines will know how unlikely it would be that these contributions should be sent from Germany. In August 1934, he and his friends were to found a new magazine called *Blather* which lasted for five issues, beginning in August 1934 and ending in the following January.

These activities virtually rule out the possibility of a prolonged stay; and insofar as the trip made any impression on his family and friends, they are agreed that it was of very short duration, probably two or, at most, three weeks.

He sent a few not very memorable postcards, none of which appears to have survived; and he had little enough to say about his experiences when he returned. He described to his family how he had seen uniformed stormtroopers beating up somebody in a laneway; and he made a few remarks about concerts and plays; but that was all. He did not discuss German attitudes, still less politics. Among his UCD friends, he made no attempt to set up as an expert on contemporary developments, even though in the months between January 1933, when Hitler became Chancellor, and the death of Hindenburg in July 1934 these were making headlines all over the world. However unpolitical or apolitical O'Nolan was, he could not have been oblivious to the ferocity, magnitude and importance of what was happening in Germany, had he stayed there for more than a few weeks. Apart from anything else, a major purge took place in the universities in February 1934, almost one in five teachers being dismissed, classes were frequently disrupted and some academic converts to Nazism went so far as to lecture in uniform.

In 1934, O'Nolan was to write an entry for a compilation called *Twentieth Century Authors*, though he does not seem to have put it in the post. In this, he refers to the supposed studentship, saying that he went to Cologne University to do linguistic research and 'spent many months on the Rhineland and at Bonn, drifting away from the strict pursuit of study.' He adds: 'In later years, I got to know Berlin very well and had a deep interest in the German people'.[32]

'In later years' would seem to refer to a time much later than that of the trip under discussion, even to the post-war era, but neither his friends nor his family have any recollection of trips subsequent to the one under discussion.

And there is another important reason for the belief that O'Nolan's acquaintance with Germany was limited to one expedition in 1933 or 1934 and that it was of very brief duration. Although not by any means the polyglot that he (and more often, Myles na Gopaleen) frequently affected to be, O'Nolan had a better than average ability to master languages. German was one of his B.A. subjects and the degree examination of course involved some knowledge of the language as well as the literature. On top of this, he claimed to have obtained a travelling studentship to do 'linguistic research'. If he had gone for any period of time in 1933 or 1934 and married there, let alone returned thereafter or 'got to know Berlin very well' in later years, his German would surely have been fluent, certainly good enough to read documents and newspapers or to conduct an ordinary conversation.

But his German was quite mediocre. His brother Kevin remembered how he came to him in the 1950s with a business letter which he hoped someone in the German Department at UCD might be found to translate; and if a fluent knowledge of German was among his accomplishments most of his friends remained unaware of the fact. In a note about the sources of his play *Faustus Kelly*, he speaks of having to take it on trust that Goethe's play was a 'masterpiece'. He found *Faust* turgid, he says, when he read it at UCD, but acknowledges that this may have been due to his knowledge of German being very poor. If it had improved afterwards, Myles would certainly have been the first to say so.

All this would be of little importance except that some commentators seem anxious that he should have had an intimate and prolonged acquaintance with Nazi Germany in order to make it seem the more extraordinary that he did not condemn Nazism in his column or elsewhere.

In fact whatever knowledge of the internal workings of Irish politics O'Nolan was to acquire later, none of his writings at this period suggest more than a superficial grasp of any politics at all; but whatever his views or lack of them, it would have been as difficult for Myles na Gopaleen as for any other newspaper correspondent to condemn the political philosophy of any of the belligerents during the war since the Irish censorship forbade such condemnations. But, as we shall see, Myles was against racism or doctrines of ethnic purity in all their forms and even kept a lookout for their local manifestations in the guise of Gaelicism.

As for the attempt to make the mythical Fraulein Ungerland into the equivalent of Wordsworth's Annette Vallon in O'Nolan's life – 'Was the real attraction of Germany something more personal than the poetry of Heine, the philosophy of Kant and the operas of Richard Wagner? ... It is curious that "Clara Ungerland" is said to have played the violin as O'Nolan himself did. Music, of course, would have provided a natural link between the young people'[33] – that can safely be left to Myles na Gopaleen too. In 1960, he was to return to the *Time* article and even to add some romantic details, though whether these were really imparted to Stanford Lee Cooper in 1943 is doubtful. According to his 1960 recollection of the tale he had told Cooper, the couple had been married by the Captain of a Rhineland steamer and his bride had died of 'galloping consumption' within the month. As Myles was to say with double truth: 'I am not the worst at inventing tall and impossible stories, but what I produced on this occasion was a superb heap of twaddle that would deceive nobody of 10 years of age.'[34]

All this is not to say that something of a possibly disturbing nature, whether in the form of a sexual encounter or otherwise, did not happen to Brian O'Nolan during the course of what was probably the only journey outside Ireland he ever made. Niall Sheridan, who was close to him at the time, believes the trip was 'an unhappy experience'[35] and his very silence about it would suggest that this may have been the case, though to express a view about whether it was so in its totality or because of something that happened during it, is only to speculate still further. The trip, in Sheridan's words, has always been 'a bit of a mystery' even to his closest friends.

After the summer vacation of 1934, though still somewhat involved in College affairs, Brian seems to have withdrawn altogether from the L. & H., but there was one further episode connected with it which had its revealing aspects. In the early part of 1935 a writer in *Comhthrom Féinne* attacked the society as a 'barbarian institution' because of the antics of the mob and castigated the then Auditor for his failure to control it. Ó Nualláin came to its defence. Writing in the issue of March 1935 he tendered some advice to participants in debate. 'Do not,' he said, 'address dock labourers on Canon Law, and if you must, speak to them in their own language. Silence them and compel their attention. Having compelled it, hold it. If you once flag, they will swamp you. But grip them at all costs, even at the expense of good speaking or "parlour language".'[36]

There is a mixture of assumptions here and a note of condescension towards both dock labourers and the mob whose jeers and laughter he had won so often that make one feel somewhat uneasy, as does the solemn tone of what follows: 'It is a weak and spineless generation. The normal people are still standing in the unhealthy draught of the doorway. They will preserve the Society by their destructive sanity and by refusing to accept spurious imitations until genuine speakers of substance and guts come along, as they inevitably must. They will continue to castigate pompous incompetents.'

But some cutting replies to this revealed that a new college generation was now in command. Writing in the following issue one undergraduate subjected Ó Nualláin to abuse which was perhaps the more galling in that some of the terms employed may have contained some element of truth. Describing him as 'venomous' and 'in love with publicity' the writer asserted that 'for Mr Ó Nualláin, "might have been" has loomed largely in his College life – larger than his bantam strutting will admit.'[37] But the reply was dignified and human. 'When Mr Fitzpatrick grows up,' it said, 'he will find that "might-have-been" figures too largely in his own little life, as in everybody else's, to be safely employed as a weapon against others.'[38]

The personal nature of this was emphasized by the fact that he signed himself for the first time in his college career 'Brian O Nolan', and as if to show that he felt it was a little late to be engaging in controversy with undergraduates, he added: 'In conclusion let me say that, academically, I have been dead for two years. When a man matriculates, he is born. When he graduates and goes away, he dies. *De mortuis nil nisi bonum.*'

UCD was not Arcadia for Brian O'Nolan. He did not find there what others found among the dreaming spires of other institutions. His experience of the true, the beautiful and even the good while there was limited, outside literature at least. But it gave him a lot just the same: the converse of near-equals, a test of his powers, much laughter and matter for future laughter, a baptism in the squalor of which he would be the exegete.

He claimed afterwards that the place had done nothing for him, academically at least. A news item about UCD in July 1958 drew from Myles na Gopaleen the statement: 'I am myself a graduate of that place and certify that I found the level of "learning and tuition" contemptible and the standards set in examination papers just a joke.'[39]

As late as 1966, Myles was to ask 'What have I to show for five years of my life' and to answer:

I paid no attention whatsoever to books or study and regarded lectures as a joke which, in fact, they were if you discern anything funny in mawkish, obtuse mumblings on subjects any intelligent person could master single-handed in a few months. The exams I found childish and in fact the whole University concept I found to be a sham. The only result my father got for his money was the certainty that his son had

laid faultlessly the foundation of a system of heavy drinking and could
always be relied upon to make a break of at least 25 even with a bad cue. I
sincerely believe that if University education were universally available
and availed of, the country would collapse in one generation.[40]

In the summer of 1934 Brian, his brother Ciarán and Niall Sheridan
became the publishers and editors of a humorous magazine called
Blather. They took an office up two linoleum-covered flights of stairs
in Dame Street, Dublin's principal commercial centre where there
were then many office buildings with poky little back rooms to let,
and appointed as business manager another former UCD student, P. J.
Hogan. The heir, when a student, to two pubs, Hogan went on to have
a chequered career at the Irish Bar. He wound up by naming his
cottage in Castleknock 'Nulla Bona', the phrase used by the Sheriff
when he returned a writ to indicate that the person against whom
judgement had been given had no goods worthy of seizure.

Blather's main principle was outrage and in this it was modelled on
an English contemporary, *Razzle*. Its first editorial declared:

> Blather Is Here
>
> As we advance to make our bow, you will look in vain for signs of
> servility or for any evidence of a slavish desire to please. We are an
> arrogant and a depraved body of men. *Blather* doesn't care. A sardonic
> laugh escapes us as we bow, cruel and cynical hounds that we are. It is a
> terrible laugh, the laugh of lost men. Do you get the smell of porter?

Blather, its editorial said, was a 'publication of the Gutter' which
would achieve 'entirely new levels in everything that is contemptible,
despicable and unspeakable in contemporary journalism.' *Blather* had
'no principles, no honour, no shame'; its objects were 'the fostering of
graft and corruption in public life, the furtherance of cant and
hypocrisy, the encouragement of humbug and hysteria, the glori-
fication of greed and gombeenism'.[41]

Unfortunately the journal did not quite live up to the description.
Blather was in its way more in touch with the politics of the day than
anything the same writers had contributed to *Comhthrom Féinne*. But
although it adverted to public events and public figures it did so in a
rather juvenile way.

The victory of De Valera's Fianna Fáil party in 1932 had been
greeted by its opponents as if it were a victory for extreme left-wing
republicanism. The truth was otherwise, but some coloration was
given to the fears of the *Irish Independent* when the new Government
released Republican prisoners from the various gaols in which they

had been held. These ex-prisoners began to rough up meetings of the Cumann na nGaedheal party, the original defenders of the Free State, now in opposition. When De Valera also dismissed General Eoin O'Duffy, who had been head of the Free State Police Force, O'Duffy formed a para-fascist organization which wore blue shirts, allegedly to protect Cumann na nGaedheal and other anti-Government meetings and secure free speech. The new Police Chief was a Colonel Broy and the Civic Guards consequently became known colloquially as Broy Harriers by analogy with a well-known hunt centred on the township of Bray, the Bray Harriers. The sort of echo these events found in the pages of *Blather* may be judged from the following:

> In regard to politics all our rat-like cunning will be directed towards making Ireland fit for the depraved readers of *Blather* to live in. In the meantime, anything that distortion, misrepresentation and long-distance lying can do to injure and wreck the existing political parties, one and all, *Blather* will do it. Much in the way of corruption has already been done. We have de Valera and the entire Fianna Fáil Cabinet in our pocket; we have O'Duffy in a sack. Michael Hayes lies, figuratively speaking, bound and gagged in our hen-house. Colonel Broy has lent us a Guard to post our letters.[42]

The attitude of *Blather* might be summed up as, 'a plague on all your parties, legal and illegal'. But this anti-political stance was not accompanied by any great bitterness of rejection, or even expressed otherwise than as an impious intention in editorials. The humour in the body of the magazine was imaginative, literary and light-hearted, as the humour in *Comhthrom Féinne* had been, rather than black or savagely satirical, as the editorials seemed to promise. There were radio programmes which guyed the programmes of the newly established Radio Athlone, fake agony columns, competitions and job guides. One of the job guides described the career of the cowboy and asserted that 'cowboys can always get a living punching steers in Ringsend', which might suggest that *At Swim-Two-Birds* was already in some sort of gestation and that Brian Ó Nualláin had already formed the habit of maturing his comic themes a long time in advance.

Blather is also noteworthy in that one of its principal sources of fun is the montage, two or more drawings or photographs being superimposed to make a unity. De Valera's head for example is depicted on the body of an athlete in singlet and shorts as illustration for an item concerning the Blather Sports. The Ó Blather, 'the famous press baron, publicist, playwright, poet, politician and press baron [sic]',[43] a much travelled creation with a wide acquaintance among the great reminiscent of Brother Barnabas and Myles na Gopaleen, figured largely in its pages.

All in all *Blather* was a noteworthy and sometimes a coruscating performance, if somewhat self-centred and lacking in direction. It did not, however, sell and it folded after five issues. Great hopes had been invested in it but they were not well founded, partly because Hogan failed to grasp that a magazine derives its income as much from its advertisements as from its circulation and although there were some attempts to drum them up no advertisement at all appeared in any of the five issues.

In January 1935 Brian O'Nolan made the fateful decision to apply for a post as junior Administrative Officer in the Civil Service. This was the cadet rank, the usual point of entry for those who were expected to go on to higher things. Candidates had to have an honours degree and a knowledge of Irish to school-leaving standard. Further to this they had to sit for a competitive general knowledge examination and an oral Irish test. The advertisement guaranteed that there would be at least three places to be filled and stated that if two or more candidates received the same placing in general knowledge, their mark in oral Irish would determine which of them got the post. The salary was £180 rising by £15 per annum to £400. There was a married scale which started at £40 more and rose to £500. There was also a cost of living bonus which began at £72 for single men and £134 for married. In those days, married women were not eligible and women who married after entry had to leave the service forthwith.

O'Nolan sat for the open exam in February and was called for interview on 1 March. There were several hundred applicants but few of them can have been as well suited by an examination in general knowledge and oral Irish as he was and he landed one of the three places. He was instructed to report for duty in the Department of Local Government at the Custom House on 29 July, on which day he signed the Official Secrets Act and also documents on 'The Use of Influence by Civil Servants' and 'Civil Servants and Politics', which was to cause him trouble later on.

Designed by James Gandon in 1781, the domed and colonnaded Custom House is one of Dublin's finest buildings and is situated virtually in the centre of the city, beside the Liffey, near O'Connell Bridge. It was largely burnt down during an attack on it by the IRA in 1921 when a large part of Ireland's public records were destroyed in the fire; but by the time Brian O'Nolan came to work there, it had been restored very much as before. The civil servants sat in oak-panelled rooms opening off long, seemingly endless, identical corridors.

To begin with, Brian was put in what was called a public office where four or five others also sat. Later he would have a room of his own. He was assigned to that section of the Department which supervised the waterworks and sewerage undertaken by Local Authorities and provided for the financing of these undertakings by way of loans and grants.

He had a stroke of luck to begin with. His immediate superior was John Garvin, who already enjoyed a reputation in the Department as a literary man and an intellectual. After the publication of *Finnegans Wake* he was to set up as a Joycean, publishing an essay under the pseudonym 'Andrew Cass' which made the identification of the character Shem the Penman in that book with Joyce himself and Sean the Post with De Valera. This brought him a reputation in Dublin as somebody who was able to interpret Joyce's obscure work and, better still, could even read it. For many years thereafter he was known to be writing a book on Joyce which was expected to contain equal insights. When this, entitled *James Joyce's Disunited Kingdom*, finally appeared some 30 years after it was first rumoured it proved a curious production, seemingly motivated by hate and largely an attempt to demonstrate that Joyce had inherited a syphilitic condition from his father and that this had accounted for the obscurities and irrationalities of his later work, including *Finnegans Wake*.

Brian O'Nolan seems to have been content to butter up Garvin to begin with, treating him as a fellow literary man and a Joycean authority. Garvin responded by teaching him the Civil Service ropes and treating him firmly but kindly. He was to say later that O'Nolan 'quickly picked up a working knowledge of our administration but it took some time to channel his rich linguistic flow within the bounds of objectivity and exactitude and to make him realize that official letters were not an appropriate medium for expressing his personality.' Garvin was frequently absent on a tribunal of which he was Secretary, but, under his tutelage, Brian soon learned to prepare letters and minute files, leaving them neatly prepared for his superior on his return to the office.

There was an incident early on when he made a note on a file of a conversation which Garvin had with the Parliamentary Secretary to the Minister of Local Government, a certain Dr Ward. This worthy had subsequently to leave politics because of his failure to declare an involvement with a County Monaghan bacon curing factory which the Government had decided to salvage. Like all politicians who have departmental duties, Ward was acutely concerned about the possible effect on his constituents of proposals emanating from his Department and after Garvin had had a conversation with him about one such proposal, O'Nolan wrote on the file 'Shown to Parliamentary Secretary by Mr Garvin in order to ward off repercussions'.[44] Needless to say when Garvin next saw the file he asked him to excise this note. O'Nolan complied.

The position the Civil Service occupied in the public mind and consciousness in Ireland in those days is now somewhat difficult to grasp. In a country where jobs had always been scarce, it offered not only jobs but almost absolute security as well; and it offered them to those without any qualification except a talent for passing examinations. It was widely believed that once 'established' in the Civil Service you were required to do little except wait for promotion and it was known that once there you were virtually unsackable.

Ireland had few institutions of any size. Even in the British days, 'a job under the Government' had been looked on as the solution for most of life's difficulties. Parents of bright offspring, more especially those who could not afford fees and maintenance while they studied for one of the professions, looked to it as a first recourse and offered special prayers that their children might be successful in the entrance examinations. Since all of the administration was centred in Dublin, it represented for many a chance to escape from the bleaknesses and inhibitions of rural and small-town life. A large proportion of the inhabitants of Dublin were thus civil servants and the rural person who had attained a job in the Civil Service and now lorded it over Dubliners was a standard joke in *Dublin Opinion* and other outlets for the humour of the time. Though there were also many Dubliners in the Civil Service, it was a joke or an allegation that Brian O'Nolan himself would deploy constantly in years to come.

Promotion in the upper levels of the Civil Service was by seniority. You could be promoted more rapidly but, given luck, you were promoted in any case; and so the watchword of most civil servants was caution. To the Service generally might be applied the words of the Polish writer Ryszard Kapuscinski in his description of the bureaucracy of the Emperor Haile Selassie:

> Whoever wanted to climb the steps of the Palace had first of all to master the negative knowledge: what was forbidden to him and his subalterns, what was not to be said or written, what should not be done, what should not be overlooked or neglected. Only from such negative knowledge could positive knowledge be born – but that positive knowledge always remained obscure and worrisome, because no matter

how well they knew what 'not' to do, the Emperor's favourites entered only with extreme caution and uncertainty into the area of propositions and postulates.[45]

Those who were attracted into the Service to begin with were very often the sort of people who would be drawn by the almost absolute job security that it offered. Not many were risk-takers or in search of variety and excitement. They found their magic in the words 'permanent and pensionable' and only a minority regarded it as part of their role to do the politicians' thinking for them or to recommend any new radical initiatives or policy departures.

To make matters worse, throughout most of Brian O'Nolan's time in the Civil Service, the Fianna Fáil party, which had come to power in 1932 with a fairly radical and innovative outlook, was becoming more and more hidebound in its attitudes. But respect for politicians was not in any case noticeably strong or prevalent among the intellectuals of the service, whose unease about their own position in the scheme of things tended to be expressed through the shared joke, the shrug, the witticism aimed at the venality and stupidity of their political masters or the pusillanimity of the Service itself rather than through forthright criticism. To be a good civil servant was to accept as inevitable much that one saw through or disapproved of; and it was certainly very different from being the darling of 'the mob' at the L. & H. or the sophisticated young writer among his avant-garde colleagues.

Yet for several years he tried to be a good civil servant and for several years he succeeded. To begin with at least, the love of order and discipline, of clearly set-out and satisfying routines, which are as much a part of youth as anarchy and sloth are, must have helped him, as well, of course, as the simple desire to please. According to regulations, one's first two years were a probationary period. After that, if one had done nothing wrong, one became 'established': practically unremovable, in line for promotion and the ultimate pension. Confidential reports of the recruit's disposition and progress were provided, usually at six-month intervals, although the first was written three months after entry.

In the first report made on him, the knowledge Brian O'Nolan had acquired of the Department's work was stated to be 'very good for a period of three months'. His personality and force of character were described as 'promising and likely to develop quickly'. His judgement was said to be 'good', as were his address and tact. His initiative, accuracy and thoroughness were described as satisfactory; his zeal and official conduct were very good. Of his power of taking responsibility it was said to be 'too soon yet to express a definite opinion', while under the heading 'General Remarks', the compiler of the report stated 'Mr Nolan has shown a real interest in his work and has rendered valuable assistance to the Section since he came.'[46] This report was signed by the Assistant Secretary of the Department of Local Government.

The next, which came six months to the day later, on 29 April 1936, was signed by his immediate superior, John Garvin. This stated that he had acquired 'a good knowledge of the work of my section'; that his personality and force of character were 'good and developing'; and his power of taking responsibility 'progressing'. Under each of the other headings he was awarded a good, very good, or satisfactory rating; and the report concluded by declaring that 'he takes a keen interest in his work and in another year should be able to take enlarged responsibility.'[47]

In the report dated 29 May 1937, which was to be the last before the question of establishment was decided on, Garvin was even more enthusiastic. 'Mr O'Nolan,' he said, 'is an efficient and painstaking officer; displays marked application to his duties and if it were possible to relieve him of some of the routine work could undertake still higher duties.'[48]

O'Nolan's record of attendance during this time bears out what is said about his zeal. In his first year, 1935–36, he was, rather astonishingly, never absent at all, even for a day. In 1936–37 he was absent for eight days but for five of these he provided a medical certificate. It is an attendance record all the more remarkable in view of the fact that his mother worried about his health during this period and on one occasion prevailed on him to see the family doctor. On hearing what this doctor had to say, she asked her husband to make representations to Brian's superiors about his being overworked.

As a senior civil servant and thus part of the network, Michael O'Nolan would have been in a position to do this, but the probability is that the representations were never made. In fact, only one small shadow fell across Brian O'Nolan's honeymoon with the Civil Service.

On 8 February 1937, after he had been a civil servant for just over 18 months, he wrote to the establishment officer:

During my recent absence from the office, I received two letters addressed to B. Nolan. This is not the name under which I entered the Civil Service, nor is it the English transliteration in use by my family. My own name is one of the few subjects upon which I claim to be an authority and notwithstanding any colloquialism countenanced for the sake of convenience in the Office, I would be glad if my own predilection in the matter be accepted in official correspondence in future. I also desire that my name be correctly entered in any future edition of the telephone guide or any similar circular.[49]

There is here, it must be said, a bit of a mystery. He undoubtedly sat the entrance examination to enter the Civil Service as Brian Ó Nualláin with an accented O, though the first document in which he is mentioned afterwards refers to him as 'Mr Nolan'. Many people in Ireland adopted the Irish form of the name with which they had been born in these years, some for good reasons, some for bad; and this practice was commoner among those in Government employ than it was among the population generally, since to be an enthusiastic Gaelgeoir, or lover of the Irish language, was looked on with favour by officialdom and believed to expedite one's chances of promotion.

But for a fellow civil servant to revert to the English form of one's name after one had adopted the Irish form, for whatever reason, would be regarded as an extraordinary liberty and tantamount to an insult. So the assumption is that either as a protest against the habit of transliteration into Irish for unworthy reasons, or out of whim, he used the English form of his name – and the more plebeian Nolan instead of the somewhat aristocratic-sounding O'Nolan at that – at some stage in the process of entering the Service. This assumption is strengthened by the fact that a note made on his file on the day he began his career simply says 'Mr Nolan reported for duty today'; also by the fact that, later on, he would sit an Irish examination as Brian Nolan when everybody else taking the same test gave the Irish form of their names, even those who usually used the English form. It certainly seems that he had up to this point acquiesced in the use of Brian Nolan as a familiar form of description and address in the office.

In any case, on 29 July 1937, exactly two years after the date of entry, the statutory period of probation, he was made an established civil servant as Brian Ó Nualláin. The document confirming his attainment of this status said that he had been 'engaged throughout the above period on writing and correspondence work appropriate to his grade and period of service and he has displayed a consistently progressive attitude for undertaking the full responsibilities of his grade.'

As if such an approving induction were not sufficiently decisive for the fates, it was on this date also that there occurred another event which was to have a profound effect on the course of his life. In the evening, while playing with his youngest daughter in the sitting room of his house in Avoca Terrace, Michael O'Nolan suffered a stroke and died within minutes.

In those days, there were no pensions for the widows of civil servants, no Children's Allowances and no ordinary Widows' Pensions. Apart from his sister Roisín, who had a job as a trainee teacher, Brian O'Nolan was now virtually the sole support of a family of twelve. His bright future was suddenly dark.

Gearóid was three years older than Brian and Ciarán a year older, but neither was earning any money. Gearóid, who had studied engineering at UCD and left without a degree, was currently unemployed. Ciarán was busy writing a novel in Irish. For two years, Brian had been a salaried young bachelor, living at home without expenses and enjoying what was in those days a considerable degree of affluence. He had emerged from UCD trailing clouds of glory and was beginning to be known in literary circles in Dublin. He had bought himself a car; and though his pleasures consisted mostly of drinking sessions with his friends, they were not curtailed by lack of money. Now everything had changed.

As his youngest brother Micheál puts it: 'In the summer of 1937, Brian, at 25, had a good job, plenty of money, he owned a Morris 8, he was a bachelor living at home, he was at the height of his powers and the world was at his feet. All this was to change for him and change dramatically.'[50] It is difficult to say how much grief he actually felt. The death of a father is always traumatic, but Michael O'Nolan had been an extraordinarily reserved man, even for his time and class. In the months before he died, he had shared a bedroom with Ciarán who was then working on his novel in Irish *Oiche i nGleann na nGealt*, but he never asked him what he was doing or why, still less to see the result of his labours.

Although much of his emotional life was centred on the Irish language, he showed no curiosity about any of his sons' writings in that language and of course died without realizing that he had begotten the first great modern prose writer in it. While Brian and Ciarán were engaged with *Blather* it was never mentioned at home, though a complete file of the magazine was found among their father's papers. His extraordinary reserve led Ciarán to write many years later:

> You might think he was free of troubles and the greater cares. But anyone who spends any time in this life understands that nobody is free of that kind of thing even if he has the appearance of it. There would have to be a lot of worry and trouble in the life of anybody who brings up a large family and lives in Ireland from the beginning of the century

until after the Great War. But if it was so, you would not know it from any impression he gave or anything he said.[51]

On the day following his father's death, Brian took some of the younger children on a drive into the foothills of the Dublin mountains. He stopped at one of the wayside pubs with which generations of Dubliners were familiar because of their 'bona fide' status, probably the Lamb Doyle's, brought them out lemonades, and tried to tell them that they would not see their father again, that he had gone to Heaven. Some of them were too young to understand. He seemed unaffected himself as he added that they must be good and do whatever their mother told them. From then on, he seems to have slipped easily enough, with some part of himself, into the role of paterfamilias.

By entering the Civil Service, Brian O'Nolan had at least postponed the dilemma of whether the vocational claims of the writer's calling should be paramount over such things as parental expectations, money to spend and the satisfaction of proving one's capacities in a sphere other than one's art. Now, in accepting responsibility for the family's welfare, he was, consciously or not, divorcing himself from one of the great myths of the 19th and 20th centuries; and one which James Joyce was said to have lived by. This was the perception of the artist as one whose primary concern is to find the mode of life which will best serve his art; even one who may, if he is thoroughgoing enough, acknowledge no duty but to his art.

It is a myth which has destroyed its share of lives, or at least cut them off from ordinary human relationships, as well as causing some of those who attempted to live by it extreme moral suffering. But it could be argued that in his case, he was, in time, destroyed by its opposite, by a too ready acceptance of the necessity of emulating the life pattern of the majority who do not have a special vocation and are not burdened by the claims of art.

In the immediate circumstances, he could not have done otherwise. Nor can the consequences of mere drift and the day-to-day postponement of decision be discounted. But his decision to enter the Civil Service in the first place was a positive one, however influenced by parental expectations, and from it derived the obligation that he now acknowledged. Stephen Dedalus's quest may have been, in words which Brian knew well: 'to find that mode of life or art in which I may express myself as freely as I can and as fully as I can ...'; but until a much later period in Brian O'Nolan's personal history there is no suggestion of a conflict in which the claims of freedom or free expression had to be balanced against other claims. When he did feel anything of the kind, it was too late.

He was now regarded as the head of the household and was the inheritor, amongst other things, of his father's keys. In those days he wore a dark crombie-like overcoat and this became the flag of residence for the younger children. Because Avoca Terrace was a large house and most of the activity was centred on the basement where the kitchen and breakfast-room (which was also, for the most part, the living-room) were, it was possible for Brian to come and go without anybody noticing; but his coat hanging on the hall stand was a sign that he was somewhere in the house. The youngest, Micheál, soon understood that when the coat was there, he could go to the hall stand, open its small drawer and find a bag of sweets that Brian almost always brought home for the children.

When Christmas Eve of that year, 1937, came round, Brian arrived home at about nine o'clock – which in Dublin then was a comparatively early hour for an unattached drinking man to leave the pub on Christmas Eve – with a large suitcase containing presents for everyone. Micheál remembers being given a box of paints.

Still, the fact that he supported everybody, while his two elder brothers brought nothing into the house, did put a strain on their relationship; and it must have galled him that Ciarán (who, throughout their childhood and adolescence, had been supposed to have the literary gift) now sat at home all day writing a detective story in Irish when he himself had been intermittently engaged for the last two years on a book which he must have known was a masterpiece.

The earliest public reference to this novel occurs in a piece which Niall Sheridan wrote for *Comhthrom Féinne* in June 1935. In this article, entitled 'Literary Antecedents', Sheridan told his readers that Brian O'Nolan was 'engaged on a novel so ingeniously constructed that the plot is keeping him well in hand.'[52] The psychological and other adjustments which his new job demanded had of course slowed his rate of progress; but the book, though it was not yet called that, was *At Swim-Two-Birds*.

The two principal devices of *At Swim-Two-Birds* were the juxtaposition of myth with sordid contemporary reality and the novel within a novel. Neither was original to Brian O'Nolan's book. The juxtaposition of fragments of mythology with ruthless evocations of the mean side of modern life had been a trick which many of the great moderns, including of course Joyce, Pound and Eliot, had used, though only Joyce had used it for comic purposes.

The novel within a novel had been used by at least two authors whose books Brian O'Nolan had read. One of these was the now almost forgotten American, James Branch Cabell, whose novels, *Jurgen* and *The Cream of the Jest*, had been passed from hand to hand among O'Nolan's contemporaries at UCD and who was subsequently to be referred to as James Joyce Cabell in 'Cruiskeen Lawn'. As so often happens it is the lesser book of the two which provides the clue.

The Cream of the Jest is about a writer of historical romances named Felix Kennaston, who invents a story set in a mythical place called Poictesme. His narrator is a humble clerk known as Horvendile, who is in love with the heroine Ezarre. At a certain point he tells her how things stand:

> There was once in a land very far away from this land a writer of romances. And once he constructed a romance which, after a hackneyed custom in my country, he pretended to translate from an old manuscript written by an ancient clerk – called Horvendile ... I am that maker of romance. This room, this castle, all the broad rolling acres without, is but a portion of my dream, and these places have no existence save in my fancies.... And it may be that I, too, am only a figment of some greater dream, in just such a case as yours, and that I, too, cannot understand ... How could I judge if I, too, were a puppet?[53]

But this, in fact, is not the cream of the jest. The real joke is that Felix Kennaston, too, is a fictional creation, the principal character in a book by Richard Fentnor Harrowby (a very Brother Barnabas-Myles na Gopaleen sort of name) who is himself merely a character in a book by James Branch Cabell.

As was so often the case in the 1930s, O'Nolan and his friends had been led to Cabell by the fact that *Jurgen* was among the first Penguins. The works of the other author from whom the idea of the novel within a novel derived needed no such introduction then, for Aldous Huxley was one of the most admired, fashionable and supposedly avant-garde authors of the decade, and his works were accordingly represented on the washstand bookshelf of the hero of *At Swim-Two-Birds*: 'The washstand had a ledge on which I had arranged a number of books. Each of these was generally regarded as indispensable to all who aspire to an appreciation of the nature of contemporary literature and my small collection contained works ranging from those of Mr Joyce to those of Mr A. Huxley, the eminent English writer.'

The work of the eminent English writer of which O'Nolan made most use was *Point Counter Point*. In this the narrator reflects on the advantages of having books, or parts of books, within a book:

Put a novelist into a novel. He justifies aesthetic generalizations, which
may be interesting – at least to me. He also justifies experiment.
Specimens of his work may illustrate other possible or impossible ways
of telling a story. And if you have him telling parts of the same story as
you are, you can make a variation on the theme. But why draw the line
at one novelist inside your novel? Why not a second inside his? And a
third inside the novel of the second?[54]

Why not indeed? O'Nolan must have thought when he read this.
One other book which critics have assumed must have influenced the
construction of *At Swim-Two-Birds* is Laurence Sterne's *Tristram
Shandy*. Perhaps it did; there is no evidence dating from that time that
Brian had read it; and though most of his sources got frequent
acknowledgement sooner or later, if only by Myles na Gopaleen,
Sterne is not among them. A quick glance at the opening of *Tristram
Shandy* could have given him the idea of alternative beginnings for a
book, however, since important influences are often lodged quickly
and off-handedly.

Some of the characters in *At Swim-Two-Birds* are modelled on
O'Nolan's acquaintances at the time. Niall Sheridan immediately
recognized himself as Brinsley when he was shown the typescript.
Niall Montgomery later fancied that he recognized himself as Kerri-
gan. Donagh MacDonagh was Donahy, the poet with whom the hero
discussed literature 'in a polished manner, utilizing with frequency
words from the French language, discussing the primacy of America
and Ireland in contemporary letters and commenting on the inferior
work produced by writers of the English nationality.'

Kelly, with whom the hero takes long and fruitless walks through
the streets and roads on the southside of Dublin, was a student called
O'Rourke, while Michael Byrne, at whose house he attends a literary
soirée, was a well-known Dublin eccentric, the painter Cecil French-
Salkeld. Like Byrne, Salkeld spent a great deal of time in his bed,
where he drank a lot of whiskey, in later life retiring to it almost
altogether and arising only on very special occasions such as the day
appointed for the annual cleaning of his murals in Davy Byrne's, a
famous pub off Grafton Street.

As has been said, there would seem to be little basis for the
suggestion that the portrait of the hero's uncle is meant to be in any
way reminiscent of Brian O'Nolan's father. And the hero's circumstances are certainly not O'Nolan's own, as throughout the period of
the book's composition he was living in his parents' house at Avoca
Terrace.

The inspiration of the name 'Trellis' for the author of the first of the books within a book had a curious origin. In the back garden at Avoca Terrace, there was a 12-foot-high trellis, the function of which was to divide the lawn from the vegetable garden. This tended to be blown down in heavy storms and was more than once a source of contention between the three eldest boys and their father. In response to his command that they should set about mending it, they considered the matter in its theoretical aspects and decided there was a better chance of it standing up if it were split into three sections. Needless to say, the trellis when divided had even less chance of remaining erect and finally a workman and his assistant were commissioned to repair it and restore it as before.

This operation left bits of it lying about which Brian decided to manufacture into a writing table. He regarded himself with apparently little enough justification as an expert carpenter but he knew how to use carpenters' tools, of which there was a box kept inside the back door. He wrote the book, using the Underwood portable typewriter which he had by now acquired, on this home-made table in the bedroom he shared with his youngest brother Micheál and called one of its key figures Dermot Trellis.

Everything was grist to his mill during the course of composition and was gleefully turned to good effect. When Sheridan showed him a letter from a Newmarket racing tipster who, like many others of his ilk, conducted his business by post, he found it intact in the next section of typescript he was shown. The same fate awaited a translation of the Latin poet Catullus he had done of which O'Nolan requested a copy. The conspectus of the Arts and Natural Sciences was a real conspectus lent him by Cecil French-Salkeld. As will happen to a writer when creatively inspired, he seemed to be lucky in the things he came across, whereas the luck really lay in having found a form which would include such heterogeneous material and make all the bits and pieces of diverse matter that he included reflect upon one another. The Greek epigraph was suggested by Garvin, to whom the book had been shown in typescript, and was from Euripides' *Hercules Furens*. 'For all things go out and give place to one another.'

By January 1938 the book was sufficiently far advanced to be shown to Niall Sheridan. He suggested shortening it, whereupon O'Nolan said he was sick of it and that Sheridan should undertake the task of shortening himself. The result was the excision of about a fifth, principally passages featuring Finn MacCool, and there is little doubt that the result was an improvement. Someone in Dublin, possibly the novelist Brinsley MacNamara, had already suggested to O'Nolan that he should acquire an agent and recommended C. H. Brooks of A. M.

Heath and Company. The letter O'Nolan now wrote was not untypical of the kind that young authors write in these circumstances.

> About a year ago a friend of mine mentioned your name to me, saying that you would be glad to look at manuscripts with a view to placing them with publishers for enormous sums if you thought they were saleable. I do not know if this is correct but I have just finished a piece of writing and it occurs to me that perhaps you would like to read through it and see what the prospects of selling it are. I haven't sent it to any publisher or agent yet. It is called 'At-Swim-Two-Birds'...[55]

But his description of the book as 'a very queer affair, unbearably queer perhaps' was more original; as was the undoubtedly ironic comment on Irishness. 'For all its many defects, I feel it has the time-honoured ingredients that make the work of writers from this beautiful little island so acceptable.'

At this stage the title was provisional and O'Nolan was already unhappy with it; but A. M. Heath liked the book. They sent it first to Collins and acquired a rejection but then fortunately tried Longman's where Graham Greene, who was already the author of *Brighton Rock* and *England Made Me*, was a reader. Greene's enthusiasm carried the day, A. M. Heath soon reporting to the author that Longman's had said they were excited about his MS and would like to meet him.

By September, the publishers had made certain observations which he was prepared to accept without demur. On the 25th of that month he wrote to A. M. Heath: 'As regards the coarseness I will undertake a decarbonizing process immediately and take steps to elucidate the obscurity of the ending and elsewhere. I hope to send you a corrected copy in about a week.'

On 3 October, he wrote a detailed reply to their suggestions, saying that before he had heard Longman's views he had 'intended to make a lot of far-reaching changes, mainly structural'; but had 'thought better of this, however, because Longman's did not seem to see the necessity for anything drastic'; and also because the 'looseness and obscurities' he would be remedying 'would probably be replaced by others'. The changes he had made were 'slight' but he thought they should 'meet the publishers' suggestions'. He then proceeded to list them:

1 Coarse words and references have been deleted or watered down
   and made innocuous.
2 'Good spirit' (which was originally 'Angel') has been changed to
   'Good Fairy'. I think this change is desirable because 'Fairy'
   corresponds more closely to 'Pooka', removes any suggestion of the
   mock-religious and establishes the thing on a mythological plane.

3 I suggest the deletion of the 'Memoir', p. 327. It seems to me feeble stuff and unnecessary. I do not mind if it remains, however.

4 I have made a suggestion at p. 333, substituting a page or so of more amusing material as an extract from the Conspectus. I do not know whether these extracts at this stage of the book are too long.

5 The Trellis ending ('penultimate') has been extended and clarified to show that the accidental burning of Trellis's M.S. solves a lot of problems and saves the author's life. I think this will go a long way to remove obscurity.

6 I have scrapped the inferior 'Mail from M. Byrne' as the final ending and substituted a passage which typifies, I think, the erudite responsibility of the whole book.

7 I have given a lot of thought to the question of a title and think 'Sweeney in the Trees' quite suitable. Others that occurred to me were 'The Next Market Day' (verse reference); 'Sweet-Scented Manuscript'; 'Truth is an Odd Number'; 'Task-Master's Eye'; 'Through an Angel's Eyelid'; and dozens of others.

If any further minor changes are deemed necessary, I am quite content to leave them to the discretion of yourselves or the publishers. I would be interested to hear whether Longman's consider the above changes adequate.

When is the book likely to appear?[56]

The amenable attitude to his publisher's suggestions and the readiness he displays to anticipate objections are again evidence of how little intention O'Nolan had of modelling his attitudes on those of James Joyce, for the master's intransigence in such matters was well-known in Dublin and had been confirmed for O'Nolan's generation by the publication of Herbert Gorman's biography.

The 'coarsenesses' referred to were in fact rather innocuous. In Brinsley's early dialogue with the narrator concerning the relative advantages of the novel and the play as modes of composition and the autonomy or otherwise of characters in the novel, the childish 'that is all my bum' was substituted for 'that is very interesting but it is all balls'. An examination of the surviving draft of this whole passage, incidentally, suggests that the book was heavily revised now that it was near publication, the revisions showing an immense advance in sophistication of technique, particularly in tone of voice.[57] The narrator's tone of cold and passionless irony, for example, was emphasized; the unrevised passages being by no means free of the sort of over-personal, near-mawkish tone which afflicts such a later work as *The Dalkey Archive*.

Of the excised passages, the 'Mail from M. Byrne' is perhaps not to be regretted:

Brinsley was here and told me about the book, it would be very good if you can bring out the idea that Trellis is neurotic and may be imagining all the queer grotesque stuff and that he is not above going out in the street in his nightshirt. Just suggest it very subtly and leave them all to draw their own conclusions – was Hamlet really mad and so on. It would not do to present him as an ordinary lunatic struggling against creatures of his own imagination, that is too worn out, like 'then he woke up' as an explanation for some otherwise inexplicable situation.

The excision of the memoir of the Pooka's father, the Crack Mac-Phellimey, is more regrettable:

His father, known far and wide as the Crack MacPhellimey, was a hard-working devil-tinker who attended fairs for the purpose of seducing farmers' boys from righteousness by offering them spurious coins of his own manufacture which (by means of a secret chemical process) had the effect of rotting the pocket or mattress which contained them and imparting a contagious dry tetter to the human body – the object of the traffic being to make the afflicted boys utter curses and ungodly maledictions.

The extension of the Trellis ending ('penultimate') was to show that the accidental burning of his manuscript by the maid rendered the rebellious characters non-existent and so saved his life. Certainly it ties things up more neatly. But the dangers of revision of a long work are illustrated by the references to Hamlet and Claudius in the 'conclusion of the book, ultimate'. Without the references in the 'Mail from M. Byrne', Claudius at least is a bit of a mystery, though Hamlet is fairly self-evident.

The mysterious title was a literal translation of the place name Snámh Dá Ean, one of King Sweeney's resting places in the original Sweeney cycle, but the fact that the author did not include a translation of the poem which Sweeney speaks there made it even more mysterious. We may be glad that Longman's preferred it to any of the alternatives he was now suggesting, though later in the same month he was expressing surprise that they did not prefer 'Sweeney in the Trees' and saying that he liked *At Swim-Two-Birds* less and less. In a further letter, he declares that he has no objection to it being retained 'although I do not fancy it much except as a title for a slim book of poems.'[58]

It was in this letter of 10 November also that he suggested the use of a pen-name. 'I have been thinking over the question of a pen-name and would suggest Flann O'Brien. I think this invention has the advantage that it contains an unusual name and one that is quite ordinary. "Flann" is an old Irish name now rarely heard.' Later he decided that he would prefer the more dour and less colourful 'John Hackett', perhaps because he had already used 'Flann O'Brien' as a *nom de guerre* in letters to the *Irish Times* attacking Sean O'Faoláin and Frank O'Connor and had fears that the Irish literary establishment might be prejudiced against the book because of it.

In fact the name Flann O'Brien was in itself a small masterstroke. It was unmistakeably and even rather poetically Irish and in being reminiscent of such well-known existing pseudonyms as Frank O'Connor, it practically made him a member of a school or movement straight away. All this increased the originality and shock-effect of the book, once opened.

He informed Longman's in response to a query that his 'full name' was Brian O'Nolan and that his nationality was 'Irish' or a 'citizen of Eire'. 'I think I should be described as "Irish" with anything it may imply. I understand the word is commonly used in such circumstances.'[59] His real name appeared inadvertently on the jacket, on the back of which Longman's quoted a perhaps rewritten version of Graham Greene's original reader's report which referred to him as O'Nolan.

Declaring that he had read the book with 'continual excitement, amusement and the kind of glee one experiences when people smash china on the stage', Greene went on to say that it was

> ... in the line of *Tristram Shandy* and *Ulysses*: its amazing spirits do not disguise the seriousness of the attempt to present, simultaneously as it were, all the literary traditions of Ireland – the Celtic legend (in the stories of Finn), the popular adventure novels (of a Mr Tracey), the nightmare element as you get it in Joyce, the ardent poetry of Bardic Ireland and the working-class people poetry of the absurd Harry [sic] Casey. On all these the author imposes the unity of his own humorous vigour, and the technique he employs is as efficient as it is original.[60]

Greene then went on to deliver what is surely still the best of all the dozens of summaries of the plot or structure of the book attempted since. 'We have had books inside books before but O'Nolan takes Pirandello and Gide a long way further. The screw is turned until you have (a) a book about a man called Trellis who is (b) writing a book about certain characters who (c) are turning the tables on Trellis by writing about him.' And he concluded by identifying what one could now see as the post-modern element in the novel. 'It is a wild, fantastic, magnificently comic notion, but looking back afterwards one realizes that by no other method could the realistic, the legendary, the novelette have been worked in together.'

John Garvin was not shown the novel until it had been safely
accepted by Longman's and in handing it over O'Nolan employed the
style of communication used on official memoranda, saying that he
was submitting it for such general and particular observations as Mr
Garvin might wish to offer and for the favour of a Greek quotation to
use as an epigraph. Mr Garvin was also asked to consider the title '*At
Swim-Two-Birds* and to suggest any alternative that might occur to
him.'

According to his own account, he read it that night at a sitting.
'Next day,' Garvin goes on, 'Brian came into my office, took note of
his offspring at my elbow, and awaited my verdict with an affectation
of the diffidence which he showed in submitting official papers.' The
rather dry response was praise for 'his achievement in artistically syn-
thesizing such a variety of themes and styles'. Garvin went on to say
that 'the title would puzzle the non-Irish reader but it seemed adequately explained in the body of the volume as a translation of Snámh
Dá Ean, the historic ford on the Shannon at Cluain Mhic Nóis.'[61]
Garvin was concerned that the work should be as explicit as possible
and it is to him that we owe the re-writing of the passage which makes
it clear that the characters in Trellis's book are annihilated when the
servant-maid burns the MS that sustains their existence.

The book appeared on 13 March 1939. After work, on the evening
of publication, O'Nolan and Garvin, who was not totally enthusiastic
about the mixture of styles in the book but was proud of his junior and
no doubt glad to be with him on such an occasion, went to the Palace
Bar in Fleet Street, near the *Irish Times* offices, to celebrate. It was a
significant choice of pub.

The Palace was the haunt of *Irish Times* journalists, of the literary
establishment and those senior members of the Administration who
liked to rub shoulders with them. Here they discussed, according to
the poet Patrick Kavanagh, such significant matters as George
Moore's use of the semi-colon and what English journals paid for
book reviews. Brian was casually carrying a copy of the new novel in
its boldly-printed non-pictorial green dust-jacket which was passed
from hand to hand. Garvin has left a characteristically unhumorous
account of the occasion which yet manages to convey some of the stuf-
finess and pedanticism of the circle as well as the intersection of literature and other things.

> Brian's literary triumph was duly celebrated. He and I left the office
> together and in the Palace Bar we joined Bertie Smyllie and Alec
> Newman of the *Irish Times*. From a neighbouring table Austin Clarke
> said that O'Nolan 'had fallen in with tradition' and quoted the 'saint-

bell of saints with sainty saints'. I murmured that Clarke himself would make a nice twin for Sweeney in the Trees. Pussy O'Mahoney came out of the snug that was there then in the back room and joined us. I asked him what would he have and he said nothing, that he carried his drink around with him, proceeding to take a glass of whiskey out of his waistcoat pocket. 'Anything,' he said, 'to escape that ranter O'Riordan, ex-D.I., RIC, out of Battersby's in the snug in there, boasting of all the IRA men he saved from the Black and Tans'. Alec McCabe, from somewhere behind me, said that O'Riordan was a bloody liar, 'and you know it, John.' Then Smyllie reverted to what was apparently his previous theme – the Rape of Czechoslovakia and the lunatic exultation on the power-crazed Führer's face as he gazed from an eminence upon the beauties of Prague. I noticed that Brian had grown silent, withdrawn into himself behind a toothy grimace, his melancholy eyes contemplating the vacuum of his glass abhorrently. He perked up a bit when I ordered a fresh round of drinks and more so when Alec Newman, who was a Trinity Scholar in Classics, enquired where he got the Greek quotation facing the alleged Chapter 1 . . .[62]

There is a strong element of predictability about the behaviour of all the characters in this account, for Austin Clarke, who was chief poetry reviewer for the *Irish Times*, was himself something of an authority on early Irish poetry; Pussy O'Mahoney, who was advertising manager for the *Irish Times*, was a well-known wit and prankster; Alec McCabe had been 'out' in the War of Independence and was a member of the first Dáil; Smyllie, Editor of the *Irish Times*, was especially interested in the Balkans and Central Europe; while the writer falls into melancholy silence when deprived of drink and notice. Perhaps what emerges as the strongest trait in the character of the author of the account, however, is a not un-endearing vanity.

The first review to appear was in *The Times Literary Supplement* which, rather surprisingly, carried a notice within the week of publication. The reviewer was a little bewildered and unable to make out who was writing about whom at certain points of the book but the notice was certainly not unfavourable.

It is all as clever as paint and by no means without interest, more particularly for the reader with an inside knowledge of Irish literary controversies at the present time . . . Altogether this is something of a 'tour de force', in which the only exceptional thing is a schoolboy brand of mild vulgarity. Whether Mr O'Brien has achieved what he set out to achieve it is difficult to say. At the beginning, his preoccupation seems to have been with the proper material and method of the modern novel, and possibly this stayed with him as he proceeded to write. At any rate, having all but exhausted, with the exercise of much ingenuity, the subject of Irish content and Irish style, will he not now sit down and try his hand at writing an Irish novel?[63]

Whatever hopes of a critical success were raised by this began to be disappointed on the Sunday following. The *Observer*'s novel reviewer was Frank Swinnerton, a latter-day disciple of the great Edwardians and certainly not enthusiastic about either modernism or experimentalism. He began, as many reviewers will, by reviewing the matter on the back of the dust-jacket. 'I see that *At Swim-Two-Birds* has been compared to *Tristram Shandy* and *Ulysses*. It is not equal to either.'[64]

He then delivered his own opinion. 'It reads as if it were the work of an Irish undergraduate, familiar, indeed, with both books and others of recent appearance, but uncertain of anything except his own humour and his wish to produce a work of fiction.' And he ended equally severely: 'Mr O'Brien has plenty of words, and writes with an immense sense of sportiveness. I did not notice, however, that he had a single original idea to express: and I should reluctantly put him among the bores.'

A few days later, a friend posted Brian an envelope from Greystones, a holiday resort near Dublin, containing a tin nameplate from one of the railway slot machines on which was punched 'F. Swinnerton'.

There was little improvement in the reviews that followed until Anthony West wrote a brief notice in the *New Statesman* in June. True, he called the book a 'self-conscious work heavily under the influence of Joyce' and said, 'Long passages in imitation of Joycean parody of early Irish epic are devastatingly dull, passages slavishly following Joyce's love of snot-green squalor are worse still.' But he went on to say that the whole thing was very funny, very good reading, and inspired nonsense which 'makes one laugh a great deal'. He was also percipient enough to notice that the work was intended as a comment on the novel form.[65]

Sean O'Faoláin reviewed the book in the journal which had been part of Brian's literary education, *John O'London's Weekly*. He identified 'Flann O'Brien' as a pseudonym and spotted the name O'Nolan on the jacket. Although he had, as we shall see, some reason to feel aggrieved, the review was not ungenerous, but on balance he tended to see the book as a display of youthful brilliance and high spirits which would lead to better things. And he too invoked Joyce. There was, he said, 'a general odour of spilt Joyce all over it.'

Whatever the reviews were like, there were consolations. In May, Niall Sheridan got married. He was spending his honeymoon in Paris and Brian saw him off at Dún Laoghaire. At the foot of the gangway, he shyly handed Sheridan a copy of the book which he had apparently concealed somewhere during the wedding ceremony and breakfast, and asked him to deliver it to James Joyce, with whom Sheridan, who had spent a year in Paris, was already acquainted, having been cordially received because Joyce had known his father at the Old Royal University. On the boat, Sheridan opened the book. The inscription on the flyleaf read:

> To James Joyce from the author,
> Brian O'Nolan with plenty of
> What's on page 305.

On page 305, the phrase 'diffidence of the author' was underlined.

At this point, Joyce had just moved into the flat at 34 rue des Vignes, on the wooden floor of which lay a woven rug given him by an admirer and illustrating the course of the river Liffey from its rising to the sea. On one wall hung the portrait of his father by the Irish painter, Patrick Tuohy. And on a coffee table was a copy of *Finnegans Wake*, which had just come out. The war, and his departure from Paris for ever, was just four months away.

When Sheridan called Joyce told him that Samuel Beckett had already praised *At Swim-Two-Birds* very highly and that he looked forward to reading it. Shortly afterwards, Brian informed Longman's that a friend of his had recently brought a copy of *At Swim-Two-Birds* to Joyce in Paris and that Joyce had already read it.

> Being now nearly blind, he said it took him a week with the magnifying glass and that he had not read a book of any kind for five years, so this may be taken to be a compliment from the Führer. He was delighted with it – although he complained that I did not give the reader much of a chance, *Finnegan's* [sic] *Wake* in his hand as he spoke – and had promised to push it quietly in his own international Paris sphere. In this connexion [sic] he wants a copy sent to Maurice Denhoff, who writes in *Mercure de France*. Denhoff's address is rue de Suresnes, Paris VIII. I wonder would you be good enough to have a copy sent to him. If a review copy is not possible, please debit me with the cost of it. Joyce was very particular that there should be no question of reproducing his unsolicited testimonial for publicity purposes anywhere and got an undertaking to this effect.[66]

Over the years, Sheridan was to vary a little his account of Joyce's reception of the book. In a letter to the publishers, MacGibbon and Kee, when they re-issued it in 1960, he said he was 'amazed to find' that Joyce had 'already read, and greatly enjoyed, *At Swim-Two-Birds*.' Joyce, he continued, 'took very little interest in contemporary writing,' but his verdict on Flann O'Brien's book was emphatic and brief. 'That's a real writer, with a true comic spirit. A really funny book.'[67] It would seem, though, that this comment was made on a subsequent occasion, after Joyce had begun to read the book, the last novel he ever read.

Certainly, Joyce was to go to some trouble to promote *At Swim-Two-Birds*. He did speak to Denhoff, suggesting he might like to review the book in the *Mercure de France*, although Denhoff's sudden death rendered this effort unavailing; and he tried to have it reviewed elsewhere. Only nine months before his death, he wrote to Sheridan again from Vichy, describing his continued efforts on its behalf.

At that time, the only Irish literary prize was one called the AE Memorial Fund, named after the poet George William Russell (AE), which was administered by the Bank of Ireland and awarded on the recommendation of anonymous assessors every five years. In 1939, the Bank took the unusual step of announcing that although the prize of £150 was to be given to the poet Patrick Kavanagh for his collection *Ploughman and Other Poems*, published in Macmillan's Shilling Poets Series in 1936, a special prize of £30 would be given to Flann O'Brien for *At Swim-Two-Birds*. Both recipients had mixed feelings about this procedure.

Besides that of James Joyce, O'Nolan also tried to elicit the interest of a best-selling popular novelist of the day, Ethel Mannin. This attempt reveals a curious dichotomy in his outlook and a confusion of values which was to be lifelong and to do him, it must be said, a not inconsiderable amount of damage. *At Swim-Two-Birds* was, in the parlance of the time, a high-brow book; but Ethel Mannin was an expert sentimental and popular author who was probably a judge of public acceptability but little else. Writing on 10 July, O'Nolan informed her that a friend had mentioned that she might read a book he had written and he had asked his publishers to send her a copy.

'It is a bellylaugh or a high-class literary pretentious slush depending on how you look at it,' he wrote. 'Some people say it is harder on the head than the worst whiskey, so do not hesitate to burn the book if you think that's the right thing to do.'[68]

Miss Mannin's response was a postcard on which she managed to lecture him about wilful obscurities, vulgarities and the pernicious influence of James Joyce; but instead of cutting his losses, he wrote to her again at length to defend himself. He began facetiously:

> As a genius, I do not expect to be readily understood but you may be surprised to know that my book is a definite milestone in literature, completely revolutionizes the English novel and puts the shallow pedestrian English writers in their place. Of course I know you are prejudiced against me on account of the IRA bombings.

But as he went on it became apparent that he was disappointed and even hurt by her expressions of dislike.

> To be serious I can't quite understand your attitude to stuff like this. It is not a pale-faced sincere attempt to hold the mirror up and had nothing in the world to do with James Joyce. It is supposed to be a lot of belching, thumb-nosing and belly-laughing and I honestly believe that it is funny in parts. It is also by way of being a sneer at all the slush which has been unloaded from this country on the credulous English although they, it is true, manufacture enough of their own odious slush to make the import unnecessary. I don't think your dictum about 'making your meaning clear' would be upheld in any court of law. You'll look a long time for clear meaning in the Marx Brothers or even Karl Marx ... The fantastic title (which has brought a lot of fatuous enquiries from bird-fanciers) is explained on page 95 and is largely the idea of my staid old-world publishers. My own title was 'Sweeney in the Trees'. Search me for the explanation of this wilful obscurity.[69]

The letter reveals a deeper disappointment than he should have felt. All his life he was to cherish a naive belief that his works would prove immediately successful, would sell in large quantities and would even perhaps make him a great deal of money; that he would become, like Ethel Mannin and even Margaret Mitchell, a rich, popular author. While this was not an ignoble belief, it was a silly one. It reveals the provincial who cohabited uneasily with the sophisticate in him; and it undoubtedly caused him pain and disappointment. What precisely he hoped to gain in the way of critical notice or sales by soliciting the approval of Miss Mannin is not clear. Probably he had some hazy notion that being a best-selling writer herself, she might help him in some way to attain the same status.

By the time *At Swim-Two-Birds* was published, its author's rank in the Civil Service had changed, as had the nature of his duties. To improve his economic position and to enable him better to support his family after his father's death, Garvin had, in 1937, recommended Brian for the vacant post of Private Secretary to the Minister, an appointment he took up in September 1937. This meant an increase in salary of £50 per annum as well as a bonus to compensate for the irregular hours and the added responsibility. He was to be Private Secretary to three successive Ministers for Health and Local Government and that he was to be found acceptable by all three proves what a clever and adaptable civil servant he was at this stage of his career. The Private Secretary's job is the 'hot seat' in every Department and it is one of the few jobs in the Civil Service which put a premium on tact, flexibility and flair as well as ordinary administrative skills.

The Private Secretary sits, literally, outside the Minister's door. He may be asked to handle the most delicate business for him, to be both watchdog and nursemaid, both bruiser and diplomat. He decides who can see his master without an appointment and may have to exercise a good deal of political judgement to do so. To a large extent the smoothness or otherwise of the Minister's relationship with his own civil servants depends on the tact and good sense with which his Private Secretary passes on messages and commands; and he must also be at home in the Civil Service ambience and keep in amicable touch with the Private Secretaries of other Ministers to avoid collisions and inter-Departmental rows.

The Private Secretary usually learns a great deal about his Minister's temperament, tastes and habits as well as about his real abilities and fitness for his job. He is witness to many a mistake, disaster and attempt to cover up, and an unremitting confidentiality about such things is expected and required of him. Something about Brian O'Nolan's own temperament is revealed by the fact that, even in later years, when he castigated his former political masters almost daily in his column, he told no stories and revealed no secrets. He was to make many a cutting remark about politicians but they were almost always couched in general terms or took as their text a publicly expressed attitude. Yet he must have seen and heard much that would bear retelling.

Even in comparatively peaceful political times, the Private Secretary's job is a taxing one and is often followed by a transfer to more peaceful havens, a fact which makes Brian O'Nolan's division of energies, including literary energies, in those years all the more remarkable.

The first Minister to whom he was appointed Private Secretary was Sean T. O'Kelly, a veteran of the political struggle for independence who had a long and successful career as one of the most prominent members of the Fianna Fáil hierarchy, second in importance only to De Valera himself and a formidable political strategist in his own right. O'Kelly was, like Brian O'Nolan, small in stature and looked like the popular idea of a leprechaun with spectacles hung on the bridge of his nose. He was a Dubliner and reckoned to be a somewhat untutored man of the people by the legal luminaries and academic wits of the Fine Gael opposition. They had found the sight of Sean T. in a frock coat especially amusing when Fianna Fáil, on assuming office, decided that, for all their revolutionary background, they should wear formal garb on formal occasions. It did not seem to occur to them that O'Kelly's common touch was partly a way of political life.

He was, however, fond of a drop, and this failing grew on him over the years. In 1944, when he succeeded Brian O'Nolan's old mentor, Douglas Hyde, in the Presidency, the largely symbolic office which had been established to provide a Head of State under De Valera's constitution of 1937, he maintained as part of his personal suite an ex-serviceman whose job it was to 'gown the President'. Gowning the President consisted principally of ensuring that there was a naggin of whiskey in the tail pocket of the President's morning coat if the function he was attending was a daytime one; or in the breast pocket of his evening dress if it was a night-time affair. As he was helped on with the requisite garment, the President would enquire: 'Am I all right now, Arthur?' To which, if all was well, Arthur would reply, 'You're all right now, sir. You're game ball now.'

In 1937, when Brian O'Nolan became his Private Secretary, Sean T. O'Kelly was still at the height of his political powers, but he was occasionally a little the worse for wear and made full use of his subordinate's diplomatic skills.

In the letter in which he told Longman's of Joyce's interest in *At Swim-Two-Birds* Brian wrote:

> I have not yet done anything about another novel beyond turning over some ideas in my head. My difficulty is to find time to get down to work of this kind. My bread and butter occupation keeps me busy until very late in the evenings at this time of the year and I do not expect to be able to start anything until rather late in the Summer and cannot see it finished until perhaps November or so. I should like to hear from you as to whether whatever is forthcoming should come quickly from the point of view of continuity in whatever fragment I have of the public mind or whether a longish interval is unobjectionable.
>
> Briefly, the story I have in mind opens as a very orthodox murder mystery in a rural district. The perplexed parties have recourse to the local barrack which, however, contains some very extraordinary police-men who do not confine their investigations or activities to this world or to any known planes or dimensions. Their most casual remarks create a thousand other mysteries but there will be no question of the difficulty or 'fireworks' of the last book. The whole point of my plan will be the perfectly logical and matter-of-fact treatment of the most brain-staggering imponderables of the policemen. I should like to do this rather carefully and spend some time on it...[70]

This novel was *The Third Policeman*. That summer, the summer of gathering war clouds and the publication of *At Swim-Two-Birds*, was enlivened for O'Nolan and his friends by a visit to Dublin from the American writer William Saroyan, whom they more or less took into their charge and made their property during his stay. Saroyan was the author of *The Daring Young Man on the Flying Trapeze*, which they all knew from the recently published Penguin edition; and he was then at the height of the rather brief reputation – as far as fiction at least was concerned; he had a more prolonged one as a playwright – which that book had established.

The Daring Young Man on the Flying Trapeze is still a remarkable work and one of the remarkable things about it is that it is, like *At Swim-Two-Birds*, an attack on the art and even on the very idea of prose fictions. Again and again in that book, Saroyan proclaims that he is not writing a story; that he does not believe in stories, that stories are falsities; and that he is merely trying to be truthful about something he has experienced. To some temperaments, the book could well have a destructive effect on the idea that it is either possible or desirable to construct prose fictions which honestly reflect experience.

But it would seem that what most impressed O'Nolan and his friends about Saroyan was that he was a successful author, that he talked money, even big money, and that he opened up a world of commercial possibility to them which would otherwise have been only a distant rumour. He brought out, in fact, that part of Brian O'Nolan's temperament which affected to believe or, more accurately, preferred to believe in the possibility of making money by writing. But he was also a very charming, free-wheeling, amusing and pleasant fellow to be with, happy to drink and talk and, as he put it, 'play the ponies' with Sheridan; and he took to Dublin and especially the parts of it they showed him immediately.

In June, Saroyan returned to the United States. He had suggested that Brian might make use of the services of his agent, Harold Matson, to find an American publisher for *At Swim-Two-Birds*; and in July, O'Nolan wrote to say that he had sent Matson the book.

> I took the precaution to ask my London agents (Heaths) what they thought of the idea and they said it was good ... I'd be very interested to hear what Matson thinks when he has seen the stuff and received a talking on the subject from yourself – I just hope something will emerge anyway.[71]

But by September, Saroyan had written to say that Matson had had no luck with the book and O'Nolan replied:

> About that book the failure of American publication comes to me as a distinct expectation. I knew all that. There is a great population in America but not enough arty-tarty screwballs to go in for stuff like that in satisfactory numbers. Joyce has the market cornered. I'm forgetting about that book. I've got no figures but I think it must be a flop over

here too. I guess it is a bum book anyhow. I am writing a very funny book now about bicycles and policemen and I think it will be perhaps good and earn a little money quietly. If I finish it, I will instantly send you a copy and then you can pass it on to Matson if you think he would not take offence.[72]

The jaunty note here – 'I guess it is a bum book anyhow' – is partly due to the adoption of the persona of the hard-boiled American professional, partly to his own confusions about the relationship of novel writing to making money. By then, in fact, *At Swim-Two-Birds* had sold 244 copies and it was to sell scarcely any more. In the autumn of 1940 when Longman's premises at St Paul's Churchyard were destroyed by German incendiary bombing, the remaining stocks were ruined, though a number of sheets survived which were not yet bound.

Six months later, in a letter to William Saroyan headed St Valentine's Day, 1940, he was able to give the American a full account of the now completed *Third Policeman*. He began with some complimentary remarks.

Thanks a lot for your letter which I got a few weeks ago. I do not know how you write and keep on writing those plays. I don't understand the way you make ordinary things uproarious and full of meaning and sentiment and make yourself appear saner than everybody else merely by being crazy. I have just been reading *The Time Of Your Life* and I think it is what we here call the business. It is fearfully funny. There is great freshness in all your stuff. It's given me a lot of ideas but I can't use them for a while because that would be copying and anyway I am beginning to think that I can't write at all – I mean, write something that would appeal to people everywhere because they are people the way you do it.[73]

The effusive tone of this makes it rather sad that in later years O'Nolan should deny that he had ever cared much for what in 1961 he would call Saroyan's 'whimsical material'; but Saroyan at least retained happy memories of his sojourn in Dublin; and when he lunched with O'Nolan's then publisher, Tim O'Keeffe, in 1964, he spoke of the reception he had got from O'Nolan and his friends with humour and affection.

O'Nolan's letter continued with an enquiry about the play for which it had been agreed Saroyan should use the title *Sweeney in the Trees*, the discarded title for *At Swim-Two-Birds*. 'I keep wondering what that new play of yours is like and how the title works into it. Has Hollywood started smelling round your plays yet?' He then went on to report the completion of *The Third Policeman* and to describe the book. Even allowing for a judicious amount of self-deprecation, the tone is surprisingly defeatist. 'I've just finished another bum book. I don't think it is much good and I haven't sent it anywhere yet.'[74]

This was not true. *The Third Policeman* had been finished and sent to Longman's in January and at the time of writing he was anxiously awaiting their verdict. He continues in the same self-deprecatory tone.

> The only good thing about it is the plot and I have been wondering whether I could make a crazy Saroyan play out of it. When you get to the end of this book you realize my hero or main character (he's a heel and a killer) has been dead throughout the book and that all the queer ghastly things which have been happening to him are happening in a sort of hell which he has earned for the killing. Towards the end of the book (before you know he's dead) he manages to get back to his own house where he used to live with another man who helped in the original murder. Although he has been away three days, this other fellow is 20 years older and dies of fright when he sees the other lad standing in the door. Then the two of them walk back along the road to the hell place and start going through all the same terrible adventures again, the first fellow being surprised and frightened at everything just as he was the first time and as if he had never been through it before. It is made clear that this sort of thing goes on forever – and there you are. It is supposed to be very funny but I don't know about that either.

And he ends with the same blend of envy and self-distrust.

> If it's ever published I'll send you a copy. I envy you the way you write just what you want to and like it when it's finished. I can never seem to get anything just right. Nevertheless, I think the idea of a man being dead all the time is pretty new. When you are writing about the world of the dead – and the damned – where none of the rules and laws (not even the Law of Gravity) holds good, there is any amount of scope for back-chat and funny cracks.[75]

All in all the letters of this period do not give the impression of a youthful author bursting with energy and self-confidence and perhaps on the verge of great triumphs. Dissatisfaction with what has been achieved and an acute knowledge of its imperfections is of course proper to the artist in any mode; but even after making allowances for this and perhaps also for the undercurrents of melancholy proper to a humorist there is a curious downbeat sadness and a lack of true élan about these letters to Saroyan which contrast oddly with the assumed zest and high spirits of some of his more public utterances of this period. As well as the self-doubts his confusions as to the purpose and possible results of fictional creation persist:

Personally I cannot get anything written that pleases me even a little but I am not trying hard and do not intend to get into ill health thinking about it ... At the same time *Gone with the Wind* keeps me awake at night sometimes – I mean, the quantity of potatoes earned by the talented lady novelist.[76]

It is of course a joke, but it is a theme to which he keeps returning all the same and it is a joke which it is impossible to imagine Joyce or, for that matter, any of the great masters of the modern movement making.

On 11 March, Patience Ross of A. M. Heath and Company transmitted Longman's verdict to him. 'We realize,' they wrote, 'the author's ability but think that he should become less fantastic and in this new novel he is more so.' Messrs Heath proceeded to try elsewhere but without success; and in late August, O'Nolan despatched a copy to Matson.

On 11 September, he wrote to Saroyan:

The other day when it was raining, I got so sick of looking at a ragged [illegible word] copy of that story I wrote about the policeman that I flew into a frenzy (the Sweeney kind), put it in a box with 2 short stories and sent the whole lot across the sea [sae?] to Matson and Duggan. Now I have to write to them and I don't know what to say because I feel (no fooling) that I've made a mess of the thing and that it's just a good idea banjaxed for the want of proper work and attention and patience. I should have kept it and redone it. It's the sort of thing that has to be right or it's no use. I feel it is very damaging to have stuff that smells sent around the publishers. If one comes along afterwards with something good, they may remember the smell and do nothing except open the windows. However, maybe they understand these things better than I do.

Matson wrote that he liked the book – which in his version was called *Hell Goes Round and Round* – but he found it impossible to place. At one point this typescript got lost and he had to ask for a copy; but still he failed to find a publisher.

O'Nolan took these rejections disproportionately hard. In spite of the cocksure and challenging attitude he maintained towards the world, his inner uncertainties were great and he was always oddly in need of reassurance about anything he wrote. As his letter to Saroyan shows, he had been deeply affected and discouraged by A. M. Heath's difficulties in finding an English publisher, although he does not mention these rejections. He should perhaps have made allowances but he had already begun to dislike the book, probably as a result of rejection. He wanted to take out the character Joe, the Voice of Conscience; and he came to believe that the whole thing would be better

recast and presented as a third person narrative. But he had not the
heart to make these changes and, as time passed, his antipathy to the
book grew.

Meanwhile, he was in a difficult position and his reaction shows not
only his deep vulnerability but his feelings about the status he enjoyed,
or fancied he enjoyed, in the eyes of his friends and of Dublin at that
time. He apparently could not bear to confess that his book had failed
to find a publisher. At UCD he had been the central figure of an
intensely admiring circle. Great things were expected of him and he
might claim to have begun to achieve them. The ripples of his fame had
spread outwards to include, as he probably thought, literary Dublin at
large, or that section of the literary establishment which attended
literary soirées or congregated in the Palace Bar and held forth under
their wide-brimmed black hats about 'coming men'.

Though the members of his own circle professed to be admirers of
James Joyce and were presumably aware of the gaps that had yawned
in the 20th century between commercial publishers and those who
insisted on going their own creative way, none of them seem to have
felt deep down that loneliness, misunderstanding and rejection were
the perhaps inevitable lot of the avant-garde. Although they
undoubtedly knew that *Dubliners* had been rejected innumerable
times and that many of the greatest works of the century had found
their way into print more or less by accident and through private
publishers, Brian must have thought that he would cease to cut such a
dazzling figure in their eyes if they knew of his rejection by Longman's and others. Then, as now, the judgements of English publishers
were relayed swiftly and in tones of awe in Dublin. Those who had
been impressed by Longman's acceptance of *At Swim-Two-Birds*
could equally be expected to take note of their rejection of its
successor.

And so he rather rashly decided to put about the story of the lost
manuscript. He told Niall Sheridan that he had mislaid it, probably on
a tramcar. He told Garvin a circumstantial story about taking it to the
Dolphin Hotel the previous night to show to someone and, between
the jigs and the reels, going home without it. 'I'm after being down
there,' he said, 'had them beat the whole bloody building and sight or
light of it's not to be found.'[77] He told the actor, Liam Redmond, a
UCD contemporary who was in touch with an English film director,
David Rawlings, and thought it might make a script, that it had been
lost on a train. And he told others an even more fanciful story about it
being blown page by page out of the boot of a car during a trip to
Donegal. Only to Donagh MacDonagh did he confess what had

actually happened and he asked him to look again at the typescript with a view to letting the author know 'what was wrong with it'. MacDonagh's answer was, 'nothing'.

Again, the sources of the book were many. It was MacDonagh who discerned the influence of Gibbon, whom Brian had been reading, in the many footnotes, of which he approved. Some part of the conception of De Selby appears to have come from the portrait of the eccentric recluse and savant, Des Esseintes, the hero of Huysmans' *A Rebours* which Devlin had lent to Sheridan who had passed it on to Brian. But of course he had always delighted in literary portrayals of dogmatic and eccentric geniuses such as Sherlock Holmes.

Later commentators have seen in *The Third Policeman* the influence of J. W. Dunne's books *An Experiment With Time* and *The Serial Universe*, which he and his circle were also reading. *An Experiment With Time* suggests that time is a dimension along which we are compelled to move blindly in one direction and at one pace. Only in dreams are we free to go forward faster. Dunne kept a record of his dreams and found that many of them 'came true'. He believed also that consciousness continued after death, and that our relationship to time then became more clearly a relationship to a fourth dimension. Dunne's books read like fairly classy hokum now but perhaps because they gave the illusion of discussing the problems which Einstein, whom nobody understood, had dealt with, they were popular in O'Nolan's circle and among Dublin intellectuals generally throughout the 1930s and 1940s.

Whatever about Brian O'Nolan, it was certainly one of the affectations of Myles na Gopaleen that he understood the theories of relativity; indeed Myles once claimed to have been 'present at the meeting of the Royal Society in London when the Astronomer Royal for England announced that the photographic plates of the famous eclipse, as measured by his colleagues in Greenwich Observatory, had verified the prediction of Einstein that rays of light are bent as they pass in the neighbourhood of the sun',[78] but he nowhere says anything about relativity that could not have been gleaned from an adequate popularization.

The gleeful reduction of all the types and modes of supposed knowledge, exemplified by the foolish De Selby, was something of which O'Nolan never tired and from which he derived a constant mordant amusement. This can be most clearly seen in the case of Myles na Gopaleen. He too is an encyclopedist who claims all knowledge for his province and can discuss hundreds of subjects, scientific and otherwise, with equal ease. Like De Selby, in terms of knowledge he is very nearly omnipotent and always infallible. Like De Selby, he is an inventor in an ingenious but always rather pointless sort of way. At the same time he has no real intellectual curiosity. He does not tremble for the outcome in any field of enquiry and the difference between him and De Selby is that he is aware of the joke. He realizes that none of these fields of enquiry really yields anything at all and he approaches them all in a spirit of mockery, knowing that none of them can add a cubit to our true stature or affect our appalling state.

As a man, O'Nolan had no real intellectual curiosity either. In spite of his mental alertness, even effervescence, he frequently complained of boredom. He pursued no subject, even speculatively, beyond fairly narrow limits. Knowledge was an entertaining province in which a clever mind might disport itself, but it had no ultimate importance. The real questions were settled and the answers known.

The Third Policeman is the only one of Brian O'Nolan's works in which there seems to be an original approach to philosophical questions involving the mystery of existence. But this is largely an illusion. Brian O'Nolan was born a Catholic and he remained one throughout his life. If he had any doubts about the faith in which he was brought up, they were on Manichaean grounds; somehow perhaps the balance of good and evil in the universe as we know it had been disturbed in favour of evil. This world was perhaps hell, or part of its empire. It is by no means impossible for a Catholic writer to combine a general orthodoxy with a Manichaean view, or at least Manichaean leanings. Heresies are, after all, branches from the parent stem; and Graham Greene has on occasion so described himself.[79] One of the most remarkable things about Brian O'Nolan's writing is the way this view of the dominance of evil coincides with and reinforces the innate nihilism of the comic vision.

Like most Irish Catholics of his generation he was a medieval Thomist in his attitude to many things, including scientific speculation and discovery. For the Thomist all the great questions have been settled and the purpose of existence is clear. There is only one good, the salvation of the individual soul; and only one final catastrophe, damnation. Though meliorations of the human condition may be looked for, perhaps even, within limits, actively sought or encouraged, they must be strictly subordinate to the primary end of existence.

Mysteries about God's purposes of course remain, but human history is to be read in the light of a battle between God and the devil for the possession of individual souls. The only important event in that history is therefore the Christian revelation. Every soul born into the world since the incarnation of Jesus Christ has had a chance of salvation; and there can be no such thing, in any important sense, as further progress. Once the revelation had been accomplished and received the stage was set. The operations of divine grace through the Christian sacraments maintain the ground won and prevent the triumph of evil, even if only partially, locally and in terms of individual salvation. But science, social organization and psychology are almost irrelevant.

Thus all secular knowledge is largely a joke. And science and philosophy are even more of a joke inasmuch as they pretend to hold out a hope that the end result of their enquiries will be to reveal something about the mystery of existence or to affect the balance of good and evil. All scientists are, to some extent, mad scientists and the archetypal scientific figure is the ridiculous De Selby, to the study of whose theories the depraved hero of *The Third Policeman* has given over his life – for which indeed he has risked his eternal salvation.

If Brian O'Nolan had any doubts about the faith in which he had been born, they were, as has been said, on Manichaean grounds, the Manichaean attitude being to him, as to some other Catholic writers, the ultimate sophistication in belief. The landscape of hell in *The Third Policeman* is, as Aidan Higgins has pointed out, unmistakeably that of the Irish midlands, where he had spent a good part of his boyhood, apparently enjoying an idyll. Hell is situated somewhere near Tullamore.

In the book there is an astonishingly casual acceptance of evil as part of the natural order of things. The hero becomes a murderer almost without anything that could be called a thought. He exhibits no remorse. 'I had got to like him and thought it was a pity he had been murdered,' he says of his victim as he contemplates him in the empty house. But he immediately adds: 'I felt relieved and simplified and certain that I would soon have the black box.'

The world of the book is a rational and even scientific one, a normal one except for the pervasive feeling that something has slipped, that the give-and-take of good and evil, which is the normal state, has been somehow disturbed. The plane on which we live has been, as it were, tilted over.

In later years when Brian O'Nolan came to re-work parts of *The Third Policeman* as *The Dalkey Archive*, he would refer in specific terms to the Manichaean belief and to the possibility that the 'awesome encounter between God and the rebel Lucifer' had, despite all we have been told, in fact 'gone the other way'. *The Third Policeman* is perhaps more lighthearted. It is also more chilling. We view things in the light of Eternity. The sun still shines on the flat and

featureless landscape of the Irish midlands. The sky is a 'light blue
without distance, neither near nor far'. You can gaze 'through it and
beyond it and still see illimitably clearer and nearer the delicate lie of
its nothingness'.

It is not suggested that Brian O'Nolan held clear, consistent and
fully thought-out views of a Manichaean kind. Apart from the
instinctual nature of the writer, he belonged to a country and a
culture where people, especially Catholics, did not 'think things out'.
Some of it was in the air he breathed. Thomistic Catholicism was the
received religion of all the educational institutions he attended,
including UCD, where the philosophy courses were designed to
confirm that everything worth knowing was in St Thomas Aquinas's
great synthesis of Catholic doctrine and Aristotelian philosophy, the
Summa Theologica, and that all the rest was vain speculation. What
is suggested is that the Manichaean view of existence provides a con-
venient label for his own *façon de voir* and that, especially on the evidence of the later work, *The Dalkey Archive*, he was quite well aware
of it and had thought about it, even if in an unstructured and inconclusive way.

The syntax of *The Third Policeman* is peculiar. It often reads like a
translation from the Irish, but it is not the poeticized version of Irish
syntax given by Lady Gregory and John Synge which had become
known as 'Kiltartan'.

'My mother I can recall perfectly. Her face was always red and
sore-looking from bending at the fire; she spent her life making tea to
pass the time and singing snatches of old songs to pass the meantime.
I knew her well but my father and I were strangers and did not converse much; often indeed when I would be studying in the kitchen at
night I could hear him through the thin door of the shop talking there
from his seat under the oil lamp for hours on end to Mick the
sheepdog.'

The basic prose style of the first person narrator of *At Swim-Two-
Birds* had sometimes read like a translation from the Irish also. At
others its very meticulousness, a sort of painstaking clarity and flat-
ness, had given the impression that English was being written as if it
were a dead language:

> That same afternoon I was sitting on a stool in an intoxicated condition
> in Grogan's licensed premises. Adjacent stools bore the forms of Brin-
> sley and Kelly, my two true friends. The three of us were occupied in
> putting glasses of stout into the interior of our bodies and expressing
> by fine disputation the resulting sense of physical and mental well
> being. In my thigh pocket I had eleven and eightpence in a weighty

pendulum of mixed coins. Each of the arrayed bottles on the shelves before me, narrow or squat-bellied, bore a dull picture of the gas-bracket.

Here, as in *The Third Policeman*, we feel that some sort of exercise in de-personalization is taking place, perhaps, in part, O'Nolan's protest against the over-personalized 'stylishness' of so much English prose, as the flat syntax which Ernest Hemingway learned from Gertrude Stein had been, but also an expression of surprise that such a language as English exists and can be made to express facts or describe appearances and feelings. Of course for humorous purposes it also provides a contrast to the idiomatic eccentricity and richness of the characters' speech and to the baroque exfoliations of the interleaved texts. Occasionally in *The Third Policeman* the two, the flat meticulousness and the eccentricity, are combined to exquisitely humorous effect: 'What is a sheep but millions of little bits of sheepness whirling around and doing intricate convolutions inside the sheep? What else is it but that?'

In the early months of 1939, when *At Swim-Two-Birds* was awaiting publication, O'Nolan and Sheridan had gleefully intervened in a controversy in the *Irish Times* about a play by Frank O'Connor which had been produced at the Abbey and unfavourably reviewed by the newspaper's theatre critic. The play had been defended by Sean O'Faoláin, who was generally regarded, along with Frank O'Connor, as the dominant figure among the writers who had appeared since the close of the Irish literary revival and the foundation of the Free State. O'Nolan used, for the most part, in this correspondence, the *nom de plume* 'Flann O'Brien', which would shortly appear on the title page of his book and, in attacking these particular targets, he and Sheridan were announcing the arrival of a *nouvelle vague* in Irish writing.

The controversy was quite sharp and it is evident now that O'Faoláin and O'Connor had identified 'Flann O'Brien' as a pseudonym but were uncertain as to its owner. O'Faoláin said the name was like 'an Easter egg with whiskers' and referred to the supposed Flann O'Brien as 'the man in the Gaelic mask'. O'Connor asked for an indication whether the person calling himself Flann O'Brien was known to the editor of the *Irish Times* and asked the editor to say whether he was also known to himself and Mr O'Faoláin. The editor replied to the first query in the affirmative; as to the second, he said he did not know; but it was evident that the question was addressed to him because some kind of conspiracy was suspected – he was also asked to call off his 'literary rapscallions' and to dissociate the *Irish Times* from the methods of 'literary gangsters'.

Perhaps the funniest of the conspirators' letters was a pained one from a Francis O'Connor who asked the editor whether he was aware that someone was writing letters 'all about artists and the Abbey Theatre' to the paper and signing his name to them. Declaring that he 'never meddled in politics or any sort of argument' the 'real' Francis O'Connor spoke of the embarrassment the letters were causing him.

The fake controversy, carried on under a multiplicity of pseudonyms, was a medium whose merits Brian O'Nolan had discovered even as a schoolboy, when he, Ciarán and others had vented their dissatisfaction about homework on the editor and readership of the *Catholic Standard*. Perhaps he had begun to suspect even then that it might have its attractions for editors too. Whether the editor of the *Irish Times* was really a party to the concerted attack on O'Connor and O'Faoláin or not, he cannot have been long in doubt that he was dealing with an energetically organized conspiracy when, early in the following year, Sheridan, O'Nolan and Montgomery invaded his pages again.

The occasion was once more a theatrical production; and the first two letters were genuine; indeed the first, asking why Dubliners were not prepared to support 'the exquisite production of Chekhov's masterpiece, *The Three Sisters*, being given by Lord Longford's Company at the Gate Theatre' reads like a simple plant for puffing purposes; but the reply, signed HP, which blames the lack of attendance at the Gate Theatre on the Irish love of American films as well as on the sort of chauvinism associated with the Irish language movement, has a different ring; and thereafter there were letters from F. O'Brien, D. C. Barry, Lir O'Connor, Whit Cassidy, Paul Desmond, Oscar Love, Luna O'Connor and others which were almost undoubtedly written by O'Nolan and his friends. It cannot be said that they read hilariously now. The principal modes were mock concern, old fogey name-dropping and comically pretentious literary criticism.

A month later the game took a new turn. Patrick Kavanagh had begun to review for the *Irish Times*. Apart from 'Flann O'Brien', Patrick Kavanagh was by far the most important arrival on the Irish literary scene in the late 1930s. Born the son of a small farmer-cum-shoemaker in the poor northern county of Monaghan, as a young man he began to publish short lyrics in AE's benign journal, *The Irish Statesman*, and these had eventually attracted the attention of literary

Dublin. The publication of his prose book *The Green Fool* in 1938 had confirmed his image as a naive and unlettered lyricist at whose expense the Palace Bar could be complacently patronizing; nor did his physical appearance when he came to Dublin and began to try to earn a living there, belie this preconception. Tall, gangling and with the seeming awkwardness of the countryman in his walk, his gestures and the set of his shoulders, he became the butt of many Dublin jokes and the comic character in many anecdotes.

Since he was actually a sophisticated and, within his limits, a well-read man, it was inevitable that his future relationship with literary Dublin should be a comedy of errors with tragic overtones. Like Brian O'Nolan, he was peculiarly attracted to journalism and even, to begin with, cherished romantic notions about it as well as the illusion that he could earn his living by it. At this time, he was writing a colloquial column in the *Irish Press* under the pseudonym 'Piers Ploughman'; and he was soon to find employment on the weekly *Catholic Standard* as a reporter, and, rather inappropriately, as a film critic.

The book he reviewed in the *Irish Times* on Saturday, 20 July 1940, was a novel called *The Hill is Mine* by Maurice Walsh. Walsh was almost unique among Irish writers, certainly among habitués of the Palace Bar, in that his books, published for the most part by Chambers of Edinburgh, sold steadily and to a very large public. He was a modest man, with few literary pretensions and Kavanagh liked him. His review began by asking the question 'What is an artist? Can a writer of best-sellers, like Maurice Walsh, be an artist?'[80] It was not a very polished piece but it asked a few fundamental questions about the nature of popularity and the relationship between success and merit. There were asides about such matters as *Gone with the Wind*, which was said to be a stupid boring book, and about the Boy Scout Movement, which moved some ordinary cranks to write letters of protest. A week later one of Kavanagh's best poems of this period, 'Spraying the Potatoes', appeared on the literary page.

This was enough for O'Nolan and his friends and soon they and others were having a great deal of sport. Much of it was only tenuously related to Kavanagh's two contributions to the paper but he was nevertheless to some extent the butt of the joke. F. O'Brien affected to believe that the heading 'Spraying the Potatoes' meant that Irish banknotes were being 'treated periodically with a suitable germicide' and went on to express what the writer felt when he realized that Mr Kavanagh was dealing with the part played by chemistry in modern farming.

I am no judge of poetry – the only poem I ever wrote was produced when I was body and soul in the gilded harness of Dame Laudanum – but I think Mr Kavanagh is on the right track here. Perhaps the *Irish Times*, timeless champion of our peasantry, will oblige us with a series in this strain covering such rural complexities as inflamed goat-udders, warble-pocked shorthorn, contagious abortion, non-ovoid oviducts and nervous disorders among the gentlemen who pay the rent.

The tone of the fake letters was unrelievedly facetious and mock-serious. There were pastiches of the recently published *Finnegans Wake*, probably by Montgomery; and read now it all seems a little tiresome. Some of Kavanagh's latterday partisans have since seen fit to interpret it in a very personal light:

Poor Kavanagh, God knows he had plenty of real problems to contend with. He must have been bewildered at this sudden eruption of quite causeless, meaningless schoolboy aggression conducted by such a frighteningly united bunch of juvenile delinquents. The message must have been clear to him – you are not one of us. You are not of our class. You have not had our education. You are not a Dubliner. Shut up or get out.[81]

The fact is, however, that though he had a long enough memory for slights and insults suffered in Dublin at this time, Kavanagh does not seem to have interpreted the correspondence in this way; and in later years anyway he had certainly no animus against Brian O'Nolan on the head of it. In his reply, which brought the correspondence to a close two weeks after it began, he did put his finger on one peculiar feature of it: the complete absence of content in the joke, such as it was. 'In my review of Maurice Walsh's *The Hill is Mine*,' he said, 'I referred to the empty virtuosity of artists who were expert in the art of saying nothing. Ploughmen without land. One of my critics said it was a wistful remark, and maybe, it was; but if ever a critic was proved right, all round, by his critics it happened this time.'[82]

Content-less or otherwise, the joke had proved immensely popular with readers of the *Irish Times*, and the editor of the paper now invited O'Nolan to contribute a column. A portly figure who was large in his physical dimensions at least, R. M. Smyllie then occupied a position of perhaps inordinate importance in the consciousness of literary Dublin, and was central to its myth of itself as a place where heavy drinkers who were also wits consumed many hours of each day in literary converse enlivened by anecdote and epigram. Although his own writings were negligible, consisting mainly of the rather rambling column which appeared on Saturdays and was signed 'Nichevo',

Smyllie wore the large black hat which was the standard uniform of the Dublin man of letters. These felt fedoras were too wide-brimmed to be available in the ordinary menswear shops and their wearers therefore had recourse to a clerical outfitters in Talbot Street near the Pro-Cathedral, which supplied them to old-fashioned Parish Priests from the country. Smyllie occasionally wore his when seated at his table in the Palace Bar near the *Irish Times* office and there might well be two or three others at the same table wearing one too – the poets Austin Clarke and Patrick MacDonogh, the novelist Brinsley Mac-Namara and others. Writing to A.M. Heath, in October of 1938, before the publication of *At Swim-Two-Birds*, O'Nolan had said that he would be glad if Longman's could be persuaded to part forthwith with the advance for the book. 'I desire to buy a black hat and other accessories,' he had said; and, rather surprisingly, he had bought one. His was not as wide-brimmed as some but it was an assertion all the same that he belonged to the Dublin community of letters.

Smyllie was always the presiding figure at his particular table and was treated with the greatest deference by the writers present as well as by the journalists. Although an authoritarian editor he was a kindly enough man and he would sit for long hours with his chosen cronies, his red face aglow with pleasure, his pipe between his teeth and his moustache sometimes bedewed with small drops of Guinness or Scotch. His arrival at the *Irish Times* office in the late afternoons has been described by Niall Sheridan:

> In anticipation of his coming, the front office was frequently occupied by a straggle of suppliants – impoverished old acquaintances to whom he gave small sums of money, crackpots seeking publicity for their crazy schemes, a well-known briefless barrister needing money for a cocaine 'fix', an elderly lady from some respectable suburb, banging her umbrella on the counter and demanding an interview with the Editor.[83]

The interview with Brian was arranged by Sheridan and took place in the Palace. They got on famously, Smyllie chuckling and grunting in approval of his new young man's flights and sallies.

The *Irish Times* was traditionally the journal of the Protestant minority, those, mostly Church of Ireland, Unionists who had been left high and dry by the advent of the Free State, an entity to whose life and development they had committed themselves with many misgivings. They still controlled more than their share of Dublin's business and industry, such as it was, and although the aristocratic element among them had lost most of its land through the division of the big estates under the various land acts, it still had sufficient economic base to continue hunting and racing horses on a fairly large scale. During the winter months the *Irish Times* carried regular reports of meetings of the Fingal Harriers and other hunts and it devoted a considerable amount of space to the various balls and reunions at which the former ascendancy still foregathered. It was a staid journal, with advertisements still on its front page, but it was the intellectuals' journal, their parish gazette, more or less by default and because the tone of the other two papers, the *Irish Independent* and the *Irish Press*, to which O'Nolan had already contributed one or two pieces in Irish, was not to their taste.

The *Independent* reflected all too clearly the Catholic triumphalism of the more prosperous farmers and the ratepayers of the towns. When the novelist Benedict Kiely joined it as a leader writer at about this time, he was told: 'There are only two subjects for editorials on this paper, the Red Menace and the Ratepayers' Burden.'[84] The *Irish Press*, which had been financed by De Valera from small subscriptions to be the organ of his Fianna Fáil Party, had a slightly more populist radical tone and its chauvinism was of a more *völkisch* nature. But its attitude to all things Irish was rather too rank and enthusiastic for the taste of intellectuals.

It was Smyllie's ambition to reduce the dependence of the *Irish Times* on the Protestant Unionist readership, which was diminishing every day; to make it the organ of the more liberal and more intellectual elements in the new state; and to modify its west British outlook accordingly. He wanted to show that it was not against the Irish language but only against the chauvinism and hypocrisy that went with it. He must have seen immediately that this potential new contributor was ideally fitted to serve his purposes; and if so, time would show him to have been right.

The two were already acquainted, for O'Nolan had been going to the Palace since before the publication of *At Swim-Two-Birds*; and indeed Smyllie had vouched for the acquaintance when challenged to do so by Frank O'Connor during the O'Faoláin/O'Connor correspondence. So it did not take many Scotches for an agreement to be reached about the column; and the first one appeared on 4 October 1940. It was called 'Cruiskeen Lawn' which can be translated as 'little brimming jug'.

It appeared in an already attenuated *Irish Times* which the war-time paper shortage would finally reduce to eight pages. The main news stories concerned the daylight bombing of suburban London by the Germans and the machine-gunning of a train in the British midlands. The RAF had replied to these sorties with a raid over Hamburg.

Neville Chamberlain had finally left public life by resigning the office of Lord President of the Council and the Germans had apologized for dropping a bomb on a creamery in County Wexford which had killed three girls. (This was to be one of the only two bombings of Irish territory during the war.)

This first column, which appeared on the leader page opposite these stories, was a bilingual joke not unrelated to events of the day. An editorial (perhaps even a plant) had spoken of the futility of Government efforts to extend the use of the Irish language:

> The task would be hard enough in normal years ... but at such a time as the present, when children all over the world are trying to keep pace with an influx of new words as a result of the war news bulletins, it becomes well-nigh impossible. Parents who confine the family mealtime discussions to conversations in Irish must find it very difficult to explain such words as air-raid warden, incendiary bomb, non-aggression pact, decontamination, and Molotoff bread-basket. Has Gaelic ingenuity, for that matter, stretched so far as to provide a really expressive and indigenous equivalent for the well-known 'Axis'?

The column which discussed this presented a comic dialogue in Irish betweeen a mother and her son who is refusing to eat his porridge until she supplies him with the Irish for such terms as Molotoff bread-basket. He expresses disbelief that there is any Irish for such contemporary phrases. There is nothing in Irish but old proverbial wisdom, 'gander's bones', he says. 'Why can't we speak English in this house?' he asks. Finally, with a box, she tells him, 'There is your Molotoff bread-basket for you.'

What follows is a small masterpiece of prevarication and obliquity. Even in this, the very first column of all, the ironic stancelessness, the refusal to adopt any real side in any argument, is evident. After giving several possible translations of 'Molotoff bread-basket', each one more roundabout and allusive than the last, 'Myles' goes on:

> The task of reviving Irish, we are told, would be hard 'unless conversations could be limited to requests for food and drink' ... Why not admit that hardly anybody ever thinks of anything else? If on and after tomorrow the entire *Irish Times* should be printed in Irish, there would not be a word about anything but food and drink. Those who find that they cannot do without 'incendiary bombs', 'decontamination', and the like, would have to get some other paper to accompany their ghoul's breakfast. The Irish would be full of *cainnt no ndaoine*, excerpts from *Séadna*, *corra-cainnte*, *sean-fhocla* and *dánta díreacha* and would embody examples of *béarla féinne* and even *én-bhéarla* or bird dialect.

In other words, the columnist is suggesting that a paper in Irish would be full of the antiquated stuff of the language revivalists – proverbs, idioms, folk tales and old sayings. And yet the editorial writer who had suggested that if the language was to have any future it must be made more contemporary is also held up to ridicule.

In the second column, which appeared six days later and was largely in English, Myles adverted to the ambiguities and uncertainties of meaning which, he claimed, were a feature of the Irish language.

> The Irish language will probably become invaluable as an instrument of self-expression in these changing times, when most of us are sure of nothing. The Irish speaker, being the most equivocal of God's creatures, expresses his ambiguous existence by two separate and dissimilar verbs 'to be' – '*is*' and '*ta*'.[85]

Characteristically he was to claim later on that Irish was the most precise of languages: 'Therein is the secret why Irish cannot be revived; the present age shrinks from precision and "understands" only soft woolly words which have really no particular meaning like "cultural heritage" or "the exigent dictates of modern traffic needs".' And throughout the lifetime of the column he was to have enormous fun with the multiplicity of definitions for a single word given by the standard Irish dictionary, that compiled by Father Dineen.

The idea of the column had been sold to Smyllie partly on the grounds that it would be desirable to have an up-to-date sophisticated contribution in Irish in the paper. But for the first three weeks there were occasional jokes and stories in English and once even a trilingual joke involving a speech by the Japanese Prime Minister Matsuoka. On 25 October there was a funny story about a dog biting a hare which concluded, 'Those who cannot read Irish may take some consolation from the fact that this is the sort of skunk-stench and scald-bosh that appears occasionally in Irish on these pages.' On the following day there was a sample lesson in Irish which explained the differences in consonantal sounds and the system of aspiration employed to produce certain sounds in Irish. The harsh words of a District Justice which condemned jazz as a foreign import were said to be justified, since the word itself contained three consonant sounds which could not be reproduced in Irish and 'the spread of Irish in England' was said to be slower than it might otherwise have been because of the difficulties of understanding and reproducing the Irish consonants, though conversely the English might be attracted, 'in a time of paper scarcity such as the present, by the advantages of the language which had a smaller alphabet and therefore would require less newsprint'.

After the first half dozen columns, the use of English became a rarity, and the column, which appeared approximately three times a week, was written almost altogether in Irish until the end of 1941. Then, when it began to appear every day, Irish and English alternated. Gradually, however, the amount of Irish diminished and from early in 1944 on it was written almost exclusively in English. After that, columns in Irish were rare although the *Irish Times* sometimes sought to persuade O'Nolan to write in Irish more frequently.

For many years, even after they began to appear every day, the columns were written in batches on Sunday afternoons. He would sit with his back to the fireplace at one end of the long polished mahogany table in the room known as the dining room in Avoca Terrace, hammering them out on his Underwood typewriter with scarcely any hesitation or apparent agonizing. During the week he made notes on scraps of paper which he carried in his pockets and the Sunday afternoon ritual would begin with the study of these. Like many writers, he used only two fingers and he hit the old Underwood with a quite unnecessary violence. But his copy was usually so clean as to cause comment among the journalists of the *Irish Times*; and it was always correctly punctuated. Over the years the initial U N D of the bold lettering which said U N D E R W O O D S T A N D A R D T Y P E - W R I T E R would become obliterated by his left thumb as it darted up to click the roller round, as likewise would the last four letters of the word 'typewriter' be erased by his right thumb as it swept up to whip back the carriage; but in these early days of joyous facility he was far from the hesitant hack described in a later column as 'slumped on his hack-chair, lolling his dead syrup eyes through other people's books to lift some lousy joke' and reminding himself of the fact that he was writing in English today and so would 'have to be a bit careful, can't get away with murder so easily in English.'[86]

Often during these early days some of the younger children would be doing their homework at the same table and it was in response to their complaints about the volume of noise he created and the vibrations of the table that he eventually placed a thick green felt cloth under the typewriter to muffle the sound and absorb the poundings. The batch of neatly typed columns (often typed on ruled Civil Service memorandum paper) would be delivered to the *Irish Times* office on Sunday evenings.

To begin with he called himself 'Myles na gCopaleen' which means Myles of the little horses, the g before the capital C being the eclipsis which the genitive case demands. At a later stage, when he had begun to cherish the hope that he would make this persona known outside

Ireland, he simplified this to Myles na Gopaleen, rather to the regret of some of the *Irish Times* staff who liked the pedantry of the eclipsis in the genitive.

The original Myles was a character in Gerald Griffin's immensely popular 19th-century novel *The Collegians* which Dion Boucicault had made into an even more popular play called *The Colleen Bawn.* In Griffin's novel Myles is a semi-heroic figure who is yet part outlaw and part picturesque peasant storyteller. He is described as having 'a broad and sunny forehead, light and wavy hair, a blue cheerful eye, a nose that in Persia might have won him a throne, healthful cheeks, and a mouth that was full of character, and a well-knit and almost gigantic person' with a 'lofty and confident, though most unassuming carriage'.[87] Boucicault broadened this character and made him more of a comic stage-Irish figure. In the column, the techniques of the television soap opera in which only gradually and after many episodes are the past lives of the characters disclosed, were employed until eventually Myles acquired a full biography.

Like 'Brother Barnabas' before him 'Sir Myles' had been almost everywhere and known almost everybody. He had worked with Clemenceau to bring about a *rappel à l'ordre* in France; collaborated with Einstein, played for Kreisler, studied under Scarlatti, known John McCormack and (of course) James Joyce. He had been born in Paris, where his father was First Consul, in 1801, in Montevideo in 1646, in Paddington Station in 1863 and at many other times and places.

He had been Provost of Trinity College, President of the Republic of Letters, even District Justice of Ballybofey. It was no wonder therefore that he refused the Professorship of Architecture in UCD and resisted pressure to take on the Presidency of Ireland; and it was a cause of dismay to many, among them his friend, the politician James Dillon, when he decided to accept an English title. Describing him as the best man in Ireland and 'my own sworn friend', Dillon said that Irish Ireland had been 'stunned and shocked by a gross and wicked betrayal on the part of their whilom champion'.

He was variously known as Baron, His Grace, His Satanic Highness but usually referred to himself as My Excellency. He was also the Sage of Santry, the Wordsworth of Ireland, the Gaelic Demosthenes, the Man in the Hat and Ireland's Own Hatchetman.

He was head of Cruiskeen Industries, a subsidiary of the Cruiskeen Corporation (the Cruiskeen Organization), which produced 'Cruiskeen Lawn' for the *Irish Times*, Director of the Myles na gCopaleen

Banking Corporation and President of Hiberno-American Air-Lions Incorporated.

And he lived of course in Santry and was known to his family and retainers as Sir Myles or the Da. So real did his residence in Santry become over the years that it was difficult for the present writer to pass the gates of Santry House without thinking of him.

Part of the inspiration of the column may have been 'By The Way', the famous 'Beachcomber' column in the *Daily Express.* 'Beachcomber' was in fact J. B. Morton. His brother H. V. Morton, a popular author of travel books, was a familiar figure in Dublin and Brian O'Nolan had met him. The Mortons were known to be Catholics and Beachcomber's satire was believed in Dublin to have a Catholic edge. Like 'Cruiskeen Lawn', 'By The Way' had a cast of characters: Captain Foulenough, Dr Strabismus of Utrecht and others. Like 'Cruiskeen Lawn', it made good use of quotations; and like Myles na gCopaleen, Beachcomber was intolerant of pretentiousness to the point of being a philistine, though the philistinism of Cruiskeen Lawn was more discursive and better informed. It was sometimes also rather humourless, but it was in keeping with O'Nolan's general outlook. Art was another thing that had to be kept in its place.

An interesting parallel to 'Cruiskeen Lawn', though probably not an influence on it, is the journalism of Karl Kraus. Like Brian O'Nolan, Kraus had a strange belief in journalism which transcended much general disillusionment. Like Myles na gCopaleen he was interested in linguistics, particularly in the way in which words exposed their users, revealed the false and ridiculous aspects of a culture and an era and permitted individuals and civilizations generally to make fools of themselves. Like Myles na gCopaleen also, Karl Kraus was a voluminous writer who scorned the idea of permanence as an end of literary activity.

The column, even while it was appearing in Irish, was an immediate and dazzling success, partly no doubt because Brian O'Nolan and his friends immediately cooked up a correspondence relating to it. Many of the letters that appeared were written by them, but such was the solemnity and hypocrisy on the one hand and resentment and cynicism on the other aroused at the time by the Irish language that it is difficult to be sure which letters are fake and which are genuine. Thus 'West Briton Nationalist', who said he was a member of the ascendancy, proclaimed his loyalty to King, Country and Empire, and said: 'I do not understand what worthy motive can inspire your "skits" on the Gaelic language and its students ... It sounds very much like fouling one's own nest,' reads like a fake now but may well have been genuine. 'I have heard many adverse comments on Irish. But you are spewing on it,' he concluded.[88]

Other correspondents accused Myles na gCopaleen of attempting 'to sabotage the propagation of the language and things Irish' and of 'hitting below the belt'. One of the more sensible letters referred quite accurately to 'the fulsome, fatuous, "sixth-standard essay" type of article which passes for Gaelic journalism in the other metropolitan newspapers' and welcomed the advent of Myles as a blessed relief.

The new column, which was seldom more than five or six hundred words in length, appeared on the editorial page of the *Irish Times* beside such features as 'An Irishman's Diary' by Quidnunc and 'The London Letter'. This was opposite the main news page whose sizeable headlines were concerned with the Battle of Britain, Hitler's meetings with Pétain and Franco and the bungled Italian invasion of Greece. De Valera meanwhile was inspecting kitchens at the Irish Army Camp on the Curragh and calling for one hundred thousand recruits to the new Local Defence Force, the Irish equivalent of the Home Guard. On the *Irish Times'* staid pictorial page, wedding photographs, mostly of Protestant couples, continued to be featured chock-a-block with those of the first meets of the winter hunting season, although there were occasionally such photographs as that of a citizen handing in his binoculars at the local police station for use by the Army.

As soon as war was declared De Valera had proclaimed Ireland's neutrality and under a new Emergency Powers Bill a Government censor saw to it that nothing in support of either set of combatants would appear in the newspapers. Until 1938 there had been British naval bases at Cobh in Country Cork and Lough Swilly in County Donegal, but these had been ceded back to Eire as part of an agreement between the Chamberlain and De Valera Governments in 1938. During the first weeks of the column's existence Churchill spoke, in response to a parliamentary question, about the heavy toll in British lives that the loss of these bases was causing, to which De Valera replied immediately that in no circumstances could they be returned. In doing so he affirmed that neutrality would be defended against attacks by either side. All Government statements and proclamations referred to the war as 'the emergency' and the phrase 'the duration of the present emergency' became a familiar one in Ireland during the years that followed. After the war, De Valera would sometimes speak of what he termed the occupation of the Six Counties of Northern Ireland by Britain as the principal reason for Ireland's neutrality.

Basically, however, the neutrality policy of the Government was popular with ordinary people simply because they did not want the country to be involved in the war.

The *Irish Times* was, like most of its readers, solidly pro-British but, even if it had wanted to, it would not have been allowed to say so; and of course Myles na gCopaleen was also subject to censorship of any views or preferences he might have expressed about the outcome of the war. In 1940 when he began his column the Germans had already overrun France, the Low Countries and Scandinavia. An invasion of England seemed imminent and even Ireland was clearly under threat. But somehow the war had not sunk as deeply into the public consciousness as one might have expected; nor had any sort of perception of the true nature of the Fascist dictatorships. Although the majority undoubtedly hoped for an Allied victory, there were numbers, particularly among nationalists, who felt the traditional sympathy towards the Axis powers that they reserved for Britain's enemies.

These feelings could not surface in the newspapers, however, and rather more strangely they were not much expressed by ordinary people in the course of conversation, even among friends. The war became, as 'the troubles' had been for so many, a subject to be cautiously adverted to in most company; and such locutions as 'the present emergency' or 'the present global conflict' as well as the censorship of films and newsreels kept it at a psychological distance. In a country in which motor cars had been, even before petrol scarcity, a luxury that few could afford, in which the vast majority of the inhabitants had never been on a ship and still fewer in an aeroplane, its physical proximity was not even clearly apprehended. In rural parts, life went on much as it had always done, with the small sprung cart or trap and the bicycle as the favourite forms of transport. There were few serious food shortages except of tea and shop-bread and though the news bulletins on the radio gave some account of how the war was progressing, there were no arguments or discussions about its causes or the aims of the participants. Even in Dublin most people adopted a neutral non-committal stance in conversation with casual acquaintances; and whatever might be understood to be going on elsewhere, it was difficult to imagine anything very violent or unusual happening at home.

Most of the drama and violence that older people had experienced had come from internal political upheavals, and the war now made them seem if anything more unlikely to recur. Shortly after its outbreak the IRA had attempted to raid an Army arms depot in the

Phoenix Park and this had given the Government an excuse to round up all its suspected members and intern them in a camp near the Army base at the Curragh. Since there was nothing to spy on, Dublin did not even have the febrile cloak-and-dagger atmosphere associated with other neutral capitals such as Lisbon and Istanbul; and although most people gave a sort of intellectual assent to the possibility of invasion it seemed inconceivable that anything would come out of the skies or appear in the bay to disturb the all too even tenor of existence.

Yet there were paradoxes. Tens of thousands had begun to emigrate annually to work in British armaments factories and thousands more joined the British Armed Forces, driven either by the need for a job or the desire to escape the boredoms and futilities of life in Ireland. As usual emigration had a psychological, indeed a psychosexual, as well as the more important economic dimension. The emigrants departed on blacked-out overcrowded boats, some of which carried cattle as well, from the North Wall, not far from the Custom House, and from Dún Laoghaire; and nobody paid much attention to their going. Like the war itself, once out of sight they were virtually out of mind.

On 18 August 1941 as a result of a Cabinet reshuffle the Ministry of Local Government changed hands and Brian O'Nolan became Private Secretary to Sean MacEntee. That he was continued in the post suggests that O'Kelly had recommended him strongly to the new Minister. No doubt his quite splendid attendance record had something to do with this, for in the year before MacEntee's assumption of the Ministry he was absent for only six days, three with influenza, two with a cold and for one day due to eye trouble.

Like O'Kelly, MacEntee was a senior member of the Fianna Fáil hierarchy. Like O'Kelly, and indeed O'Nolan, he was small in stature; but he had none of O'Kelly's reputation for geniality and forebearance and was in fact a rather dirty political infighter with a wounding tongue who was frequently involved in unseemly exchanges in the Dáil. Like his Private Secretary, he was a Northerner, a civil engineer from Belfast who had become involved in Nationalist politics almost by accident, a fact which his political opponents seldom allowed him to forget. The allegation that he would have joined the British Army in 1916 had he not missed a train at Mallow, was one of the Dáil's running jokes.

Less widely known was the fact that he had begun life as a poet and had published a little green bound book of romantic verses full of the worst clichés of the Irish literary revival. That his critical faculty had improved with the years was shown by his determination to buy up any copies of this which from time to time surfaced in the book shops.

O'Nolan and MacEntee seem to have got on well together, which was just as well, for, like Divney and the nameless hero of *The Third Policeman*, they were compelled to spend long hours in each other's company. One of the Private Secretary's duties was to accompany his Minister to the Dáil on occasions when a Bill sponsored by his Department was being shepherded through that assembly. When the Minister was actually speaking or when that worthy had to remain in the Chamber to listen to points made or unexpected questions raised in Debate he sat in the Private Secretary's pen, a railed-off area near the Government Front Bench. These hours in the Dáil were excruciating for Brian O'Nolan since Dáil debates in those years were mostly on an abysmal level. The art of oratory seemed to have vanished entirely from the land with the passing of the old Irish party; and except when exchanges became especially heated and caution was thrown to the winds, the more colourful phrases of Irish speech were banished in favour of the jargon and the officialese which allows politicians to say nothing at great length.

To make matters worse MacEntee was benevolently aware of his Secretary's literary talents and he occasionally employed him as a speech writer or as one to whom the task of improving a speech written by somebody else in the Department could be entrusted. A study of that personage's utterances now yields no clue as to what might or might not have been written or rewritten by Brian O'Nolan and it is likely that he merely decided to please his employer by tightening up the normal style in which these orations were composed or perhaps by employing a better type of cliché. Small wonder though that he became such a great collector and connoisseur of clichés himself. MacEntee boasted that his Secretary knew his inmost thoughts and could express them better than he did himself. Probably these thoughts were so predictable that the Secretary's task was an easy one. The real matter for surprise is that he still retained his keenness for the job and even felt a certain amount of cordiality towards his master. Of course he was still learning about his own capacities and there is no doubt that he took, as he was entitled to do, a certain amount of pride in them. And the importance and the delights of mere role-playing must not be underestimated.

During 1940 and 1941 Brian O'Nolan's interest in the Irish language, its nature and possibilities was perhaps greater than it was ever to be again. The language movement was by then almost half a century old, the Gaelic League having been founded with Douglas Hyde as its first president on 31 July 1893. In the years that followed there had been immense popular enthusiasm for the revival of Irish and at the time when Michael Victor Nolan was courting his bride-to-be in Strabane, young people all over the country were flocking to classes and of course to céilidhes and concerts as well. Nearly all the leaders of the 1916 rising had been touched and invigorated by contact with the language, and after 1916 it became incumbent upon all politicians to affect some knowledge of it. Pearse had said that the Ireland which was to come would be not free merely but Gaelic as well; indeed he considered Gaelicization as important as the attainment of political freedom, for English was for him and many of his contemporaries a badge of servitude; and large numbers of people certainly hoped that the achievement of independence would see the beginning of a united national effort to make Irish the everyday language of the Irish people.

It was not to be. The first Free State Government had made Irish a compulsory subject for the school-leaving certificate and it became necessary to have some knowledge of it in order to obtain an official position of any kind. Strangely enough, from that moment on the fervent enthusiasm of the first generation of language enthusiasts began to give place to widespread cynicism and apathy. The Irish people do not take kindly to compulsion and they have a keen eye for all forms of venality and jobbery.

After the establishment of the Free State the language began to be seen as the preserve of the careerist and the job hunter. This perception was not far wrong. As we have seen, civil servants thirsting for promotion made sure to use the Irish forms of their names and so did many employees of the new State broadcasting service. Politicians were wont to begin their speeches with two sentences of pidgin Irish and then to continue 'and now for the benefit of those who don't know their native language I will continue my address in English.' Worse still to many intellectuals was the fact that the language was associated with the puritanism and the moral witch-hunting which had unfortunately become part of Catholic nationalism. Those who believed that Irish youth of both sexes, but especially young Irish women, were, unless corrupted by foreign influences, naturally more virtuous than the youth of any other nation on earth, saw in the language a possible line of defence for chastity and purity and they insisted somewhat against the facts that in its literature the language had always been the repository of pious and chivalric feelings.

Writing in the monthly review *Ireland Today* in 1938, O'Nolan's friend Niall Sheridan had said that the language revival movement was characterized by a humourless bigotry that was completely un-Irish. 'All those who cherish Irish for the culture it enshrined are being gradually antagonized by the methods of the revivalists. The intolerance and bigotry displayed by its leaders have alienated all those to whom the language is not a trade.'[89] No doubt O'Nolan shared these views which were those of the intellectual côterie to which he belonged.

Yet he was on the horns of a dilemma and from him a deeper and more complex response was called for. Undoubtedly he despised as they did professional Gaelgeoirs, a genus of which he met plenty of representatives in the Civil Service and elsewhere. Certainly he had a deep contempt for what passed as contemporary literature in official language circles. In 1957 he was to write: 'The Government sponsored "Gúm" publishing house maintains a downpour of novels, poems, essays, plays in Gaelic; scarcely a soul buys or reads them because they are composed chiefly of embarrassing dreeder and prawnshuck.' And later still he was to write: 'The Stationery Office has over the years published many books in Irish, translations and attempts at novels. I would say that 90 per cent of these are worthless and ten only middling.'

He had a keen sense of the ridiculous aspects of the language movement and was anxious to dissociate himself from the clodhoppers who made common cause with the job hunters and place seekers in its ranks. Early in 1940 before 'Cruiskeen Lawn' was begun he addressed a letter to Quidnunc, the author of the 'Irishman's Diary' column in the *Irish Times*.

> It is common knowledge that certain categories of Irish speakers are boors. They (being men) have nuns' faces, wear bicycle clips continuously, talk in Irish only about *ceist na teanga* and have undue confidence in Irish dancing as a general national prophylactic ... Hence some self-consciously intellectual citizens are anxious to avoid being suspected of knowing Irish, owing to the danger of being lumped with the boors. There is, however, a *non sequitur* there. A knowledge of Irish does not necessarily connote adherence to the social, cultural or political philosophies of any other Irish speaker.[90]

Propaganda for the language was often part of a general call for a purer ethnicity. Language propagandists tended to be the sort of people who approved of book censorship and wanted to ban the – supposedly – depraved English Sunday newspapers as well as, in some cases, foreign dancing, foreign games and allegedly immodest women's clothing. Myles na gCopaleen, at least, was in no doubt as to where he stood on these issues. About the quite serious call for the banning of English Sunday newspapers he was to declare in the 1950s: 'It seems to me that all national publications, of whatever country, gain in vitality by a process of interaction with imported papers. The same is true of Irish people's blood. It is more and not less foreigners we want here and there is no limit to our requirements of foreign mental germination.'[91]

Later he was to return to the topic. 'There is, in fact, not half enough foreignism in this country,' he was to declare. In the 1940s there was a small outcrop of para-fascist organizations which made the usual calls for a ban on foreign cultural imports in order to safeguard the moral and cultural purity of the Irish people. Although it is dangerous to confuse the opinions and reactions of Myles na gCopaleen with those of Brian O'Nolan and although Myles na gCopaleen will usually be found to be on several sides of a question at once, there is no mistaking the flash of steel in this:

> I was recently held up again at a Dublin street corner by a small crowd who were listening to a young man with a strong North of Ireland accent who was aloft on a little scaffold.
> 'Glún na Buaidhe,' he roared, 'has its own ideas about the banks, has its own ideas about amusements, has its own ideas about dancing. There is one sort of dancing that Glún na Buaidhe will not permit and that is jazz dancing. Because jazz dancing is the product of the dirty nigger culture of America, the dirty low nigger culture of America ...'
> Substitute Jew for nigger there and you have something new and modern. But what pained me was the fact that nobody present laughed.[92]

The column went on to pour scorn on the 'mystical relationship' which was said to exist, 'between the jig, the Irish language, abstinence from alcohol, morality and salvation.'

But whatever his reservations about the sinister undercurrents of the language movement and about the various obscurantists, careerists and establishment hypocrites who had brought enthusiasm for the revival of the language into disrepute, Brian O'Nolan understood quite well that its final disappearance would be a cultural tragedy. Whatever irony Myles na gCopaleen may have brought to his frequent insistence that it was a more sophisticated and precise means of communication than English and uniquely fitted to the ambiguities and dichotomies of the Irish mind, Brian O'Nolan also gave repeated expression to his belief in it both as an instrument of literary communication and as a repository the loss of which would be more than merely linguistic.

Much of the hypocrisy and much of the controversy surrounding the language centred on the position of the Gaeltacht areas in the natural scheme of things. These were the areas, mainly in the West, where Irish survived as a living day-to-day language. Pearse, De Valera and the legendary Michael Collins, a victim of the Civil War, had all rhapsodized over the Gaeltachts and their people. In *The Path to Freedom*, published in the year of his death, Collins had written: 'It is only in the remote corners of Ireland in the South and West and North-West that any trace of the old Irish civilization is met with now. To those places the social side of anglicization was never able very easily to penetrate. Today it is only in those places that any native beauty and grace in Irish life survive . . . '93

In the early days of the Revival these areas had been happy hunting grounds for linguists and language enthusiasts. Then Yeats, Lady Gregory and John Synge had conspired to make the lifestyle of the people of the western districts the envy of more complex and cosmopolitan literary types. Governments both native and foreign added hordes of inspectors and instructors to the traffic in and out of the Gaeltachts. Shortly after Fianna Fáil came to power in 1932, the Government began to pay a bounty per head to families whose children spoke Irish and it subsidized fishing and agriculture. After independence, middle-class Dubliners, many of them careerists who wanted to learn Irish for the sake of advancement, others more simple or starry-eyed, holidayed in the Gaeltachts in large numbers or sent their children there to do likewise. Yet the Gaeltachts remained ghettoes which were also slums whose economic problems were virtually insoluble. Their inhabitants could not be accommodated within the mainstream of Irish life unless they lost the language and the traditional ways that marked them out as superior mortals. So, however romanticized by language enthusiasts, Gaelic racialists and bourgeois holidaymakers, the people of the Gaeltachts continued to emigrate to Boston and Springfield, Massachusetts.

Brian O'Nolan himself had been encouraged to go to the Donegal Gaeltacht as a boy and had continued to do so as an adult. He had the excuse that his father was one of the first enthusiasts to become familiar with the Rosses and the adjoining districts, and that he had in any case been born and brought up very near it in Strabane. But by 1940 when he began to meditate on a comic novel about the Gaeltacht, to be called *An Béal Bocht*, he had come to recognize quite clearly how romantics, conservationists and racialists can combine to stultify and degrade the objects of their enthusiasm.

But of course the book would not have presented itself to his creative faculty in the form of such a thesis nor was it written to prove such a point. It was the product of a not uncommon form of literary inversion. The Gaeltacht, and in particular the Blasket Islands, had by now produced quite an amount of literature. There were the Donegal novels of Séamas Ó Grianna who called himself 'Máire'; the auto-biographies of Muiris Ó Súileabháin, Peig Sayers and, above all, Tomás Ó Criomhthain, whose book *An t-Oileánach* or *The Island-man*, had created a minor literary sensation when translated by the Oxford enthusiast, Robin Flower. With all these, O'Nolan was familiar. His father was an admirer of Ó Grianna's novels and they were much spoken of in Donegal.

An Béal Bocht has been regarded as a satire on them, on *An t-Oileánach* and on the Gaelic literary tradition in general. Myles na gCopaleen said afterwards (and after all *An Béal Bocht* is his book not Flann O'Brien's) that he read *An t-Oileánach* soon after it was published – 'about 1930' – and that it disturbed him so much that he put it away, 'a thing not to be seen or thought about and certainly not to be discussed with strangers'. Nevertheless 'its impact was explosive. In one week I wrote a parody of it called *An Béal Bocht*.'[94] On another occasion he declared, 'I had scarcely put down this great book – *An t-Oileánach* – until I was engaged on a companion volume of parody and jeer. There, if you like, is the test of great writing – that one considerable work should provoke another. It is held that the *Aeneid* provoked the *Commedia*.'[95] According to his own account in 'Cruis-keen Lawn', during the time that the book was 'in course of com-position – a mere month or so – news leaked out and a famous firm of Dublin publishers asked me whether it would be possible for them to be permitted the privilege of publishing it.' The firm was Browne and Nolan which published school books and some general titles; Myles went on to favour his readers with extracts from their reader's report:

> I can safely assert that in an experience of sixty years this is quite the craziest piece of Irish I have ever met.
>
> What most surprises me is the self-assurance of its author – a man who demonstrates twenty times on every page that he is the veriest tyro in the Irish language. For want of knowledge he cannot begin, or continue or finish a sentence properly. Constructions such as he writes have never before been seen in Irish, and one earnestly hopes that nothing of the kind will ever be repeated. The late Stephen McKenna at one time proposed to write a book:
>
> HOW TO WRITE IRISH
> by
> ONE WHO CAN'T
>
> and here, I am convinced, we have an author who could take up his project with every hope of success.[96]

According to Myles, the reader's report went on to object to the episode about the stinking pig and to say:

The author may reply that the whole thing is an extravaganza, but if every word of his text were a *genuine* pearl, jem [sic] or jewel, the inferiority of the Irish would dam the production...
    My advice to you is – to spend none of the firm's money on this work.

In fact Browne and Nolan's reader's report was moderately enthusiastic and was, on the whole, in favour of publication. Its general conclusion was that the author had the 'making of a fine book' which would make the public laugh but that it would be a pity to publish it as it stood. 'The author has struck a new note in Gaelic literature, he has done it well but could do it much better. He should cut out the objectionable things and give us a couple more chapters like chapter IV.'[97]

The typescript was returned to the author along with this report and once again O'Nolan displayed a rather surprising readiness to bowdlerize his work according to a publisher's wishes. 'I have cut out completely all references to "sexual matters" and made every other change necessary to render the text completely aseptic and harmless,' he wrote.[98] He demurred however at certain of the other suggestions. 'It seems pointless to say that people in the West do not keep pigs in their kitchens because nothing else in the book is true and does not pretend to be. Similarly in regard to the chapter on housebreaking. Most readers will know that the people of the West do not live by breaking into each other's houses (and presumably stealing each other's washing). Apart from being absurd it is obvious that such an economy would be physically impossible.' He went on to say that he was 'satisfied that the thing is now safe from any puritanical objection but not sufficiently lifeless to prevent myself from whipping up a controversy in the papers about it under a thousand aliases. It is funny enough and I think it should sell if it can be published before *der Tag*...'

Sex is such a rarity in O'Nolan's work that it is a pity that the excised passages no longer exist. The probability is that they were pretty harmless; but in any case Browne and Nolan were still not satisfied. Now they returned the book with a note asking him to call at their office. When he did so he was told simply that their reader, Richard Foley, did not understand it and would not advise publication. Fortunately there were other publishers including The National Press, in spite of its grandiloquent name, a small, new firm recently founded by Pádraig Ó Canainn, who wrote to him on 17 June. 'We have definitely decided to undertake the publication of *An Béal Bocht* and will proceed with the setting up at the earliest opportunity.'[99] It was agreed that O'Nolan should receive 10% on the

first 1000 copies and 12.5% thereafter. The National Press declared
their readiness to publish before the autumn and O'Nolan immediately began to advertise the book in his column. This had actually
carried several adumbrations of its themes since November of the
previous year and also many references to Corca Dorcha, the fictional
Gaeltacht area in which it is set. Myles na gCopaleen now pretended
that he had received many enquiries from readers about this place and
stated that all curiosity would be satisfied in a forthcoming book
which would be published at 25 shillings before Christmas. In fact the
price was 3 shillings and 6 pence, by post 3 shillings and 9 pence, and
the date of publication was 3 December 1941.

On 28 November he had written to The National Press acknowledging the receipt of a rough proof copy of the book which he said looked
fine. 'I will try and work a big review by myself in the *Times* and do
what I can with the other dailies,' he wrote. 'If the book doesn't
provoke a row with the Die-Hards I will have to whip one up by
showers of pseudonymous letters to the papers.'[100] That the book had
been published under his columnist's pseudonym of course gave him
far more licence to puff it and praise it than he would have had if it had
appeared under his own name or even as Flann O'Brien; and on 12
December after the reviews had begun to appear Myles na gCopaleen
wrote:

> I am rather pleased with the reception given to my book, *An Béal Bocht*.
> It is gratifying to know that an important work of literature receives in
> this country the recognition that is its due. Scholars, students, men-
> about-town, clerics, T.D.s, ladies of fashion and even the better class
> corner boys vied with one another in grabbing the copies as they poured
> from the giant presses. How long will the strictly limited edition of
> 50,000 copies last? A week? A month? Who can tell? Suffice it to say that
> you cannot order your copy too soon. Paper difficulties make it
> doubtful whether another edition of 50,000 will be possible in our
> generation at any rate.[101]

The book itself, he said, was 'fine stuff' and he told his readers to
beware of imitations. 'Refuse all substitutes. Every genuine copy bears
the name, "Myles na gCopaleen".'

The reviews were very favourable, perhaps because Myles na
gCopaleen had already done much to make a certain amount of
sophistication *de rigueur* among a certain type of reader of Irish. Some
read it as a satire on Gaeltacht autobiographies and others as a much
needed satire on the Gaelgeoiri who infested the Gaeltacht and
patronized its inhabitants. There was also, however, a certain amount
of disapproval, most of it on the predictable grounds that the people of

the Gaeltacht had been caricatured. Richard Foley, who had turned the book down for Browne and Nolan, reviewed it unfavourably in a journal called the *Irish Library Bulletin*; and a reviewer in *The Bell* who did not find the episode of the inspector being fooled by the pigs dressed as children at all funny, concluded with the rather meaningless statement 'Whatever may be said about the Gaeltacht, it was never merely cheap.'[102]

Among those who read the book was Frank O'Connor, who by now was well aware of the identity of Flann O'Brien and doubtless also of that of Myles na gCopaleen. He now wrote to the editor of the *Irish Times* asking for the assistance of readers in the biography of the late Myles na gCopaleen which he said he was engaged upon: 'I should be particularly grateful for first hand accounts of his tragic boyhood in Corca Dorcha,' he wrote, 'as I need hardly say that it was those gloomy years described in *An Béal Bocht*, which gave his mind its melancholy slant and finally unhinged it entirely.'[103] Jack Carney, who was a friend of Sean O'Casey's, suggested that O'Nolan might like to send the famous playwright a copy and it was duly despatched. On 2 April 1942 O'Casey replied:

> Many thanks go to you from me for sending me a copy of your *Béal Bocht*. Lots of things come my way, loudly or silently calling for a good word (though I seriously declare before God my word is no more than the opinion of an intelligent man), and rarely deserving one (in my opinion); but yours is a happy exception; though, I am sure, many in Corca Dorcha won't say the same. There is, I think, the swish of Swift's scorn in it, bred well into the genial laughter of Mark Twain. It is well that we Gaels should come to learn that Gaels do not live by Gaelic alone, though, of course, no Gael can really live without it. The birth of the boy is well done, his home and all that therein is – a vicious bite at the hand that never fed it; with the Sean Duine Liath in the middle of the moil, a Gaelic Polonius, with his Creed of 'As it was in the beginning is now and ever shall be': the reek of the Penal Laws and all that followed them, over the lot. The chapter on the coming and going of the Gaedhilgeoiri is delightful, and the Féis that followed grand. How often have I seen and sensed things similar! The scene and the description of the scene where the young man stands to watch the sea on page 62, is fine. I like your book immensely.[104]

O'Casey lived in England, having gone into exile after the rejection of the *Silver Tassie* by the Abbey Theatre and its presiding genius W. B. Yeats. Like many of his generation he had learned his Irish at Gaelic League classes in the years before the First World War, but he was fluent in the language and had, like Brian O'Nolan, an admiration for Tomás Ó Criomhthain's book. That *An Béal Bocht* was a satire

on Ó Criomhthain's work or at least a comic inversion of it did not
bother him. Nor need it bother the reader. All literature exists in a
polarity between the heroic and the abysmal view of life.
Ó Criomhthain's book presents the heroic, salted by a sort of everyday realism; O'Nolan's the abysmal, energized by the outrageousness
of its comedy. Both are 'true' though it might be argued that
O'Nolan's was the more true for its time.

But in the end all questions of the book's origins, satiric or otherwise, are irrelevant. The starting point may have been O'Nolan's
irrepressible comic sense, working on the Donegal Gaeltacht novels
that his father admired, and even on *An t-Oileánach* which he so
admired himself, combined with his satirist's view of the Gaelgeoirs
who had made the Gaeltacht areas their preserve. The result is something much greater.

Patrick C. Power, whose translation, published in 1973, was the
first, has said:

> In *The Poor Mouth* Myles comments mercilessly on Irish life and not
> only on the Gaeltacht. Words such as 'hard times', 'poverty', 'drunken-
> ness', 'spirits' and 'potatoes' recur in the text with almost monotonous
> regularity. The atmosphere reeks of the rain and the downpour and
> with relentless insistence he speaks of people who are 'facing for
> eternity' and the like. The key-words in this work are surely 'down-
> pour', 'eternity' and 'potatoes' set against a background of squalor and
> poverty.[105]

In fact one might go further than this. In describing, in these
extreme comic terms, the life of the Gaeltacht, or, as Patrick C. Power
suggests, a sort of ultimate Irishness, the state of being Irish, Myles na
gCopaleen succeeds in conveying, again albeit in extreme comic
terms, a view of the human condition. Like his compatriot Samuel
Beckett he arrives at this view by ruthless and relentless exaggeration,
an unnerving *reductio ad absurdum*, or at least a reduction to the final
essentials of need and satisfaction, the barest and worst circumstance
possible. Like Beckett he confronts the final squalor of our bodily
existence, and through it perhaps of our spiritual existence, by a
method which compels an acknowledgement that when all the noble
and carefully constructed things have been said and done this is what
is left: the struggle, the misery, the clinging to the sheltered side in a
life which is, in the end, nasty, brutish and short. The method by
which he arrives at this view is the ancient method of the comic artist:
the tall tale, the puncturing of pretence, the refusal to tolerate illusion;
but in this book at any rate, unlike some other comic writers, he never

weakens. Like Beckett he is scarifying all through, and the result is an unrelentingly bleak view of human existence which is also a comic triumph.

An Béal Bocht was perhaps the only one of Brian O'Nolan's earlier works for which its author retained his affection. Mention of it in subsequent years always pleased him and would cause him to laugh or chuckle with pleasure. Myles na gCopaleen returned to it again and again in his column, lauding its virtues and adverting to its success. (It was not in fact as great a success as he claimed. In three years about 1,100 copies were sold.) Usually, however, when he praised his books, he did so in the wrong terms, describing them only as a swipe or a jeer at something when of course they were more than that; and *An Béal Bocht* was no exception. In his reply to Sean O'Casey, written almost immediately he received O'Casey's letter, he said: 'It is by no means all you say but it is an honest attempt to get under the skin of a certain type of "Gael", which I find the most nauseating phenomenon in Europe. I mean the baby-brained dawnburst brigade who are ignorant of everything, including the Irish language itself. I am sure they were plentiful enough in your own day.' He went on to say that he saw no prospect of reviving Irish 'at the present rate of going and way of working' but that he agreed absolutely with O'Casey that it was 'essential, particularly for any sort of a literary worker. It supplies that unknown quantity in us that enables us to transform the English language and this seems to hold for people who have little or no Irish, like Joyce. It seems to be an inbred thing.'[106]

He told O'Casey that he had been reading his 'last book', by which he may have meant the first volume of his autobiography *I Knock at the Door*, published in 1939, 'with great interest and enjoyment'. He concluded: 'It is a pity you do not come to Ireland – an odd time for a look around. The recent revival of *The Plough* at the Abbey was an enormous success. I am about to start trying to write a play called "Faustus Kelly". Kelly sells his soul to the devil in order to become a T.D.'

There is no need to search very far to find reasons for an ambition to write plays. Everybody in Dublin wrote plays, including many people who were not writers at all. And they usually offered them to the Abbey. Playwriting was much discussed on both sides of the family when Brian was younger. His uncle Eugene had written at least one play which was never performed; his uncle Fergus was the author of one which had achieved the dignity of production and of others in collaboration with his father which did not. Niall Montgomery had urged him to turn *At Swim-Two-Birds* into a play and William

Saroyan had, with his permission, used the rejected title of that book, *Sweeney in the Trees*, for a successful play of his own. In the summer of 1939 he had often discussed playwriting and the profits to be made from it with Saroyan. After the completion of *The Third Policeman* and before he had heard of its rejection by Longman's he informed Saroyan that he was 'thinking of making a crazy play out of it'.

He had by now become acquainted with Hilton Edwards and Mícheál MacLiammóir who had founded the Gate Theatre, a more cosmopolitan and experimental venture than the Abbey and more or less in opposition to it. A homosexual couple who lived together and gave famous parties in their house in Harcourt Terrace, Edwards and MacLiammóir had introduced a much-needed note of sophistication into the Dublin theatrical scene. They were a contrasting pair as Edwards was very English and MacLiammóir professionally Irish, the one an immensely competent tradesman, the other a theatrical showman who was also something of a ham. They had produced Denis Johnston's early expressionist plays, including *The Old Lady Says No*, which, under another title, had been rejected by the Abbey and returned to the author with that phrase written in pencil across the cover, the old lady in question being Lady Gregory. A sketch of O'Nolan's, *Thirst*, was put on at the Gate as part of their Christmas show at the end of 1942. Later that year he was evidently still thinking of trying to adapt *The Third Policeman* for the stage because he wrote to Hilton Edwards that he had an idea for a play about 'horrible concepts of time and life and death that would put plays like *Berkeley Square* into the halfpenny place.'[107]

But *Faustus Kelly*, as he made clear to Edwards, was written deliberately as an Abbey play. The Abbey had been living for many years off kitchen and middle-class drawing-room or, to be more exact, parlour comedies, usually set in rural or small-town Ireland and making fun of the manners and aspirations of rural and small-town people. These pleased audiences because they gave them an opportunity to laugh at the sort of milieu from which they themselves had just escaped. In writing a comedy set in small-town Ireland which, he told Hilton Edwards, was 'meant to be an uproarious play',[108] O'Nolan was thus following what was by now an established Abbey tradition. His mistake perhaps was to give his play altogether too much edge.

In his letter to Hilton Edwards, he said that he had sent the play to the Abbey but had not yet received a reply. In fact, by the date of his letter, he had; and the Abbey had shown sufficient interest to suggest some alterations, in particular a strengthening of the devil's part to

Right: A studio portrait of Brian's mother, Agnes
Courtesy of Micheál O'Nualláin

Below: Michael O'Nolan, Brian's father, taken at his graduation from Queens, Belfast
Courtesy of Micheál O'Nualláin

Above left: Strabane,
County Tyrone, taken from
the river

Above: Brian O'Nolan's
birthplace in Strabane, taken
in the 1960s. It is the dark
house in the row

Left: The Copper Beeches,
Tullamore. The young Brian
is third from the left. The
picture was taken by a
travelling photographer,
1921-2

Courtesy of Micheál O'Nualláin

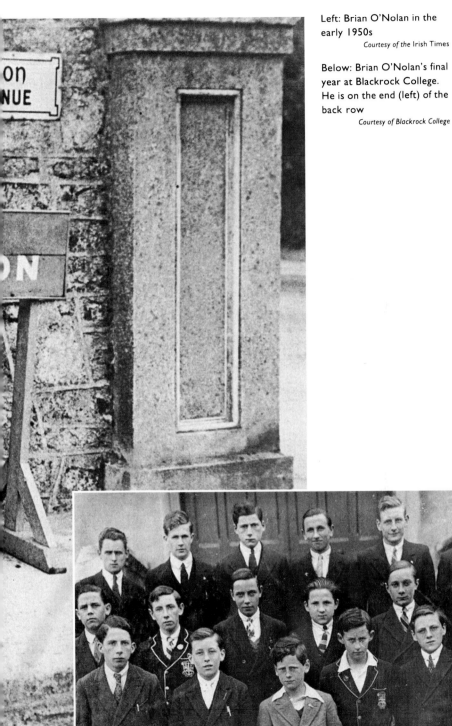

Left: Brian O'Nolan in the early 1950s

Courtesy of the Irish Times

Below: Brian O'Nolan's final year at Blackrock College. He is on the end (left) of the back row

Courtesy of Blackrock College

The Bloomsday
celebrations, Dublin,
16 June 1954

Left: Brian O'Nolan (centre)
between Anthony Cronin
(left) and Patrick Kavanagh
Courtesy of the Irish Times

Right: With 'Con' Leventhal
Courtesy of John Ryan

Below left: Film maker John
Ryan, Anthony Cronin
(centre) and Brian O'Nolan
Courtesy of the Irish Times

Below: Horse-drawn cab,
hired specially for the
Bloomsday pilgrimage,
passing the Martello tower
at Sandymount
Courtesy of the Irish Times

Left: With his sister, Nuala, and her husband, Paddy O'Leary, on his last visit to Strabane

Courtesy of Micheál O'Nualláin

Below: A relaxed conversation with Brinsley MacNamara

Courtesy of the Irish Times

show what other forms of temptation he might get up to; a prologue to clear the way for the rest of the action, a shortening of many of the speeches and the pointing up of dramatic effect. With his usual amenability, O'Nolan declared his readiness to accept their suggestions and on the same day that he wrote to Hilton Edwards, he told them, 'I shall now revise the whole thing quickly and send it in.'

The play sprang directly from O'Nolan's exposure to the clownish oratory, the sedulous self-seeking and self-promotion of the politicians in the Dáil. Many years later, he was to write: 'For some seven years my duty as a Private Secretary necessitated almost daily attendance at Leinster House. Garrulity is a feeble word to describe what I encountered in Dáil Éireann ...'[109] In the play, Kelly, who is a local Councillor with ambitions to become a member of the Dáil, sells his soul to the devil in return for a promise of election. A sub-plot concerns a Mrs Crockett whom Kelly wishes to marry and who is, as usual with O'Nolan's female creations, somewhat improbable. His own first acquaintance with Dr Faustus, that 'shady man', as he was to call him, had been when he was a student at UCD. Having taken German as a subsidiary subject for his degree, he had found himself 'pitched headlong into Goethe's masterpiece'. This was a description that he made clear he was taking on trust for he himself found it, as he said, 'turgid'; while he was prepared to admit that this was possibly due to his poor knowledge of German, it is also the case that about this time he began to develop a considerable resistance to most of the acknowledged masterpieces of literature.

The play opened to a full house on 25 January 1943, with a strong Abbey cast. F. J. McCormick, the theatre's leading character actor, played Kelly and Cyril Cusack, who had been a contemporary of O'Nolan's at UCD, the Town Clerk. Other parts were filled by such well-known Abbey actors as Eileen Crowe, Ria Mooney, Liam Redmond (whom O'Nolan also knew well from UCD), Michael J. Dolan, Brian O'Higgins and Denis O'Dea. Joseph Holloway, an avid first-nighter who had attended every opening night in Dublin for years and kept a diary of his impressions, was there. He had already been to see the play in rehearsal and found it 'dry'. He observed that the house was 'crowded and expectant' and attributed the general air of expectancy and good humour to the fact that Myles na gCopaleen had a large following because of his *Irish Times* column. But besides the well-wishers, there were also those who hoped for an old-fashioned Abbey row, reminiscent of those that had taken place at the first nights of the *Playboy of the Western World* and *The Plough and the Stars*.

In the event Holloway found the play itself 'all talk and no play'. Much of it, he thought, 'was witty and pointed, but after a promising first act – a meeting in the Council Chamber – it became all blather and high-falutin' oratory' which reminded him of a famous stock Irish comedy *The Eloquent Dempsey* by C. J. Boyle; the difference, he said, being that 'Boyle used his gas bag of an eloquent spouter with more dramatic inventiveness.' He thought the central idea of Kelly selling himself to the devil in order to become a member of the Dáil 'a droll one' but he was of the opinion that 'the author allowed his characters to talk all the dramatic possibilities out of the idea.'[110]

Patrick Kavanagh was in the audience and, according to Holloway, he agreed that the play was not a success, adding 'I hate all bloody vulgarity.' As his writings in the *Standard* show, Kavanagh was extraordinarily puritanical at this time and vulgarity was one of the words he used rather inaccurately to describe what he found objectionable in language or subject matter; but it is difficult to see what he meant in this instance. Some years later, he was to tell the present writer that he thought the first act of *Faustus Kelly* the best thing 'little Myles' had ever written.

By and large, the critics agreed with Holloway. But the first night audience seemed to feel otherwise and there were many enthusiastic calls for the author at the final curtain. These were answered by a gentleman, dressed as the traditional stage Irishman with pipe, caubeen and cutaway coat, who did a little bit of a jig and then silently vanished. Holloway and some members of the audience disapproved of this extension of theatricality into the author's appearance on stage; but in fact the gnomic figure was an Abbey actor. The play had been billed as the work of Myles na gCopaleen and it was that mythical personage who was now taking a bow, not Brian O'Nolan.

Brian had provided some members of his family with tickets, entertained them to dinner in The Bailey, the well-known steak-house and bar off Grafton Street, and then decided to make himself scarce, watching the performance from the back of the stalls so that there should be no public identification of Brian O'Nolan with Myles na gCopaleen. In writing this satire on politicians, he was conscious that, as a civil servant, he was in an ambiguous position. It was the first time that the shadow of this ambiguity had fallen across any of his work. 'There are certain political implications in it which, as a State employee, I am not too sure about,' he wrote to Ernest Blythe, the Managing Director of the Abbey.[111] Blythe himself was a former politician, who had been in Crumlin Road gaol in Belfast in 1918 with O'Nolan's uncle Eugene. Now he was notorious as the ex-Minister for Finance who had taken sixpence off the old age pension in 1932 as an economy measure and thus paved the way for the victory of Fianna Fáil.

The play ran for two weeks, doing fairly good business, and in after years, as his rancour towards politicians increased, O'Nolan alleged that Blythe had closed it down in response to Government pressure. He was also to make high claims for it, but, in doing so, to reveal some of his own doubts at the time.

> Why did we all, including myself, think it so bad? In that now distant year, I thought I had gone too far, that the play (though straight farce) had hurt too many people, and that that sort of thing doesn't pay in this country. I also thought it exaggerated some notorious national failings. Re-reading it in this different age, I am convinced I was right, but that the work takes on a new importance by reason of life and facts catching up on it. It had an unsuspected oracular and prophetic content.[112]

He was by then (1954) of the opinion that it was 'a masterpiece, saturated with a Voltaire quality, and penetrating human stupidity with a sort of ghoulish gusto.' It is not as good as that; but it is better than the critics were prepared to admit. That a play should be a verbal construct can hardly be held to be a valid objection to it, or, if it is, the claim could equally be held against *Hamlet*. Nor is dramatic interest necessarily a matter of confrontations and discoveries. The critics would have had a more telling point if they had said that the ancient art of storytelling is neglected in *Faustus Kelly* after the opening scenes. Like most of Brian O'Nolan's works, *Faustus Kelly* is rather static. It is what the characters say, rather than what they do, that provides the fun. The technique, as it frequently is in Irish writing, is self-revelation through modes of speech. One instance, Kelly's speech to Captain Shaw about the English, is uncomfortably close to the Citizen's famous speech in Joyce's *Ulysses*. The derivation may have been unconscious, but in 1943 Joyce was still the property of a very small côterie in Dublin and so the coincidence passed unnoticed.

Six weeks after the closure of *Faustus Kelly* O'Nolan's second major foray into the theatre took place. This was the Edwards–MacLiammóir production of his version of the Czech writer Karel Čapek's famous *Insect Play*, which opened at the Gaiety Theatre on 22 March and ran for a mere five nights. The suggestion that O'Nolan should adapt this had been made by Hilton Edwards and was probably inspired by the company's success with expressionist drama, for they had done not only Denis Johnston's expressionist plays but also works by Ernst Toller and others.

O'Nolan worked from a translation that Edwards provided him with. He changed Čapek's ineffectual and beautiful butterflies into drawling and effete wasps and gave the play local colour by making his crickets Cork men and his beetles Dubliners. All in all the *Evening Mail* was not far wrong when it said that he had used the 'original framework ... to "put across" some rather banal topicalities more appropriate to the variety stage'[113] than to the serious theatre. The thrust of the satire, if satire it was, was obscure to most, nor did he succeed in making his insects representative of the human condition in the way the original he was working from does. Even the note of despair about human existence which is undoubtedly behind it lacks theatrical resonance. The play was not a success with audiences and so the theatrical ambitions that O'Nolan certainly cherished around this time were disappointed.

In March 1943 Brian O'Nolan was promoted to the position of Acting Assistant Principal Officer in the Department of Local Government. This represented rapid advancement and the minute confirming his appointment said, 'Not alone is he qualified, but he is the best qualified of the eligible Officers serving in this Department.'[114] He was now to be in receipt of £400 per annum advancing by £15 annually to £500, which was, for a single man with no responsibilities, quite good money at that time.

But of course, though indubitably single, he was not free of responsibilities. Gearóid, still an unqualified engineer, had now gone into the Irish Army, an expanded force which was supposedly capable of defending the country for a few hours in case of invasion. He made, though he was eventually commissioned, by all accounts but a poor soldier; but at least he was no longer a dependant. Neither was Ciarán, who was now earning a modest living as an Irish-language journalist, a trade, or rather a disinterested vocation, which brought in surprisingly little in a country supposedly devoted to the restoration of the Irish language. A bachelor of somewhat irascible disposition, Ciarán had a streak of quixoticism in his character which gave his life a certain nobility. Roisín, as a teaching nun in the Dominican Order, was also self-sufficient, and Fergus had just become a doctor and was serving in the RAF. But responsibility for the other children, for his mother and for the upkeep of the house in Blackrock still fell on Brian. The additional needs and responsibilities of married men were acknowledged by the Civil Service through the existence of a special pay scale; but officialdom did not recognize any other kind of responsibility, however incurred, and so he got no extra money for being in effect the father of a large family. He often complained about this to colleagues, comparing his situation adversely to that of married men who had fewer mouths to feed but received more money with which to do it.

In the month he received promotion, the Minister for Local Government appointed a tribunal to enquire into the causes of a fire which had swept through an orphanage in Cavan run by the order of nuns known as the Poor Clares and had claimed the lives of 35 children. There had been local rumours that the nuns had kept the doors of the dormitories locked until it was too late because they did not want the rescuers to see young girls in their night-clothes; and the whole conduct of the rescue operation had given serious cause for concern.

The tribunal was to ascertain the cause of the fire and to make any recommendations in relation to it which it thought proper. It began its sittings on 7 April at the Courthouse, Cavan. Brian O'Nolan, or, as he is referred to in the official report of the proceedings, Brian Ó Nualláin, 'an official of the Department of Local Government and Public Health', was nominated to be its Secretary.

In all 64 witnesses were examined at 11 public sittings, eight of them held in Cavan and three in Dublin. The Attorney General, the Mother Abbess and the Poor Clare Nuns, the Cavan Urban District Council and the Electricity Supply Board were all represented by batteries of senior and junior counsel; but it is noteworthy that the General Solicitors for Wards of Court, that is to say the children, were represented only by solicitors. The duties of the Secretary were described in a Departmental document – to make 'detailed summaries of the evidence and assist in the preparation of the report'. The same document also stated that the 'work was done mainly after official hours'. In fact the Secretary had to sit through many hours of sometimes very distressing and repetitive evidence, the gist of which he had to set out for the consideration of the members of the tribunal, and he also had to sit through their subsequent deliberations. The report was presented to the Minister on 17 September 1943 and published shortly afterwards on grey wartime paper.

It is, as one might expect, a model of conciseness and lucidity. It found that the fire which started in the laundry on the night of 23 February after the children had gone to bed was, in all probability, caused by a defective flue 'which could not have been discovered or anticipated by reasonable care'; but the loss of life was caused by a number of factors including panic and want of training in fire fighting and evacuation procedures.[115] The recommendations mostly concerned themselves with safety surveys of such premises, the provision of emergency exits and the institution of fire drills, fire fighting and evacuation exercises. Many were dissatisfied with the report, including, probably, O'Nolan. When he met one of the counsel involved, the subsequent Chief Justice and Presidential candidate T. F. O'Higgins, in one of the local pubs during the hearings, they composed a limerick together:

> In Cavan there was a great fire;
> Joe McCarthy came down to inquire,
> If the nuns were to blame,
> It would be a shame,
> So it had to be caused by a wire.

There was and still is reason to believe that the tribunal did not challenge some of the evidence it heard closely enough, particularly that given in relation to the doors of the dormitories and whether they were locked or not; and none of the counsel employed had any interest in doing so either. So rumours have persisted in the locality ever since and local people still believe that children were herded into one of the dormitories and left to die there when it would have been still possible to get them out. If there was any sort of a cover-up of which he was aware, Brian O'Nolan, whose reticence in relation to matters that he had official cognizance of was always remarkable, never adverted to it. He did, however, afterwards speak of the harrowing nature of the evidence presented about events that night and the impression it had made on him. It should be remembered of course that the tribunal was not set up to enquire into the way orphanages and industrial schools were run at the time by the religious orders, but only into matters pertaining to the fire. As the transcript makes clear, from such evidence as he heard, none of the allegations that have been made since about the way the Poor Clares ran the orphanage would have come to his notice.

In the immediate aftermath of the fire, O'Nolan was involved in a dispute with the Department. He claimed that there were five days' leave owing to him which he had been unable to take because of his involvement with the tribunal and he wished these days to be carried over into his next leave year. The reply was that in the Department of Local Government it had always been the rule not to allow such leave accumulations. A gratuity of £30 was however recommended for the amount of overtime he had to do as Secretary of the tribunal. In the event he got £15.

In March of this year, just before the tribunal was set up, he had applied for the post of Acting Assistant Principal Officer in what was known as the Wireless Broadcasting Section of the Department of Posts and Telegraphs. In his application he claimed not only to have 'a wide experience of official work' but 'also ... considerable experience as writer and publicist – a sphere with which the work of the Broadcasting Section might be expected to be concerned',[116] and the application is evidence of some dissatisfaction with the course his life was taking and the all too clear division between his creative and other activities. The Wireless Broadcasting Section controlled the activities of Radio Éireann; and he evidently hoped that he might end up as a producer or even as an active broadcaster. His application was accompanied by a recommendation from his own Department which stated that he had 'a good experience of local Government work' and was Private Secretary to the Minister. He was described, no doubt with every justification, as 'highly competent and efficient' and in May of 1943 he was called for interview.

The questions asked at this were mostly based on the Statistical Abstract, a publication which enshrined statistics relevant to the State's workings, its economy and demography; and one account of the interview, very likely O'Nolan's own, had it that a member of the interview board asked him how many railway engines there were in the State. When he gave the correct figure his questioner looked down at the Abstract on the desk in front of him and shook his head, whereupon O'Nolan replied, 'You are looking at the wrong column.' In any case he did not get the job.

This failure to achieve a transfer out of the Department of Local Government into the somewhat more relaxed and, in one sense or another, more creative atmosphere of the broadcasting station, though a minor episode, he certainly felt as a rebuff; and as time went by it may have affected his attitude to the State Broadcasting Service, though it must be insisted that most of what he said about its bureaucratic outlook was objectively justified. He had some reason to feel aggrieved and some reason also to feel that the gaps between his various existences were widening.

Within the narrow confines of wartime Dublin and its intelligentsia his column was now quite famous; and in that year, 1943, the *Irish Times* was moved to publish a selection of columns set out in a double column format with Irish on one side and English on the other. The cardboard cover was a simulacrum of an *Irish Times* front page. 'Myles na gCopaleen Crowned King at Tara,' 'Dáil Dissolved By Royal Decree,' the headlines read. Despite the inclusion of Irish on an equal basis in this book, Irish columns had by now virtually ceased. The main themes of the column had however become established.

There was the Research Bureau with its diabolically apposite illustrations, many of these lifted from a Victorian *Cyclopedia* that Brian had found in the Custom House and appropriated as his own, others from such publications as *The Boys' Book of Inventions*. Some were drawings of his own or montages combining various elements from various sources. The Research Bureau had made its first appearance in 1941 and most of the other running jokes were now well established features. The Plain People of Ireland, perhaps modelled on Beachcomber's Prodnose, made regular interjections. The Brother buttonholed his bewildered but polite interlocutor at many bus-stops. The lives and adventures of Keats and Chapman were gradually revealed and the Catechism of Clichés, begun in 1942, continued to grow, a cliché being defined as 'a phrase that has become fossilized, its component words deprived of their intrinsic life and meaning by incessant usage.'[117] The Book-handling Service and the Escort Service were already functioning and Steam-men were being regularly catered for with discussions of single expansion jobs, compounds, poppet valves, simples, and the beautiful Manley superheats that had come in about 1921.

As with other subjects, his knowledge of steam locomotion was not so extensive as it pleased him to suggest, but his interest in it went back to Strabane, which was an important railway centre with a multi-platform station. The O'Nolans had also lived near the Great Southern works at Inchicore, and in Herbert Place the three eldest boys had had an extensive Hornby railway system which was subsequently laid down in Avoca Terrace. In a later 'Cruiskeen Lawn', he was to say of a famous railway engine: 'I know the Maedbh. I helped to design her and, when in 1949 the boys dreamed up an alleged Great Southern and Western Centenary, I drove her from Dublin to Cork at the company's request ... To be allowed to drive the train I had to join about six trade unions, and the cost of that transaction came out of my own pocket.'[118] The *Irish Times* published a photograph of the engine pulling into Cork with a begrimed Myles in overalls and an engineer's cap on the footplate; but in fact he had boarded the train at its last stop on the way and his presence in the driver's cab caused some ill feeling. When he made the claim in his column, a correspondent wrote to say: 'As regards Myles' claim to have driven this engine on her centenary run to Cork, I am informed that he boarded her without official authority by means of a subterfuge at an intermediate station.'

Myles na gCopaleen's vintage early columns all appeared against a background of wartime Dublin. It was a city in the last grip of the paralysis which Joyce had thought its principal characteristic. Trams, as in Joyce's day, still had their terminus at Nelson's Pillar where they changed trolley before starting for Blackrock, Dalkey and the red-bricked Victorian suburbs of Rathgar, Terenure and Rathmines which were the city's outer limits. Some trams were open-topped, especially on the line that Brian O'Nolan used to come in from Blackrock to the Custom House in the morning; and the streets through which they swung were so silent that both the hissing of the trolley on the overhead wire and the ting-a-ling of the bell that the conductor used to signal to the driver could be clearly heard as they approached. The bells of cyclists, hordes of whom pedalled through the streets of the city centre, the clop of hooves and the ring of steel wheel-rims were other familiar sounds, for the horse-drawn traffic which had never quite disappeared had come into its own again. The famous Dublin growlers and jaunting cars queued for fares outside Jury's and the Shelbourne, and horse-drawn drays and delivery vans had also been given a new lease of life.

There were still slums, overcrowded tenements the squalor of which was accentuated by the fact that their architecture was classical Georgian: the broken fanlights and the doorways from which the door itself had often been removed for firewood (as perhaps had the stair balusters) asserting the values of proportion and harmony against the greed of landlords and the desperation of their tenants. Though Fianna Fáil Governments after 1932 had launched serious housing drives and succeeded in moving a large part of the population to the new concrete-paved suburbs of Kimmage and Crumlin, these slums still crowded close on the city centre so that the swarming children of the poor were everywhere; and close to the city centre too were streets where tiny shops sold a penny or twopence worth of almost everything from tea and sugar to bundles of firewood. The Georgian streets and squares which retained their character were largely given over to lawyers and doctors, but there were flats in the upper storeys of many of the houses and a few were even still occupied by a single individual or family.

Most of the professional and administrative middle classes lived in the large red-brick houses of the Edwardian and Victorian suburbs of Ballsbridge, Rathmines, Rathgar and Terenure. And in a sort of inner ring of still older residential areas there were myriads of digs where thousands of students and civil servants of junior rank enjoyed full or partial board, often sharing a bedroom with two or three others. Many of these civil servants were confirmed bachelors and would spend their entire lives in digs, perhaps graduating to more comfortable circumstances and favoured status, but still propping the evening newspaper

up against the sauce bottle at the evening meal and coming down to
breakfast with hangovers after a night of pint drinking.

The amusements of this city were few. It had the largest cinema seating
capacity per head of population of any city in Europe, and on Friday
and Saturday nights long queues would form outside the Savoy and
the Carlton, the Metropole and the Theatre Royal. Besides the
cinemas the only places where couples could go were the dance halls,
the Olympic and the Classic, the Four Provinces and the National,
though these were more often the haunt of males and females who
went with companions of their own sex and eyed each other warily
across the floor before striking up an acquaintance which might end in
a long walk to where the girl lived and some heavy courting beside her
hall door. And of course there were the pubs in every non-residential
street and on every corner, sometimes having corners named after
them, Doyle's on the north side and Leonards and Kelly's on the
south. In an article he wrote in 1940 – one of three documentary pieces
for *The Bell*, covering the dog-tracks, the dance halls and the pubs –
Flann O'Brien had given a list of them. There were the new Lounges
and Select Lounges, Doran's of Marlborough Street, which although
he could not say so, was supposed to be a haunt of sin, Neary's and the
Waterloo Bar. The best of these, he said, were 'quiet and comfortable,
softly lighted, and a boon to any sensible, tired person who wants a
stimulant without being jostled and who does not concern himself
with social trends or think that a well-dressed woman in a pub is an
outrage that imparts a sourness to the drink.' The others, though,
afforded an insight into the meaning attached to the word 'modern' by
many publicans. 'They think that it means just tubes – tubular chairs,
repellent alike to eye and seat, tubular lighting, tubular effects in
decoration ... The ugliness of such a tavern cannot be completely
offset by the fact that most of the customers appear to be film-stars or
that the man who serves you is a bell-hop from New York.'[119] He
praises Davy Byrne's of Duke Street because it is not yet a lounge and
because like the Bailey on the other side of the street and the
underground Bodega in Dame Street, it is one of a small number of
'licensed tabernacles' which had been sanctified by the attendance of
famous figures of the recent past, among whom he names 'the Bird'
Flanagan and 'the Toucher' Doyle, both renowned Dublin 'characters', as well as literary and political celebrities such as Orpen,
Gogarty, Griffith and Joyce.

    Many of the pubs he mentioned had been well sanctified by his own
presence by that time. Grogan's of Leeson Street and Higgins's of

Pembroke Street had been familiar to him since his student days, and Grogan's, with its gaslights and marble-topped tables, figures largely in *At Swim-Two-Birds*. The Scotch House on Burgh Quay was a more recent haunt. This spacious and well-kept establishment with its glass and wood partitions was famous for its excellent whiskey; and to a confirmed Irish whiskey drinker, which Brian O'Nolan had now become, the quality of the drop, in wartime and thereafter, was all important. The Scotch House was also strategically situated for it was only a couple of hundred yards from the Custom House although on the other side of the river, and it had, like many Dublin pubs of the era, a side-door for elusive patrons who did not wish their ingress or egress to be too noticeable. In years to come he would spend more and more time there, even during office hours; for the moment it was a handy pub for a 'curer' or a dropping in place after work.

And it had another attraction also. Situated near O'Connell Bridge and near various bus and tram stops, it attracted a large passing trade, composed mostly of solitary individuals who were supposedly on their way home or had business to attend to. As was usual in Dublin they often got into converse with one another or with the barman, even over large intervening spaces, and the Scotch House was therefore a first-rate listening post. To it, more than to any other place, are owed the thousands of examples of the talk of anonymous and forgotten Dubliners contained in the column and elsewhere. He was to spend countless hours alone there, becoming, as quiet solitary drinkers often did, the person addressed, at whom, again often over surprising distances, complaints, anecdotes, theories and character sketches of public figures were aimed. The Scotch House was to achieve over the years a great number of mentions in 'Cruiskeen Lawn'. When it was auctioned in the late 1950s Myles na Gopaleen was to suggest that a clause should be entered in the contract of sale which would read 'the emptors guarantee that insofar as the conduct of the Scotch House hereinafter is concerned, Myles na Gopaleen shall, as a human person antecedent to all positive law, be permitted to pass and re-pass and where necessary pass-out on the premises.'[120] Fortunately the new owner, Hugo Dolan, was to realize that in acquiring Myles na Gopaleen along with the premises he had gained a valuable asset.

Not far from the Scotch House along the quay and across the wide but then comparatively traffic-free expanse of Westmoreland Street was the Palace Bar; and thither, when he had stoked up enough to overcome his extreme natural shyness, Brian would sometimes go next. With the advent of the war the importance of the Palace in the

Dublin literary scheme of things had, if anything, increased. To foreigners and exiles, such as Cyril Connolly, Louis MacNeice and John Betjeman, coming from a blacked-out and frequently bombed London, where the only literary pubs were the Bohemian hang-outs of Fitzrovia, the Palace seemed an extraordinary place, as indeed it was. The urgencies, brutalities and curtailments war had brought seemed very far away there. In spite of the eccentricity of many of its habitués and their occasional feuds, its big back room was a snugly respectable, placid and complacent shelter. It was also totally male, by a custom never challenged rather than by any rule of the management. Whiskey was in unlimited supply and was copiously consumed until the very last months of the war when stocks began to run a bit low. Nor, with the exception of Kavanagh and Brian O'Nolan himself, both of whom were conforming as best they could to the accepted mode, was 'that queer thing, genius' often present to disrupt the party. The conversation was literary but heavily anecdotal. Good puns were highly regarded and the studied witticism, that great stultifier of natural conversation, was much admired. R. M. Smyllie presided over the gatherings, largely by virtue of the fact that he edited a newspaper which published book reviews and a poem on its Saturday book page. A famous cartoon of the period, by the New Zealander Alan Reeve, shows a crowded room with, at the back, Patrick Kavanagh rising with big hand outstretched as if in protest, from a table at which sit Brian O'Nolan and his friends Liam Redmond and Donagh MacDonagh. But he is the only figure in the room who displays any real animation. Smyllie glances half apprehensively over his shoulder as if in fear that something Kavanagh might do or say would threaten his placid rule, but the others pay no attention, secure in the knowledge that they can command table-service, that the management will guarantee freedom from intrusion by unwanted unknowns and that all can go home by tram at closing time to safe middle-class havens.

Bruce Williamson, a young poet who joined the *Irish Times* at this time and was eventually to become its literary editor, remembered Myles as a 'phantom' figure who used to appear on the edge of the company, making 'an invisible outer circle of his own'; a 'rather solitary person' who might spar gently about something or other and make a few remarks, 'sometimes disobliging, occasionally funny'. He was not a conversationalist and when he spoke at length it was often to illustrate a 'citizen's grievance' by way of humorous anecdote. His appearance was 'very ordinary' and he certainly did not stand out in a crowd.[121] Later, Brendan Behan was to say of him, 'You had to look twice to see if he was there at all.'

Nevertheless, Myles na gCopaleen was now a considerable figure in Dublin, as was Flann O'Brien and, to a somewhat lesser extent, Brian O'Nolan or Brian Ó Nualláin. True, the reputation of the former was confined more or less to *Irish Times* readers; and only those who were to a greater or lesser extent in the know connected him with Flann O'Brien or the Civil Service. But perhaps the best way to illustrate the degree of reputation that this corporate figure enjoyed outside a small circle of initiates in 1944 is by autobiographical reminiscence.

Around this time, the present writer was in digs in Mespil Road. It was summer and, as Patrick Kavanagh was to put it,

> The eerie beat of madness in Europe
> Trembled the wings of butterflies along the canal.[122]

On 6 June a fleet of over 4,000 ships had landed an allied invasion in Normandy. There had been heavy fighting near Caen where the invasion was held up and the first V1s, a new German weapon, had begun to fall on London. Among the residents in this digs was a school teacher, a Mr Heffernan. A fairly typical denizen of such a house, he was a bachelor in his mid-thirties who played bridge at the Teachers' Club in the evenings and was by way of being a bit of an intellectual. We occasionally lent each other books and one day he lent me a library copy of a novel with a green dust jacket. On the back was printed a tribute from Graham Greene, whose *England Made Me* I had just read and whom I had read about in a piece by Walter Allen in John Lehmann's *Penguin New Writing*, then a source of much illumination to such as I. As a first-year student in UCD I was in search of sophistication, in art and, to some limited and timorous extent, in life. I bought the *Irish Times* whenever I could afford it because the *Irish Times* was a symbol of liberation from the values of one's *Irish Independent*-reading forbears and of graduation to intellectual Dublin; and in it I read Myles na gCopaleen whose column was by far the most sophisticated production one could find or hope to find in any native publication; indeed, like others, I bought the newspaper largely in order to read it.

When Mr Heffernan told me that Myles na gCopaleen was in fact Flann O'Brien, the author of the book he was lending me, my interest was immediately increased. Mr Heffernan went further; he told me that *At Swim-Two-Birds* was its author's only novel to date apart from one in Irish, a sort of in-joke for Gaelgeoirs; that it had been a 'flop', and that this accounted for the rancorous or, as he put it, cantankerous nature of the column. Though he enjoyed being in the know and letting other people know he was in the know, he did not seem to be *au*

fait with the author's private life though he did say that his name was
O'Nolan (which indeed was on the jacket) and that he was a civil
servant. Handing the book over, Mr Heffernan assured me that it was
'great gas', but apart from this, Graham Greene's glowing tribute and
the knowledge that its author was Myles na gCopaleen, it came to me
innocent of any critical foreshadowing or recommendation, even then
a rare event where contemporary writing was concerned, perhaps now
almost an impossible one.

In search of sophistication, a commodity then rare in Ireland, I took
to it straight away for, whatever else it was, it was indubitably
sophisticated. It was also unmistakably avant-garde, which, in my
view, was not the same thing as sophistication but was equally to be
valued. Inherent in its general cynicism seemed to be the assertion that
the present was more important than the past; that the past was
something of a joke. As Graham Greene said, 'it filled one with the
kind of glee one experiences when people smash china on the stage'. It
was irreverent; and while one was full of romantic reverence for all
sorts of things in Ireland in the 1940s, one thirsted for irreverence too.
And of course besides all this, it was very, very funny.

It had other qualities too which I can only describe as life-related or
related to the life one lived and knew. Its hero was a student at UCD,
as Stephen Dedalus had been, though this hero, unnamed throughout
the book, was of a blessedly more cynical turn of mind. He seemed,
apart from anything else, to be cynical about the physical facts of
existence, the necessary disguises and conventions required for social
acceptability. His medium was squalor. He stayed in bed a great deal,
as indeed did Dermot Trellis, his creation and the author of the book
within the book, but it was not just that he was lazy or deficient in a
sense of personal hygiene. His attitude, and the attitude of the book
generally, seemed closer to the truth, to a truth about physical
existence, than did that conveyed by the works of other, more
athletically minded authors.

In Mespil Road we students lived three to a room, though Mr Heffernan had a little first-floor return room to himself. As the war drew
to a close, there was an epidemic of scabies in Dublin which was
particularly virulent among people living at close quarters in digs.
That summer too, as the allied forces at last penetrated into Germany,
the censorship that had so long blotted out the physical facts of the
war was lifted. The first films from Belsen and Buchenwald were
shown on cinema screens, revealing the images of wasted bodies and
seemingly enlarged heads that no-one afterwards could ever forget.
However comic and peripheral Flann O'Brien's book might seem to

those who demanded a more literal commentary on public events, these not unrelated facts, the domestic squalor of the war and the more horrible squalor of the camps, seemed somehow to confirm his vision of things.

And they seemed to vindicate the book's cultural honesty as well. A time was coming, towards the end of the long drawn out post-war era, when the English university wits would shock the critics by mocking the cultural pretensions of the society in which they lived. Flann O'Brien's hero, for whom the name of Rousseau would be forever associated with the sight of a little man shaking his divested, vomit-covered coat and rubbing it along the wall, had been there before them. And although one was not to know it then, he was there before many other things as well.

He had deconstructed his own text long before deconstruction was ever heard of and he had obeyed the deconstructionist injunction to reject 'the literary/non-literary opposition as an absolute distinction' before it was ever uttered. The moment can even be dated. It was when Niall Sheridan showed him a letter from V. Wright, the backer's friend, of Wyvern Cottage, Newmarket, Suffolk, which began: 'Dear Friend and Member. Thanks for your faith in me, it is very comforting to know that I have clients who are sportsmen and do not lose heart when the luck is "the wrong way"'; and he immediately decided to incorporate it into the typescript. He had also anticipated some of the basic tenets of post-structuralism, though they were not to be enunciated for many years to come. Professor Terry Eagleton describes some of them as follows:

All literary texts are woven out of other literary texts, not in the conventional sense that they bear the traces of influence but in the more radical sense that every word, phrase or segment is a re-working of other writings which precede or surround the individual work. There is no such thing as literary 'originality', no such thing as the first literary work: all literature is 'intellectual'. A specific piece of writing thus has no clearly defined boundaries: it spills over constantly into the works clustered around it, generating a hundred different perspectives which dwindle to vanishing point.[123]

This would not of course have been news to the hero and not-quite-ultimate author of *At Swim-Two-Birds*, who had given it as his opinion that:

The modern novel should be largely a work of reference. Most authors spend their time saying what has been said before – usually said much better. A wealth of references to existing works would acquaint the reader instantaneously with the nature of each character, would obviate tiresome explanations and would effectively preclude mountebanks, upstarts, thimble-riggers and persons of inferior education from an understanding of contemporary literature.

But Brian O'Nolan was also, in 1939, a post-modernist, even though 'post-modernism' is not supposed to have begun until the late 1960s and did not become an identifiable literary mode until much later still. Writing in 1982, Professor Frederic Jameson, a high priest of post-modernism, said:

> The second feature of this list of post-modernisms is the effacement in it of some key boundaries or separations, most notably the erosion of the older distinction between high culture and so-called mass or popular culture ... so-called paraliterature with its airport paperback categories of the Gothic and romance, the popular biography, the murder-mystery and the science fiction or fantasy novel. They no longer 'quote' such 'texts' as a Joyce might have done or a Mahler, they incorporate them.[124]

And even more apposite to Flann O'Brien's first book are Professor Jameson's remarks on the place of pastiche and 'blank irony' in post-modernism:

> One of the most significant features or practices in post-modernism today is pastiche. I must first explain this term, which people generally tend to confuse or assimilate to that related verbal phenomenon called parody. Both pastiche and parody involve the imitation, or, better still, the mimicry of other styles and particularly of the mannerisms and stylistic twitches of other styles ... Pastiche is, like parody, the imitation of a peculiar or unique style, the wearing of a stylistic mask, speech in a dead language: but it is a neutral practice of such mimicry, without parody's satirical impulse ... pastiche is blank parody ... [It] is to parody what that curious thing, the modern practice of a kind of blank irony, is to what Wayne Booth calls the stable and comic ironies of, say, the 18th century.

Of course, as I have said, such concepts as structuralism, post-structuralism and post-modernism were far in the future as the war drew to a close, the allied armies fanned out through Normandy and cab horses clopped peacefully over the sunlit setts and cobblestones of Dublin. Yet one reader at least formed the impression that with the publication of *At Swim-Two-Birds* something drastic and, in a sense, irreparable had happened to literature in general and the novel in particular.

No more than those other concepts, the designation anti-novel had not been invented then; and, like structuralism, the declared anti-novels of Robert Pinget, Alain Robbe-Grillet and Nathalie Sarraute were not to come into existence until the late 1950s; but to one uninstructed reader, himself despairing of literary forms and seeking the courage of his contempt for some literary conventions, Flann O'Brien or Myles na gCopaleen or whoever he was seemed to have gone a long way towards the abolition of the illusionist novel of dramatic structure.

A simple but essential part of this abolition had been his elevation of the quite banal and the totally inconsequential to a central place in his work. Of course at that time the present writer had not read *Ulysses*, for there were very few copies around in Dublin and he did not yet move in the circles in which they were treasured. But even if he had, he might have seen that Flann O'Brien had gone much further than Joyce in freeing the banal and the inconsequential from its place in the plot of his book, and in its structure. Nothing in *Ulysses* is as free from the shackles of Joyce's own particular kind of consequentiality and his underlinings of significance as is the story of the jumping Irishman or the discussion of the fiddle as an instrument in *At Swim-Two-Birds*.

Perhaps what struck the present writer first about them in that far off era though, was their simple accuracy: it was only later that he recognized that the authenticity of the conversations between Furriskey, Shanahan and the others was only possible because these interchanges did not have to be constrained to an outcome dictated by the exigencies of a plot or even a structure. But probably even then he recognized it as obsessional, on a par with a painter's obsessional depiction of an object for its own sake and not for its extra-pictorial interest or value. There is really no reason, except the categorical imperative to preserve the passing thing, the ephemeral motif, the seemingly insignificant that all art labours under, for Flann O'Brien's wish to preserve the speech of the Dublin lower middle class of the 1930s and 1940s. Sometimes of course his transcription of it answers the mysterious purposes of the humorist as well:

After the cheering had died down, said Lamont, my man Bagenal strolls around and turns his back on the Sergeant and asks for a cigarette and starts to blather out of him to his friends. What does my Sergeant do, do you think, Mr Shanahan.

I am saying nothing said knowing Shanahan.

By God you are a wise man. Sergeant Graddock keeps his mouth shut, takes a little run and jumps twenty-four feet six.

Do you tell me that! cried Furriskey.

Twenty-four feet six.

3

The Dubliner

In the immediate post-war period official literary Dublin removed itself, black hats and all, across Westmoreland Street from the Palace to the Pearl, on the head of some difference of opinion with the management of the former about whiskey or cheques. This brought them the width of a wide street nearer to the *Irish Times* and seemed, if anything, to increase Smyllie's dominance over his tame literary men. But whatever interior trepidations they felt, the demeanour of everybody here was assured and calm. There were no literary enmities and few expressions of cosmic, or any, angst. Everybody aimed at the confidently delivered witticism, mildly deprecatory rather than cruel or hurtful, but often involving a pun on somebody's name. Only an occasional eruption by Patrick Kavanagh, whose tolerance for his fellow poets and writers was becoming as frayed as theirs was for him, but whose behaviour was partly constrained by the hope of employment, disturbed the general placidity; though the advent of the Northern poet W. R. Rodgers and his colleague Douglas Cleverdon from the BBC to do one of their celebrated radio programmes about Joyce, Yeats, Synge or the other luminaries in whose afterglow everybody lived would create a certain excitement.

But the Pearl was now only one of Brian O'Nolan's ports of call. These still included the Scotch House, which was near enough to the office for him to nip out for several quick ones drunk slowly during working hours; and this he was increasingly beginning to do. It was some time in the late 1940s that he made his famous reply to Garvin, who had cautioned him in a friendly fashion against tale-bearers in the Custom House. 'You were seen going into the Scotch House,' Garvin said. 'You mean I was seen coming into the Scotch House,' returned Brian. The comment reminded Garvin of a story told him by an elderly member of the staff when he had come to the Custom House in the 1920s. This man knew John Joyce and one day in the Scotch House met him in the company of a young man whom Joyce senior introduced as his son Jimmie. When performing the introduction, John Joyce described his friend, Mr Tully, as a Clerk in the Custom House. 'You mean,' said the young man, 'he's a Clerk out of the Custom House.'

Two bridges upriver in Essex Street was the Dolphin, a hotel which boasted only eight bedrooms but had a famous open charcoal grill in the dining-room on which a never-failing supply of steaks was cooked during the war. This was managed by Jack Nugent, a member of a famous racing family, and was a haunt of racing people on their way back from the Phoenix Park, as well as of rugby enthusiasts, known as 'Sport Kings' or 'Alickadoos'. Since rugby in Ireland is very much a game of the business and professional classes these were heavily represented in the clientele of the Dolphin, but Brian O'Nolan had always a chameleon-like quality and was capable of the sort of anecdotal small talk that enabled him to fit in after a fashion with company which was not at all literary or intellectual. Even his black hat was dual-purpose, counting as orthodox literary garb in the Pearl but with a brim not too wide to prevent its passing as an ordinary felt hat in the bar of the Dolphin. As an old Blackrock boy he was adept enough to display some knowledge of rugby or at least to contribute a pun or two employing the name of a player and he also had his talent for seeming more erudite than he was on almost any subject. When Ireland won the Triple Crown in the 1948/49 season he celebrated the occasion with a column which incorporates a long list of names of 'Sport Kings' who had allegedly chartered a mailboat and gone over to Cardiff 'to beat, by sheer lungpower their living daylights out of the Welsh.'[1] Why he should have bothered to go through such charades is another matter, perhaps only to be explained by the loneliness of genius, sometimes felt most acutely in literary company.

During this period of enthusiasm for rugby, Douglas Gageby, then just out of the Irish army and working on the *Sunday Press*, used to go into the Scotch House at 11.00 or 11.30 in the morning with a colleague, Dick Wilkes. In the large upstairs lounge there almost every morning they would see Brian O'Nolan, or Myles as they soon began to call him. He was nearly always alone, at most in the company of a fellow customer or two, members of the Scotch House's very varied set of regulars, many of them 'hard chaws' according to Gageby. They soon got to know and like Myles and they formed the distinct impression that he was an enthusiast for the game of rugby; so much so that when an international match was in prospect Wilkes had the bright idea of asking him to write a piece about it for the sports pages of the *Sunday Press*. O'Nolan readily agreed provided they could clear the pseudonym Myles na gCopaleen with Bertie Smyllie; but wary of being let down, they prepared a substitute piece, not contingent on the result of the game, which they could use if necessary.

On the Saturday Brian duly turned up at the Scotch House and he and Dick Wilkes set off for the game at Lansdowne Road, without overcoats but with the miniature bottles of whiskey known as 'baby

Powers' clinking in every pocket. When they got back to the *Sunday Press* office at 5.00 Brian sat down at the typewriter; but after half an hour or so it was clear to Wilkes that nothing printable was going to result and so the substitute piece was used instead.

After so much enthusiasm it is, according to one's viewpoint, sad or cheering to have to record that in later years his affection for rugby waned and that the game itself, its friends and supporters and the Irish Rugby Football Union (IRFU) became targets of incessant attack in 'Cruiskeen Lawn'. Some of these late attacks were on the grounds that the IRFU had decided to play matches against a South African team in spite of many protests, but their tone, alas, suggests that Brian felt one stick was as good as another to beat Sport Kings and Alickadoos with.

He found another sort of companionship in Neary's of Chatham Street, just off Grafton Street, and in Sinnott's, nearby on South King Street. The back door of Neary's communicates by a lane with the stage door of the Gaiety Theatre, which is just opposite where Sinnott's used to be, and in either of these pubs he was liable to find Jimmy O'Dea, who was certainly much more of a kindred spirit than the lawyers, dentists and accountants he consorted with in the Dolphin. A true artist in his own métier, Jimmy O'Dea was the great Dublin comedian of the era. He was a sad-eyed, gentle man whose very short legs seemed to make it difficult for him to keep his feet on the ground even when seated on a small stool at one of Neary's copper-topped tables. Offstage he was courteous, receptive and not averse to allowing those he drank with to do most of the talking. He gave an impression of vulnerability, with a demeanour which masked the tremendous reserves of energy and ebullience he put into the portrayal of his gallery of Dublin characters, including the famous Biddie Mulligan, and to anybody who admired them both the sight of the two Dublin comedians, both small men, sitting together, was a memorable one. Jimmy seemed to wish to appear very ordinary in the pub and this was equally, though he did not always manage it, an ambition of Brian O'Nolan's.

His last port of call on an ordinary drinking day would very likely be O'Rourke's of Blackrock, where he might find his friend, the painter Sean O'Sullivan, who, having likewise survived the perils and entrapments of other places, was also on his way home to bed. Until his bedtime began to be much earlier in the evening Brian would sometimes see out the end of licensed hours in O'Rourke's and then often repaired to the nearby house of a customer, Paddy O'Connor, a former Guard, to sit over cards and a bottle of whiskey.

With the end of the war, petrol had become available again in Ireland and private cars were allowed back on the roads. Brian had bought himself a post-war Ford Anglia to replace the Morris of the pre-war years but he was always a poor driver and was constantly in trouble. It was around this time that he told Garvin a story to account for an injury to his new acquisition. They had been drinking together after office hours and at pub closing time Brian offered to drive his superior home. On the way back he was struck into at the junction of Rathgar and Rathmines, by 'a fellow heading for bona fide country'. A caped and glistening Guard then emerged from a doorway where he had been sheltering from the pouring rain and suggested that they should follow the culprit. This they did to such good effect that they caught up with him and even passed him as he headed for Templogue; whereupon Brian stopped, the Guard got nimbly out and waved the other down. A few moments later Brian was surprised to see him salute while the offending driver sped off, but when the Guard returned he said, 'I was very lucky there sir. I was just going to summons him when I discovered he was the son of a High Court judge.'

'Well, do you know who I am?' Brian demanded.

'I don't sir.'

'I am the Private Secretary to the Tánaiste, the Minister for Local Government and Public Health.'

'Glory be to God. Will we follow him again, sir?' the Guard exclaimed.

Being a bad driver O'Nolan was sometimes inept in city traffic and one day as he drove along Eden Quay towards O'Connell Bridge his failure to obey the injunctions of a large pointsman caused a considerable snarl-up. The pointsman waved him to the side of the road, but as is usual in such circumstances took his time about coming to the car. When he finally chose to do so and pulled out his notebook Brian said, 'I will have you know, Guard, that I am the man who wrote the road traffic regulations.'

'Well indeed then, I am not one bit surprised,' the Guard replied wearily. 'And you made a right hames of them too.'

The end of the war had if anything accentuated Ireland's peculiar isolation and the contrasts between it and rest of the world. True there were now more visitors from abroad and newspapers, films and magazines were no longer subject to the special wartime censorship, though they were still censored on supposedly moral grounds. But the pietism, conservatism and patriotic archaism of Ireland seemed more oppressive than ever and the paralysis of its economic and social life more complete.

In 1948 Fianna Fáil was defeated in an election for the first time in 16 years and De Valera, who had established a record as the longest-ruling continuously re-elected European head of Government, fell from power; but the coalition which replaced Fianna Fáil and gave the civil servants of the Custom House a new set of political masters, though partly composed of Labour Ministers, soon showed itself to be as reluctant to effect social change as its predecessors had been. Post-war Ireland was a repressive, puritanical place in which even old-fashioned European liberalism seemed a dangerously innovative doctrine. There were regular condemnations of non-existent Communists and almost equally invisible free thinkers by the bishops, whose Lenten Pastorals, sometimes occupying two whole pages, were reprinted in full in the newspapers. When not occupied with the latest red scare, these were still filled with condemnations of the evil forces at large in modern life, such as Hollywood films, English Sunday newspapers, lounge bars and dance halls.

Myles was always professionally leery of both liberalism and social progressivism. As a linguistic critic, he was impatient with cliché; and as one who believed in definition, he was distrustful of the often ill-defined assumptions which underlay such views. His criticism of them was from a standpoint which is recognizably Catholic; and though thus the same as the bishops', it was philosophically more respectable, being of the kind others have derived from the thinking of the 17th-century Catholic philosopher Blaise Pascal. Since most human activity was pernicious or harmful, social busybodys could only make the state of mankind worse instead of better. Self-interest, self-deception, hypocrisy and fraud bulk large in all human affairs; and however much Myles na gCopaleen might devote himself to exposing them, his basic assumption is that they will continue to do so; nor does he ever show any gleam of admiration or enthusiasm for the countervailing modes of human behaviour, be they gallant, generous, visionary or, come to that, rational.

Of course a professional humorist is to be forgiven if he is seldom starry-eyed; but in Myles' case the tone of resigned irony and weary contempt is so strong as to convey the impression that he believes the world will always be governed by maladroit, shabbily corrupt, parochially unlettered people whom the satirist can reprove but cannot change. True, the Ireland of the 1940s and 1950s was largely so governed, but Myles' social pessimism was more than a product of local history or local conditions.

In a late 'Cruiskeen Lawn' – admittedly coloured by the discomforts inherent in his own situation towards the end – he wrote: 'It is seemly and proper that a man should exert himself politically to reduce and even seek to abolish hardship and hunger, but if he has the courage to raise his eyes and look sanely at the awful human condition, taking the world as his field of appraisal, he must realize finally that tiny periods of temporary release from intolerable suffering is the most that any individual has the right to expect. Cheerful? No, today's essay is not meant to be.'[2]

Even if the dreams of social planners were realized the world would not be much of a place to live in. As the war drew to a close there was, in Ireland as elsewhere, much talk of post-war planning, social insurance and welfare services. Myles' view of what the planners might succeed in bringing about resembled that of Huxley and Orwell:

> I solemnly warn Pat to look out for himself. Hospitals are being planned for him, clinics, health centres, stream-lined dispensaries. I can see the new Ireland all right, in mime-hind's eye. The decaying population tucked carefully in white sterilized beds, numb from drugs, rousing themselves only to make their wills in Irish. Outside, not a stir anywhere to be discerned – save for the commotion of funerals hurtling along the vast arterial roads to the vast arterial cemeteries – planned by architects, need I say – where tombs and tomb-stones are prefabricated in plastics. It is my considered view that Paud keeping step with world hysteria in the belief that he is being 'modern' is a woeful spectacle, is nowise funny. He has got himself a lot of graphs and diagrams and is beginning to babble about 'built-in furniture'. Give him just a little rope and he will demolish any decent houses he may have and go and live in insanitary 'prefabricated' shells, the better and the sooner to qualify for the new glass-brick sanatorium.[3]

The war reinforced his basically pessimistic, Manichaean view of human nature. For the most part he chose not to comment on it, even within the limits allowed by the censorship, but when he did, what he said was in keeping with a view of human nature as eternally wicked and governed by original sin: 'War is to be understood only in terms of man; man only in terms of war. There is no third war. There is only one war and to think that it will cease within the borne of humanity's tenure of the soil is to think as one thought in the nursery ...' There was in fact little difference between war and peace: 'When the world is at peace, horror camps are not photographed.'[4]

Yet the explosion of the first atomic bombs over Nagasaki and Hiroshima seems genuinely to have shocked him. He devoted three successive columns to the bomb in August 1945 and his horror was so great that it seemed even to strain his own general expectation of evil.

In 1944 the Ministry of Local Government had proposed to extend to the employees of local authorities the establishment and pension rights already enjoyed by civil servants. The draft of a Bill to effect this was drawn up and circulated within the Department. Among the desks it traversed was Brian O'Nolan's and he used the occasion to write a lengthy memorandum. It is in many ways a cry from the heart, one of the few occasions on which the views of the real man are expressed clearly and unambiguously on a matter of great importance to him. It calls in question the structural and moral basis of the Civil Service itself; and it is also a fascinating example of his style of memorandum-writing at its very best.

He begins sarcastically and somewhat in the manner of his column by saying that the draft might be taken 'to contain a statement of the advanced official thought of 1944 on human and social issues, such as are necessarily involved in the idea of superannuation. Considered as such, the draft is ominous.' In the discussion of the main part of the Bill, the memorandum took on a more personal note, revelatory of the position in which he found himself. The draft, he said, proceeded on the assumption that the civil servant was in a sort of heaven to which every sane person would wish to seek admission.

> This admiration on the part of civil servants for the Civil Service system is most significant. The Civil Service superannuation code at present in operation in this country is a semi-penal system devised in another age by the British Treasury to ensure docility and progressive emasculation on the part of its servants. It is unjust, cynical and immoral but achieves its purpose so well that many of its dupes have come to regard it as a divinely ordained norm; any pension system incompatible with it is bad but a system conforming to it is not only good but represents the final fulfilment of all legitimate human aspiration. Psychologists recognize that in conditions of exceptional morbidity the sufferer conceives his disorder to be a precious possession and a great delight; he pities others who are not subject to it and will consider that he is conferring an enormous favour by communicating it to them.
>
> The draft proposes to reinforce and perfect in relation to local officers superannuation provisions similar to those in operation in the Civil Service. In the Civil Service the entrant commences his career with a period of 'probation' ... The formally prescribed period of probation is his first official invitation to be timid and 'good'...[5]

From what follows, it is evident that he had given some serious thought to the question of leaving the service.

The entrant to the Civil Service from the outset suffers a cut of about
15% in his pay in respect of 'pension liability'. Such a deduction could
be defended only if it were in the nature of an assurance premium, which
would guarantee the officer or his representatives in certain eventuali-
ties a pension or lump-sum which would not vary according to the
number of premiums paid or the time at which the contingencies
provided against materialized. This is what any prudent person would
arrange himself if the state agreed to let him manage his own private
affairs and his salary.

However, the fact was that civil servants got no pension at all if any
reason, including 'inescapable personal circumstances', compelled
them to quit the Service before they were eligible for pension, that is to
say before they had been there for 40 years or had reached the age of
65.

The entrant's first ambition is to succeed in keeping his nose clean for 10
years. He is then 'pensionable'; i.e., he cannot voluntarily leave the Civil
Service without suffering great financial loss. His next goal is retirement
at the age of 65 or after 40 years' service. He now knows he is in for life
and moreover that the previous pension, rosily maturing over the years,
can be wiped out by a single serious lapse. He becomes a mouse.

He went on to attack the existence of differentiated scales and to claim
that they were loaded in favour of the married state. The fact that,
although the supporter of a large family, he received less money than
married men of similar rank who had the benefit of the 'married scale'
was a constant topic of complaint in Brian O'Nolan's conversations
with his colleagues. He now spoke out against what he believed to be
the philosophical basis of the regulations which favoured married
men.

The State's kindly protection of its wards goes further. The State makes
it clear through the infamous differentiated scales, that all its male
servants should be married because:
  i. this condition is more hygienic;
  ii. the propagation and management of large families (additional
      bribes are given for this activity) has a steadying, not to say
      prostrating effect;
  iii. marriage usually connotes the hire-purchase of a suburban house,
       another valuable 'anchor' for a person with a fixed income.

Private as well as official life is thus regulated in detail and this is the
sinister paternalism that is so much admired.

Then he broadened the attack even further, to include the position
of the Civil Service in the Irish scheme of things. The truth of much

of what he says here, especially his argument that the economy of the
country was already dangerously unbalanced by the existence of such
a large Civil Service and that a country of the size and population of
Ireland could in no circumstances afford any addition to what he
called 'the Civil Service caste', has only been admitted very recently,
after the lapse of nearly 40 years.

> Already the bulk of the country's intellectual material passes into
> the Civil Service as a matter of course. Once there, it is deliberately
> debased and dehumanized but it is lost forever to the proper service of
> the nation ...
> The bulk of the material in Parliament at present is dangerously
> mediocre and the considerable problems of the future can be hopefully
> attacked only if the attitude to those forced to enter the administrative
> services is emancipatory rather than restrictive. People of intelligence
> whose parents have no money have virtually no other choice. Children
> of the well-to-do enter the professions and the majority are too
> absorbed by their lucrative work to make any contribution to public
> affairs. The only other considerable class is the business community.
> Business experience seems to confer an *ex parte* and unduly materialistic
> mentality; businessmen in public life have not been impressive. The
> administrator, on the other hand, has uniquely useful experience of the
> structure and function of the modern civil organism. It would be
> difficult to imagine a better deputy than a man who has served for 20
> years as a County Manager and who retired in his prime (say at 50) to
> take a hand in public affairs.

These are quite sensible observations but they occur in a document
through which Brian O'Nolan's own feelings of frustration and
entrapment shine quite clearly. He ends by suggesting that virtually
the whole Bill should be scrapped and replaced by voluntary pension
arrangements with appropriate salary increases for those who elected
not to have a pension. An even more personal note is struck in the
suggestion that all officers should be permitted to retire at any time
they chose after one year's service, 'short service pensions to be abated
in a manner that would compensate the local authority for the loss of
any experience accumulated in its service by the officer who resigned.'
Of course he is speaking here of the servants of local authorities but
it is clear that he is thinking of his colleagues in the Civil Service proper
in his conclusion that the majority probably want more and more
'security' irrespective of what civil disabilities are inherent in such a
system. 'This is a pernicious and craven attitude and the minority for
whom it does not hold should be given the most solicitous consideration.'
What he wanted was evidently some method of release which would

allow him to enjoy his accumulated pension rights. It is typical of something in his mentality, also in the mentality of the time, that it would have irked him to quit without them. If he were to leave, the quite considerable sum by then deducted would come in handy; but, apart from that, a meticulous, book-keeping side of him would have grudged the state the profit it made on the 15% deductions plus accumulated interest. That he seriously hoped to change anything or to do more than relieve his own pent-up feelings of frustration and inhibition is doubtful. He was too experienced a civil servant for that. Most of the provisions of the draft were to be incorporated in the new legislation which became law some time later.

A view of Brian O'Nolan's career as it seemed to literary and intellectual Dublin in 1947 is recorded in a piece by Thomas Hogan which appeared in *The Bell* in that year. Hogan's real name was Thomas Woods and he was, like O'Nolan, a civil servant, constrained, like O'Nolan, Conor Cruise O'Brien and others, to write under a pseudonym. Like O'Nolan also he was a heavy drinker and though a voluminous writer of book reviews and other critical pieces under his assumed name, he too was acquiring a reputation for unfulfilled brilliance which would last until his death in the 1960s.

Hogan's piece was headed simply 'Myles na gCopaleen' and it made no distinction between the works O'Nolan had published under various pseudonyms, treating them as if they were all by the same author. It described this writer's *oeuvre* as 'Ireland's greatest contribution to buffoonery since Daniel O'Connell'; said that he had been writing for about 15 years; and characterized his contributions to students' magazines as 'crabbed wit, embellished with copious pedantry'. It dismissed *Blather* as an example of 'post-graduate silliness ...' which had announced with charming accuracy in its last issue that 'if feeble twaddle like this is to be admitted to the pages of this publication, we frankly cannot see any future for it'.[6]

Hogan's article then went on to describe *At Swim-Two-Birds* as 'a work heavily influenced by Joyce', many parts of which were 'variations on the Cyclops episode of *Ulysses*', although it remained in many ways the author's best work. It informed its readers that Myles na gCopaleen had written two full-length plays, one an adaptation of Čapek's *Insect Play*, and *Faustus Kelly*, 'the first act of which was the funniest thing seen on the stage since *Charlie's Aunt* but which fizzled out deplorably in the remaining acts,' and also a book in Irish, *An Béal Bocht*, 'a parody on Gaelic autobiographies, which is so neat that it is occasionally as dull as the originals.'

But to most people, Hogan went on, Myles was known as the author of 'Cruiskeen Lawn', a column that had been appearing regularly in the *Irish Times* since 1940. In the development of the column three periods might be distinguished. The first was that of 'the Gael who is at the same time an anti-Gael, or more correctly perhaps, the anti-Gael who is also a Gael'. This was 'a mildly good joke for a while but it quickly palled and could have had as little success as *Blather.*'

The second and third periods might be classed under the heads of Humour and Satire respectively. To the humorous phase belonged the Keats and Chapman stories, the dialogues relating to the Brother, the Book-Handling Service and so on. Myles' humour, Hogan maintained, was highly intellectual, for the most part purely verbal and mock Joycean rather than really Joycean, 'resembling that form of harmless and dull word play indulged in by people who think they are parodying Joyce'. Nevertheless the primarily intellectual element in the humour was like Joyce's in that it was tortuous and beset with *arrières-pensées*, showing 'distrust for the direct statement and tending naturally to the circuitous and involute ... It is very easy to picture him as our ancient monk, immured in his cell, patiently and with great pedantry, tracing the elaborate and sinuous embellishments of some old text.' His deviousness was such that he was inclined to lose himself in the labyrinthine ways of his own mind and sometimes vanish 'down a dark tunnel from which emerge sounds like the babble of an old man of the sea. At certain periods there have been in "Cruiskeen Lawn" long stretches of contorted mouthings, full of vague leers and jeers. They appear to recur spasmodically – the quartan ague of the over-clever.'

Latterly, Hogan concluded, Myles had become more of a satirist than a humorist. As such, he was 'essentially destructive, like Goethe's Mephistopheles'. This was partly due to the ambiguous position he occupied in the *Irish Times*. The proper subject of a satirist, if he wanted to be of any worth, must be 'the great stupidity of the mind of the mass'. But it was to be expected that the *Irish Times* would 'sneer at the Irish people', or so at least the Irish people were likely to think, and therefore Myles was forced to lean the other way, to be on the side of common sense and the common man against intellectuals. Needless to say he was superior to most of the intelligentsia because he was intelligent; but his general position was weakened by the fact that he really belonged to that camp himself. He carried 'the mark of the beast' and showed clearly 'the influence of his environment – the denigratory atmosphere of certain back-rooms inhabited by the native "high-brows".' Finally, concluded Hogan, 'His growth is thwarted by the debility characteristic of the ... post-coitum depression of a city that did once produce something. Myles is our type – he is the active embodiment of Dublin's, and Ireland's, destructive element. His best work, *At Swim-Two-Birds*, is far behind him and the line of his present work is brilliant but futile.'

This 1947 view is fairly typical, albeit of the limited circle of Civil Service and academic intellectuals to which Hogan belonged, of which indeed he was a central and much admired figure; and it is interesting in several respects. It provides the spectacle of one essentially un-creative member of the Dublin intelligentsia attacking another for being, as he thinks, of the same ilk. It attaches the Joycean label to virtually all of Brian O'Nolan's writings, under whatever name, except for *An Béal Bocht*, which is said to be a rather boring in-joke for language enthusiasts. (Mr Heffernan, it will be remembered, was of the same opinion.) It propounds a view of the column as rather cantankerous and sterile which, in spite of the fact that they continued to read it, was becoming the accepted notion in such circles in the late 1940s. Although O'Nolan was still only 36 the article cruelly asserted that his best work was 'far behind him', and from now on, this too was to become the accepted view in the circles in which Thomas Hogan moved.

These people were all aware of Myles' history up to this point. They knew of his UCD career and of the admiration he had commanded among a clique of cronies. They knew his drinking habits and, though heavy drinkers themselves, were prepared to be knowledgeably dismissive about the effect on his talents. They were beginning to doubt that the early promise and the early achievement had been so real after all and to invoke the word Joycean, with its implied tribute to the great dead exile, to conjure away their own previous enthusiasm for the work of somebody who was now a familiar in their midst.

Dublin has always preferred exiles, the mystery men of the boule-vards of foreign parts who are rumoured to be the recipients of foreign accolades, to the familiars of Grafton Street and its environs, who are cast, as it thinks, in its own image. From now on the legend of early, unfulfilled brilliance, the all too easily sustained judgement of alco-holic decline and the denigratory Joycean label were to become Dublin's currency of dismissal where Brian O'Nolan was concerned. If it is possible for a man to have several albatrosses round his neck at once, he had them.

And of course he had run into creative difficulties. *At Swim-Two-Birds* was, as far as most people knew, his last novel in English, and *At*

Swim-Two-Birds had established a position from which he could neither advance nor decently withdraw. It had been a brilliantly conceived undertaking; but as far as the writing of novels was concerned, it was also brilliantly and deliberately nihilistic. His very achievement now combined with a peculiar relationship with his audience to make a further foray into prose fiction difficult. What he had done made advance or retreat within the boundaries of the novel a dilemma, the choice really being between a more extreme outrage or a perhaps humiliating retreat. In their virtuosity, originality and even mere cleverness, *At Swim-Two-Birds* and 'Cruiskeen Lawn' were extraordinarily difficult acts to follow.

And in any case the column was by now having an effect in channelling his creative urge into a mode of discourse enlivened by dialogue rather than into modes of dramatic narrative or the fictional presentation of life and circumstance. He had never had a facility for plot-making in the ordinary sense. The brilliant structure which sustains *At Swim-Two-Birds*, the story within a story, could hardly be repeated. And he carried round with him as a secret even from his friends the knowledge of the rejection of *The Third Policeman*, the typescript of which still lay on the sideboard in the more or less unused dining-room in Avoca Terrace. To employ a metaphor related to the book itself, an unpublished novel can be for some writers almost like a major crime, weighing on the spirit and setting up a neurotic block to further development. A few years later Patrick Kavanagh was to say to the present writer, 'That poor little na gCopaleen has never found a myth that would carry all the stuff in his column, that would lift it on to a creative plane' and the remark is a perceptive one, both about the process of creation and about O'Nolan's dilemma.

Of course the word 'creative' begs certain questions, as possibly does the word 'imaginative'. In our time there has been an elevation of imaginative or creative literature in its narrower definitions over other kinds: epistolary, discursive, rhetorical, autobiographical, polemical or whatever. The reputations of the great essayists have declined as the reputations of the great fiction writers have increased. Imaginative or creative literature better suits the purposes of the critic. He prefers a bit of an enigma, a mystery, a construct, something that doesn't do its own interpreting. Whatever creative satisfaction Brian O'Nolan got from his column and however brilliant it continued to be, from now on across it would fall the shadow of the novels he was apparently failing to write. This affected his own view of his achievement as well as that of those who had perhaps a prurient interest in what they termed his failure. And of course he was ambitious for a wider success than a column in an Irish newspaper could afford him, in the rather naive hope that he might make money out of it as well as simply desiring a broader, more international fame.

In the January of the year in which Hogan's piece appeared in *The Bell*, O'Nolan drove his Ford Anglia into the back of another car at a set of traffic lights on the Stillorgan Road and broke his leg. According to his friends the matter was 'squared' or 'fixed', probably through a friend in the judiciary, but it meant that he was to be absent from work until 30 September, for much of which period he was only on half pay. It also led to a long-running feud with the Guards at Blackrock Police Station who had been responsible for attempting to bring a prosecution in the first place. It is difficult now to separate folklore from fact about this feud but one story is attested by O'Nolan's friend, Tommy Conolly, for many years one of the best-known seniors at the Irish Bar.

Conolly was O'Nolan's passenger one night some time in the early 1950s when they were stopped and taken to Donnybrook Garda Station. O'Nolan insisted that he was not drunk and, as was the law in those days, a doctor was sent for to carry out the usual tests – walking the white line, picking articles off the floor and pronouncing difficult words. There was a delay of over an hour before the doctor came and, during this hiatus, a change of desk sergeant. The new man, who did not recognize his prisoner, seemed civilized and amenable, and when O'Nolan suggested that Conolly should be allowed to go out and fetch him a drink, he raised no objection. It was still early in the evening and Conolly, who had been keeping his friend company in the charge-room, went over to Long's and returned with a naggin of whiskey. He handed it, unopened, to O'Nolan, who, looking the sergeant straight in the eye, unscrewed the cap, raised the whiskey to his lips and drank it off virtually in one gulp. 'Now,' he said, 'you can get all the doctors you want.' When the case came to court, O'Nolan's solicitor pointed out that the doctor's testimony was useless. O'Nolan's condition when examined was no proof of his unfitness to drive when brought in.

The District Justice threw out the charge and O'Nolan left the court in jubilation. But the Guards were not pleased, for, apart from anything else, the case, though unreported, had set a headline. When the word got round, many drivers took to carrying a naggin of whiskey with them which they would consume immediately when stopped by the Guards.

Another well-known story has O'Nolan and a friend parking a car outside Trainor's, the famous bona fide pub at Goatstown. The friend takes the keys and the car is carefully immobilized by the removal of the distributor cap. After several drinks, O'Nolan staggers out to the car, sits for a while in the driver's seat and then returns to the pub as if he had changed his mind and decided that he needed another. He repeats this performance several times, pantomiming more extreme drunkenness as the evening progresses. Naturally this behaviour comes to the attention of the Guards and when he next makes his little trip to the driver's seat, they arrest him. He is taken to Donnybrook where he admits to being drunk but when the case comes to court, he denies that he was in charge of the vehicle and calls his friend to prove this as well as the fact that it was not at the time mechanically propelled. The case is dismissed; and this time the Guards are even more seriously discomfited.

In his defence, it should be said that these stories belong to a more innocent era when a more lenient view was taken (especially of course by fellow drivers) of those who drove while under the influence. And lest evil should be thought to have triumphed over good, it should also be emphasized that the Guards were the victors in the end, when, as a result of being stopped and charged on the way home to where he then lived in Merrion Avenue, O'Nolan's licence was finally taken away. As if to give the *coup de grâce* to his driving career, within a week another inebriated driver ran into the back of his car while it was parked outside his house, rendering it a total wreck. He never drove again.

Until the car accident his attendance record at the Custom House though not so impeccable as in earlier days had not been sufficiently bad to cause any comment among his superiors or impede his chances of promotion. In 1946, for example, he was absent on 24 days for which he produced medical certificates. Eight were due to what was described as an ischio-rectal abscess and 16 were due to fibrositis; there were only two uncertified absences in that year. On 17 February 1948, he was promoted to Acting Principal Officer in the Department, his salary being £1,030 which was set to rise by £31 per annum to a maximum of £1,155. His protector John Garvin became Secretary of the Department towards the end of 1948.

On 2 December in that year Brian O'Nolan married Evelyn McDonnell in the church of Our Immaculate Lady of Refuge in Rathmines. This was the parish church of his bride, who was then sharing a flat in nearby Belgrave Square with a girlfriend. There were no guests other than the witnesses. At the time of her marriage, Evelyn McDonnell was a civil servant, a typist in the section of the Department of Local Government in which her husband worked. She had become a civil servant almost by accident; she detested the Service; and it had certainly never been part of her plans to marry a colleague.

A north County Dublin farmer's daughter, she had been educated at the Loreto Convent in St Stephen's Green before spending a year at a convent run by the same order in England. She then decided to leave and return to Ireland, where she found that her 'next sister' had received high marks in a Civil Service entry examination. More or less in a spirit of rivalry and because she was uncertain what to do next, she took the examination herself; and when she got one of the first places in Ireland she accepted the job offered to her. She was posted to the Roads Section of the Department in the Custom House where her superior was Brian O'Nolan.

She soon learned of course that he was Myles na Gopaleen of the *Irish Times*. All the girls in the office knew that, though there were many who did not understand his column. She thought it brilliant and she also found his letters, memoranda and notes on the files which passed through her section admirable in their unusual directness and absence of jargon.

But she did not feel that any glamour attached to him as a writer and still less as a rising civil servant. In fact she was not, to begin with anyway, especially attracted to him. She agreed to go out with him because he asked her to. She had gone out with others before, 'the way girls do'. She was an intelligent, forthright girl with a directness of manner which some men possibly found disconcerting. By the time of his marriage Brian was already a heavy drinker but she did not know that then. 'I suppose he must have been,' she has said.[7]

They had been going out together for about a year before they were married, though not many people seem to have been aware of the relationship. They would drive in his car to the hotel in the Glen of the Downs and other places near the city where they could have a meal and a few drinks. On some occasions they would go together to the theatre or to symphony concerts. On one of their very first dates he had spoken of marriage. She thought he was joking, but soon he returned to the subject and she found she had to take him seriously.

To say that his friends were surprised by their marriage would be an understatement. Most of them regarded him as simply uninterested in women; many of them had heard him make remarks which suggested an active hostility to the other sex. In a country where celibacy was not regarded as an unnatural or inexplicable state, he was regarded as a natural celibate.

The couple spent the first night of their honeymoon at the Glen of the Downs hotel, where the proprietor was a friend of Brian's. Then they drove on to west Cork, staying at various hotels and guesthouses for the rest of the time. Evelyn noted that in spite of his shyness he quickly got into conversation in pubs and hotel bars, often telling stories or making a few opening remarks which would gather company around them. He had taken some books with him, which he leafed through in a desultory fashion: among them Sean Ó Faoláin on the short story, Francis Stuart's just published *Pillar of Cloud* and Robert Farren's *The Course of Irish Verse*. Through the rest of December these would appear in his column, variously guyed, as books he had received for Christmas.

On the first night of their return to Dublin they called at Avoca Terrace. Brian, who had had a few bottles of stout, fell asleep in an armchair while Evelyn sat on the floor by his knee. The younger children noticed how fond of him she seemed to be. The couple went to live in the house he had already bought at 81 Merrion Avenue, not far from Avoca Terrace and so close to his old haunts in Blackrock that O'Rourke's and Levy's were still his locals.

It was not long before the extent of his drinking became apparent to Mrs O'Nolan, but she never lost her respect for her husband in 18 years of marriage; indeed some of their friends thought that she deferred to him too much. She realized quite early that she was dealing with an unusual and in some ways very difficult human being, but she realized too that he had uncommon abilities. She read books and respected his literary ambitions; and in spite of the many difficulties of their life together and the shortage of money later on, she even had a feeling of security because she believed that he could manage things and that 'nobody could ever get the better of him'.[8]

The marriage meant a slight improvement in Brian's financial situation, for he now moved on to the famous 'married scale', of which he had spoken so much and with such bitterness to his colleagues in the Custom House. Since at the same time his family responsibilities were now, in the nature of things, beginning to decrease, its first years were reasonably prosperous. To begin with the house in Merrion Avenue was rented – he had in fact taken a lease on it some months before. Later, in 1953, he was to purchase it by way of an Educational Building Society Mortgage for £1250.

The fact that the couple went to live in Blackrock reinforced the many other continuities of habit and association which survived his marriage. For one thing, his friends Sean O'Sullivan and Richard McManus lived nearby and these were, in many ways, his greatest intimates. O'Sullivan was a fashionable society portraitist who, like himself, had an increasing drink problem and who also like himself was acquiring the reputation of being a brilliant failure. His early work, particularly his drawings of some of Dublin's best known literary figures, if not very original, shows a certain flair and sensitivity, but his portraits in oils were to grow coarser and less inspired as he took on more commissions to paint the supposed luminaries of Irish society and drink got the better of him. In the 1940s he had signed a contract with Ponds Cold Cream to provide drawings of 'famous Irish beauties' who supposedly used their product. These appeared in the Ponds advertisements in the newspapers every week and this made O'Sullivan a very well-known figure. Commissions crowded in on him from people who thought that a commission for an oil painting might also result in a pencil sketch appearing in 'Famous Irish Beauties'.

O'Sullivan was a man of considerable culture who had studied in Paris, spoke both French and Irish fluently and was fond of quoting poetry in his cups. He had drawn the end papers for *An Béal Bocht* and was one of the very few people with whom Brian O'Nolan discussed his circumstantial and personal problems. Dickie McManus seems in some ways to have been Brian's alter ego: a gregarious extrovert who was intellectual enough for companionship and had a great sense of humour but who had none of the morbidities and self-doubts to which writers, and perhaps humorists in particular, are so often subject.

In 1950 Pantheon Books of New York decided to re-issue *At Swim-Two-Birds*. This resulted from a recommendation by James Johnson Sweeney, a well-known Irish-American connected with the Guggenheim Museum, who was also an enthusiastic Joycean and a collector of Joyce's manuscripts. The book appeared in March of the following year, in a handsome pocketable edition of 3,000 copies; but the reviews, though enthusiastic enough, were uncomprehending and sales were moderate. Though O'Nolan, who does not seem to have attached any great importance to the event, did not know it at the time, this was the beginning of a comeback. His book would slowly but surely acquire a word-of-mouth reputation among discerning Americans, particularly among sophisticated New Yorkers, some of whom sought him out when in Dublin.

In that year also a young Dubliner, John Ryan, who belonged to one of Dublin's merchant families, owners of the familiar Monument Creameries, founded a monthly review which he called *Envoy*.

Envoy had an office above the Monument Creamery in Grafton

Street but McDaid's pub in Harry Street, just across the road, was the editorial hang-out. McDaid's was a narrow high-ceilinged place whose proprietor had made unsuccessful attempts to turn it into a lounge, with leatherette seats against the walls and an odd cork-topped counter which was soon pockmarked by cigarette burns. It had become the headquarters of one of Dublin's bohemias, though that word scarcely fits, for this one had the Irish virtue of being uncategorizable, composed as it was of many different kinds of layabouts, piss artists, idle rentiers, distressed gentlefolk and dissident, breakaway or retired subversives. Now, with the advent of the magazine, McDaid's took on a more literary or rather anti-literary character.

Patrick Kavanagh was the best-known local contributor to its pages, writing a monthly Diary which was in large part an attack on the poets and novelists who were acceptable at Smyllie's table. He had dealt with them before, in his satirical poem, the 'Paddiad', published in the famous English literary review, *Horizon*, during the war.

> Paddy Mist and Paddy Frog,
> Croaking nightly in the bog ...

But however stinging this was, it could be shrugged off. The implications, the 'meaning' of poetry, can always, as Thomas Hardy observed, be shrugged off. But the habitués of the Pearl found the poet's humorous, sophisticated and ironic prose considerably more disturbing; and it was largely his Diary which marked out *Envoy* as the first radical point of departure in post-war letters in Ireland.

But the author of the Diary was also delighted with the new ambience of McDaid's and with the company he found there, declaring that among some of the younger contributors to the magazine he had found the sort of friends he had sought in all his years in Dublin. He paid at least one visit every day to the *Envoy* office and would then cross over to the pub. He would peer round the door for a moment or two before entering, reach his chosen company in two or three giant strides and demand attention at once with a generalization or an anecdote.

Soon Brian O'Nolan, or Myles, as everybody in the pub, including the barmen, called him, was a contributor to the magazine also, the general editorial aim being to foster a counter-trend of sophistication and cosmopolitanism against the debased Celtic twilightery and the forms of rural picturesque which, it was felt, still held sway in established literary circles. Alas, we were not to know that Celtic twilightery and the rural picturesque are hydra-headed monsters which survive all attempts to extirpate them either by precept or example. Many of the contributions to *Envoy*, including Kavanagh's, had a strong anti-nationalist coloration, a more or less humorous form of protest against the tattered and cliché-ridden nationalist triumphalism with its endless references to the 'War of Independence' and 'our unique Gaelic culture' which was the official ethos of the country; and it was to *Envoy* that Brian contributed the story 'The Martyr's Crown'.

Like all his works it had been in gestation for quite a long time and in fact the first version of the story dates from January 1940 when it was called 'For Ireland Home and Beauty'. The 1950 version is immensely superior to the first, which was more anecdotal and had a trick ending beyond the ending after the manner that O. Henry had bequeathed to commercial short story writers everywhere. In the following year, 1951, John Ryan asked Brian O'Nolan to edit a special James Joyce issue of *Envoy*. This was a brilliant idea. All his writing life Brian O'Nolan had had the word 'Joyce' firmly attached to him, almost, one could say – if the metaphor was not otherwise so inapt – like a tin can tied to a dog's tail; and it is no wonder that he frequently reacted to it with annoyance.

Samuel Beckett recalls meeting Brian O'Nolan in Niall Montgomery's house shortly after the publication of *At Swim-Two-Birds* and telling him that Joyce had read and liked it. In a letter to Anne Clissmann in 1967 Beckett said that O'Nolan's reply was 'best forgotten';[9] but in Berlin later on, he decided to tell all and twice repeated O'Nolan's reply to Aidan Higgins, the second time with what Higgins called emphatic distaste. 'His reply was the following,' Beckett said, ' "Joyce, that refurbisher of skivvies' stories!" '[10] It is charitable to assume that O'Nolan had already begun to hear too much about Joyce's influence on his book from its readers in Dublin, whether friends or enemies.

There are nearly a hundred references to Joyce in the 'Cruiskeen Lawn' column over the years. Many were attacks of varying degrees of seriousness on Joyce's work; others were pseudo-biographical, usually referring to 'poor Joyce' or 'poor Jimmy Joyce'. Some were denigratory of American scholarship. One was a discussion of the difficulties of translating *Ulysses*, a task on which Myles himself was said to be engaged and of which a sample was actually given. Often, with particular reference to *Finnegans Wake*, Joyce was said to be a wilfully obscure writer, or even an incoherent one, whose experiments had been destructive of the English language.

From UCD days on, O'Nolan and his friends had always been inclined to take the art for art's sake view of Joyce as a semi-demented genius whose books were great fun for the initiate but had not much extension into life. Allied to this view was one which reflected their own situation generally. Joyce was bedevilled by his Irish Catholicism and set out to free himself from it by a series of shock tactics which had the merit, in his own eyes, of shocking other people as well. He wound up by writing a private language, and his writings, though impressive for their obsessional quality, were onanistic and could even be taken as an example of the futility of artistic endeavour. O'Nolan was certainly encouraged to take this view of Joyce by his friend, Niall Montgomery, and he rarely departed from it; although once in a late 'Cruiskeen Lawn' he admitted that all that are needed for the understanding of *Ulysses* are 'intelligence, maturity and some knowledge of life as well as letters.'[11]

O'Nolan's own editorial contribution to the special issue of *Envoy* was a piece called 'A Bash in the Tunnel'. This is a superb joke in itself and it ranks with the earlier 'Drink and Time in Dublin' as the funniest of O'Nolan's writings on the subject of alcoholic addiction. In 'A Bash in the Tunnel' the protagonist possesses a key which gives him access to the dining cars of the Great Southern Railway and their liquor supply and is accustomed to avail himself of this facility by locking himself in the lavatories of cars parked overnight and drinking himself sozzled. On this particular occasion the night seems very long but he gallantly drinks through it. Only when his supply comes to an end does he discover that at some stage during his bash the car has been shunted into a tunnel and that he has been there for weeks. This, the author winds up, is a paradigm of the situation of the artist in Ireland:

> Sitting fully dressed, innerly locked in the toilet of a locked coach where he has no right to be, resentfully drinking somebody else's whiskey, being whisked hither and thider by anonymous shunters, keeping fastidiously the while on the outer face of his door the simple word ENGAGED.[12]

This tall enough tale is prefaced by some remarks about Joyce which are resumed after its telling with the statement: 'I think the image' – of the man drinking obliviously in the tunnel – 'fits Joyce.' The thesis enunciates, with startling clarity, what might be called the O'Nolan–Montgomery view of Joyce and it has a double aspect. The first is of the demented artist, engaged on an enormous *acte gratuit*: 'James Joyce was an artist. He has said so himself. His was a case of Ars gratia Artist.' The second, enunciated also in the opening paragraph, is of the equally demented Catholic, or ex-Catholic. 'He declared that he would pursue his artistic mission even if the penalty was as long as eternity itself. This appears to be an affirmation of belief in Hell, therefore of belief in Heaven and God.'

The first aspect of Joyce is re-emphasized towards the end in the statement that 'Perhaps the true fascination of Joyce lies in his secretiveness, his ambiguity (his polyguity perhaps?), his leg-pulling, his dishonesties, his technical skill, his attraction for Americans.' The second, the view of Joyce as a lapsed believer, occupies more space and is more forcefully presented: 'It seems to me that Joyce emerges, through curtains of salacity and blasphemy, as a truly fear-shaken Irish Catholic, rebelling not so much against the Church but against its near-schismatic Irish eccentricities, its pretence that there is only one Commandment, the vulgarity of its edifices, the shallowness and stupidity of many of its ministers. His revolt, noble in itself, carried him away.'

Both views are sad and reveal something of the sadness of O'Nolan's own position. Neither takes account of Joyce's broad humanity, his determination to extend both the ordinary recorded area of human experience and the reclaimed area of poetic compassion, his ultimate assent to life and its purposes. The first view stems from O'Nolan's own philistinism, his reluctance to regard the sort of dedication to art which he himself had refused as other than deluded or, alternatively, false and pretentious; the second springs from his own brand of Catholicism, with its dark, deterministic tendencies.

True, there is a third view, expressed often enough by Myles na Gopaleen, which declares an admiration for Joyce's 'dexterity and resource in handling language', his 'subtlety in conveying the image of Dublin and her people' and his 'accuracy in setting down speech authentically'. But this view also, however much fellow feeling it may convey, is, taken on its own, too reductionist. Less so perhaps is that of Joyce as primarily a humorist; but in the *Envoy* essay, the praise of Joyce's humour is given a rather startling coda, which again says more about O'Nolan himself than about Joyce.

> The number of people invited to contribute to this issue has necessarily been limited. Yet it is curious that none makes mention of Joyce's superber quality: his capacity for humour. Humour, the handmaid of sorrow and fear creeps out endlessly in all Joyce's works. He uses the thing, in the same way as Shakespeare does but less formally, to attenuate the fear of those who have belief and who genuinely think that they will be in hell or in heaven shortly, and possibly very shortly. With laughs he palliates the sense of doom that is the heritage of the Irish Catholic. True humour needs this background urgency: Rabelais is funny, but his stuff cloys. His stuff lacks tragedy.

In 1950, the year before the special issue of *Envoy*, Ewan Phillips of the Institute of Contemporary Arts in London had written to O'Nolan about a projected Joyce exhibition. He asked for a copy of the Longman's Green 1939 edition of *At Swim-Two-Birds* (there was then no other) and also the originals of any correspondence he might have had with Joyce. O'Nolan replied on 24 May.

Dear Sir, In reply to your letter of the 14th regarding the proposed Joyce Exhibition in London, I enclose a copy of the book you mention. It is not mine and I would like to get it back in due course.

In regard to letters from Joyce, he asked me some years ago to make some confidential enquiries on business and related matters. Apart from the fact that the letters are of no literary interest whatever, I don't think it would be proper to exhibit them publicly. Yours sincerely, Brian O'Nolan.[13]

This was a spoof. Joyce had corresponded with Niall Sheridan but not with him; and there is of course no mention of any personal acquaintance in the special issue of *Envoy*.

In 1950 also a copy of a Paris publication edited by Maria Jolas, *The James Joyce Yearbook*, arrived in Dublin. This contained the text of a supposed interview with Joyce's father, John Stanislaus Joyce, which had been written by an un-named Dublin journalist and, though the editor of the *Yearbook* did not say that, was found among James Joyce's papers after his death. In it, the old man is in characteristically boastful humour, happily rambling on about his youth, his fame as a singer, his athletic prowess, his son's brilliance as a debater in the Literary and Historical Society and other matters; and exhibiting a great richness of phrase and idiom as he does so. Internal evidence suggests that he was responding to questions supplied by his son. If one had any doubts about the authenticity of the interview they would be on the grounds that it is all a little too much in character and too picturesque in tone and idiom.

The publication was brought to Dublin by an American professor, John V. Kelleher, who took it straight to Niall Montgomery. It was gleefully received and Kelleher was quite happy to fall in with Montgomery's suggestion that they should immediately seek out Brian O'Nolan and show it to him. They found him in a pub (un-named) and Kelleher noted that his reaction was also gleeful and knowing. Gradually Dublin gossip began to attribute this interview to O'Nolan, or possibly to a collaboration between O'Nolan, Montgomery and Sheridan. It was assumed that it was completely made up and that they had intended to fool whoever was credulous enough to be taken in by it. O'Nolan never denied that he was one of the authors of the interview and the legend became well-established. On 25 February 1956, Quidnunc referred to the interview in his 'Irishman's Diary' column in the *Irish Times*. The supposed interview, he said, was 'a brilliant fake'; and he added, 'I have good reason to believe that its author was James Joyce's literary foster child, Flann O'Brien.' Except that being described in these terms cannot have pleased him, it seems obvious that O'Nolan encouraged Quidnunc to believe that he had been the author of the *Yearbook* piece and that it was entirely a joke.

Of course, as we have seen, O'Nolan and Sheridan had gone to see John Joyce a year or two before his death; but Sheridan has assured the present writer that they were not the authors of the supposed interview, which 'bore no relation to the atmosphere, mood or feeling of the real occasion.'[14] He also assured Richard Ellmann that nothing was written up afterwards by either of them and that Brian O'Nolan never sent any account of their visit to Joyce. In fact both to Ellmann and the present writer he has been adamant that Brian O'Nolan was never in communication with James Joyce and never had any direct acquaintance with him. Yet, as we shall see, on at least one occasion towards the close of his life Brian O'Nolan would claim such an acquaintance. The figure of Joyce hung over his life like a sort of cloud from which the apocalyptic vision could come or had come. Like all revelations, it was resisted, distorted and, in part, rejected; but there was no disputing the fact that it had been vouchsafed.

In the early 1950s Brian's relationship with the *Irish Times* was not happy. There had always been rows because his copy, though admirably clear, was difficult both to sub and to set; and unfortunately the more alert the sub or meticulous the typesetter, the more his puns, his jokes and his deliberate mistakes were 'corrected'. This had led to a stream of letters to whoever was subbing the column over the years, the terms of abuse employed being already familiar from their use in the column itself – 'cornerboy', 'thullabawn', 'thooleramawn', along with the odd 'gobshite', 'bastard' and other terms. The novelist Jack White, who to begin with was the junior in the editorial department responsible for subbing Myles and later features editor, afterwards wrote, 'In terms of sheer scurrilous abuse I have never seen anything quite like those letters.'[15]

And besides changes and alterations, there were cuts and rejections. It was a standing editorial order that Myles' copy was to be closely scrutinized for libel, scurrility and double meanings. Columns found to offend were drastically cut, or thrown whole into the waste-paper basket. He was the more aggrieved by this procedure because there was a rule that he was to be paid only for what was printed. Through the 1950s, he was paid in any case only two guineas a piece, but because the rate of rejection was so high he did far more work than he was paid for. This was a constant source of contention which was even more infuriating to Myles since he would never admit that he had libelled anyone, even when libels did slip through.

One of these occasions of libel had been in the 1940s when Myles attacked the Institute of Advanced Studies, founded by De Valera to give substance, according to his enemies, to the general belief that he was a great mathematician manqué and happy only in the company of the most eminent mathematical brains of the world. Among these was the Nobel Prizewinner, Erwin Schroedinger, who indeed came to Dublin at De Valera's invitation to head the Institute. Schroedinger had given an address to the Institute on 'Science and Humanism' in which, as Myles understood him anyway, he said that there was no logical basis for the belief in a First Cause. At the same time, another luminary of the Institute, the Celtic scholar T. F. O'Rahilly, advanced the hypothesis that there were two different Christian missionaries to Ireland who had been confused historically as one figure, St Patrick. The Institute, Myles wrote, in a witticism much admired in Dublin, was seeking to show that there were two St Patricks and no God.

When the Directorate of the Institute sued, the matter was settled out of court, the *Irish Times* agreeing to pay £100 in damages. Only £50 was ever paid but the matter rankled in the editorial memory.

By 1952, Smyllie, who had always been a heavy drinker, was showing the effects. His health was failing, he was frequently in hospital, and he was becoming wilful and erratic in his judgement, which had always been, in Jack White's word, 'arbitrary'. Quarrels were inevitable, particularly since Myles' judgement of possible libels in his column was also less good than it had been and he was increasingly reckless. According to Jack White, 'He took extravagant pride in his ability to circumvent the law of libel; and in fact he attracted singularly few actions, considering the nature of his material.' For these reasons and also because the column was becoming ever more polemical, a larger number of pieces than before was being rejected and Myles was reacting with greater anger to the editorial veto.

As in most quarrels, both parties were probably in the right. But the *Irish Times*, in O'Nolan's view, compounded its offences by apologizing to the Board of the Abbey Theatre for a piece in January 1952 which, the Board claimed, implied that they were lining their own pockets out of the State subsidy to the theatre. The newspaper had also been considerably alarmed in April and May 1951 by the tenor and extent of its columnist's attacks on T. F. O'Rahilly's brother, Alfred O'Rahilly, who was then President of University College Cork, and several cuts were made in his copy.

What is surprising, considering the nature of his complaints, is how much he was actually allowed to get away with, the eminent Professor being described as 'a Cork thooleramawn' and 'a Cork gawshkogue' among other things. An *Irish Times* editorial had commented on the resignation of Dr Noel Browne from the Coalition's Ministry for Health after his Cabinet colleagues had rejected a welfare measure which was to become known as the 'Mother and Child Scheme'. Browne was then the 'new man' of Irish politics and had already established himself in many people's eyes as an idealist whose motives were unusually pure, a reputation he was never quite to lose in spite of several changes of party allegiance in the ensuing years. It was widely and correctly believed that the rejection of the Bill was forced on the Cabinet by pressure from the Catholic Bishops led by Brian O'Nolan's old mentor, John Charles McQuaid, Archbishop of Dublin, and the *Irish Times* said so. O'Rahilly then foolishly attacked the newspaper in the *Catholic Standard*, where he described its editor as a 'megalomaniac journalist' and the *Irish Times* as a Protestant organ which had a 'tradition of episcopophagy'. Myles, somewhat surprisingly, took up the cudgels in defence of his editor. He had, in some ways, a soft target, since O'Rahilly, although President of University College Cork, was justly regarded as a member of the lunatic right and had been an intellectual apologist for the now discredited Blueshirts; but he was in any case in dazzling form throughout the exchanges that followed and had easily the best of them.

He began by questioning O'Rahilly's credentials. 'An M.A. by gob? I, too, am an M.A. of the same wretched university and can prove documentarily (by producing the preposterous "thesis") that the degree, like the university, is a fake. There is, however, nothing fake about being President of any of its colleges.' In his second article he seized delightedly on the fact that O'Rahilly had chosen to sign himself 'Dr Alfred O'Rahilly, M.A., D.Sc.' 'Note in passing that the sage is a doctor at both ends, which is a most unusual distinction.' He had great fun with the fact that O'Rahilly had called him a hired humorist. He did not deny that he took money, but, he said, 'I formally deny that hired or otherwise, I am a "humorist". I am a most serious and thoughtful commentator, and a large number of persons and interests have found much of what I have written far from funny.'[16] And O'Rahilly's claim that he was exalting himself into a 'super-bishop' provoked one of his most famous witticisms. 'Really,' he said, 'I have no ecclesiastical ambitions ... I am merely a spoiled Proust.'

All in all the controversy, which he kept going over seven columns, showed Myles at his agile best. He made full use of his persona and was serious and flippant, playful and vicious just as it pleased him. But, though Smyllie was basically loyal, the affair did not improve his relations with the paper generally and for the rest of 1951 he was absent from its pages quite often, sometimes appearing only once or twice a week and in November not at all.

It was in any case a year of illness and he was absent from the office a great deal also, but much that he did write was killed. According to Jack White, 'The board ... would have seen him go with no regrets: they found him something of an embarrassment. But the readers missed their "Cruiskeen Lawn" ... ' In 1952 O'Nolan asserted several times that he had made his positively last appearance in the columns of the paper; and Jack White, who lived nearby in Blackrock, was repeatedly employed as mediator, sometimes meeting him in Levy's or O'Rourke's and sometimes going to his house or going back there afterwards. He found him, in drink, as most people did, 'extravagant and even bombastic'; and remembered that on one of his diplomatic missions, 'When we went back to his house he confided to me that he had it in his power to make a revelation that would blow the entire Irish language movement sky-high.' White found it difficult to believe that Brian himself took this kind of thing seriously, and concluded, 'It was a performance which had to be staged, even for an audience of one.'[17]

In the Custom House, even more than in the *Irish Times*, all was not well. In 1948 Brian's friend and protector, John Garvin, had become Secretary of the Department and in that year O'Nolan had been put in charge of the Planning Section. Here he dealt with appeals to the Minister against the decisions of tribunals and local authorities who had turned down planning applications. It was work in which he could perhaps see the worst side of politics and its relationship to the Civil Service, for here, if anywhere, were the opportunities for the 'back stairs intrigue' which was later to be a recurrent topic in his column.

It is only fair to say that others who worked in the Planning Section claim they saw none of it; but it was anyway work in which too many others could see the worst side of him, for there were frequent meetings with local authority officials and members of the public at which he was inclined to be sarcastic, aggressive or even obviously drunk. Legend has it that around this time there were numerous denigratory references to his former Minister, Sean MacEntee, in 'Cruiskeen Lawn'. Alas for legend, an examination of the column in the years before 1953 discloses no such attacks. There were to be several later, after he had left the Civil Service; notably one in 1956 when 'the public nostrils' were said to be 'enstenched' by MacEntee's attitude to the taxation of ministerial salaries. Frequent even at this time however were slighting references to the culture and capacity of public representatives generally; and herein lay part at least of the rub.

Fianna Fáil was a populist party with a strong rural base and a rough and ready political philosophy. Though the principal opposition party had also a traditionalist rural wing, its leaders were lawyers, academics and urban sophisticates. References in the column to public representatives of deficient general culture and rural origin therefore tended to be interpreted by many, including the victims themselves, as references to members of Fianna Fáil.

Civil servants were specifically forbidden to engage in political controversy or party politics by a circular drawn up after the change of Government in 1932 which Brian O'Nolan had signed on his appointment. This stated that 'The nature and conditions of a civil servant's employment should, of themselves, suggest to him that he must maintain a reserve in political matters; and not put himself forward on one side or another and, further, that he should be careful that he do nothing that would give colour to any suggestion that his official actions are in any way influenced, or capable of being influenced, by party motives.'[18]

While the Coalition Government which came to power in 1948 remained in office, O'Nolan was safe. But, however laxly or generously these regulations might be interpreted or however willingly the difficulty of establishing that the civil servant Brian O'Nolan was in fact Myles na Gopaleen was embraced by politicians who felt that abuse of 'pultogues', 'gawshkogues', 'turnip-snaggers' and others was directed at Fianna Fáil rather than themselves, in the nature of things the day was coming when it would be more dangerous. And in any case the regulations forbade a civil servant to comment on politics at all, stating as a matter of specific direction that, 'An official should not make any verbal statements in public (or which are liable to be published), and shall not contribute to newspapers or other publications any letters or articles, conveying information, comment or criticism, on any matter of current political interest, or which concerns the political action or position of the Government or any member or group of members of the *Oireachtas* [Legislature].'[19]

When Fianna Fáil were returned in the elections of June 1951 the new Minister for Local Government was a Cavan man, Patrick Smith. He was a typical rural rough diamond of the party and a veteran of the struggle for independence who was not lacking in qualities – he was one of the few politicians in the history of the state to resign on a matter of principle. But he could be expected to have less admiration for Myles' literary merits than the gourmet MacEntee or the dyed-in-the-wool Dubliner Sean T. O'Kelly had had. And so it was to prove.

There was now also an obsessional element and a more undisguised contempt in Myles' attacks than hitherto. In the latter part of 1951 he had noted that the clock on the premises of a Pearse Street coal merchant, Andy Clerkin, was stopped. He affected to find this significant because Clerkin was Lord Mayor and should have enough civic spirit to get his clock going again so that citizens passing along Pearse Street might know the time. The campaign that followed was nothing if not repetitive and soon the column began to be headed ACCISS, which purportedly stood for 'Andy Clerkin's Clock Is Still Stopped', a statement that appeared virtually every day, whatever the ostensible subject.

Initiates knew, however, that Clerkin, a Senator and a member of Fianna Fáil as well as Lord Mayor, was a man of a few words who could sometimes seem a little slow-witted; that he had a wife called Cis who seemed to be a stronger and more capable personality than himself; and that when baffled by this or that he had a habit of bringing the discussion to a close by saying, 'I'll axe [ask] Cis'. Dublin, which is always full of initiates, got the joke immediately; but Clerkin, who was a man of power and influence and, as Lord Mayor and a member of the corporation, had direct dealings with the Planning Section of the Department of Local Government, was less amused. There was even an ACCISS salute which readers of the column were encouraged to give him on public occasions, one arm being extended vertically and the other horizontally to symbolize a stopped clock.

On 26 October the *Irish Times* published several photographs of the stopped clock, one of which showed their correspondent Myles na Gopaleen gazing at it in disapproval. This was a mistake. On the occasions when there had been complaints to the Minister and Garvin had found it necessary to defend his junior he had always fallen back on the claim that the column was the work of several hands and that since O'Nolan's friends Niall Montgomery and Niall Sheridan often wrote it, there was no way of proving that Brian O'Nolan had written the offending piece. Although Brian was not to know it, the photograph showing him looking at the clock was now placed in his file.

But Myles na Gopaleen's writings were not the only factor in the concern now being expressed about Brian O'Nolan's position in the Civil Service. T. J. Barrington, who was Personnel Officer in the Department and was subsequently to be its Secretary, often had to relay to Garvin, however reluctantly, complaints about his attitude to members of the public and the unsettling effect his behaviour was having on the Department's staff. Since the Department had in any case a bad image among those members of the public who had any dealings with it, and a campaign involving circularization of relevant personnel had recently been embarked on to improve it, these were regarded as serious matters.

As head of the Planning Section, Brian O'Nolan was not under immediate supervision and of course he had a room to himself in the oak-panelled corridors of the Custom House. This meant that to an even greater extent than hitherto he could keep his own hours. For some years now his attendance record had been increasingly deplorable and even when officially present he had spent much of the day in the Scotch House, a place which Myles na Gopaleen referred to in his column as 'my office', a joke in which many of his colleagues saw nothing funny whatever.

Besides one or two female assistants, who covered for him as best they could and to whom, for this reason, he was surprisingly cordial, he had a number of subordinates to whom he was known as 'the horse'. One of these was a young man called Michael Phelan who had joined the Department of Local Government after the war and was very excited to learn that the author of *At Swim-Two-Birds*, a battered copy of which he had cherished for years, was also a member of the staff. He even nourished some hopes of literary converse or some elucidations of the mysteries of the creative process. Alas, it was not to be.

> A full 18 months passed and I never saw him officially. He never looked in, even to count us, and I do not recall that I even saw him entering or leaving his room which was 30 feet away. We prepared our work and passed it through the Higher Executive, one Lyons, who in turn cleared it through Mr Ó Nualláin, to give him his Civil Service title. Lyons was a discreet man of the old school and in those days *esprit de service* would have made it untypical to pass comment on the moods or behaviour of a superior. Nevertheless he was cordial and if Ó Nualláin had ever spoken meaningfully to him on any subject, even the staff or the work, he would

have passed on the news. I think it would be safe to say that Ó Nualláin never even knew of our existence, or cared.[20]

In the course of time, Lyons fell ill and Phelan became the Section Head's immediate subordinate. It was now his task to induce his superior to attend to pressing business, and to elicit his approval or otherwise of important documents.

> Some days would find Ó Nualláin at his desk, but only for minor periods, staring gloomily ahead and blindly signing the documents presented. Others would find him at his typewriter, firing furious bursts at another target and violently resenting interruption.
> 'Mr Ó Nualláin, Mr So and so has phoned about the ... '
> 'F ... So and so!'
> 'But the County Council feel that we should ...'
> 'F ... the County Council! F ... the whole f ... ing lot of them.'

Sometimes Phelan would be fearful of interrupting a train of thought that might never be resumed. When he did so, his superior's response was often to throw his head forward and bury his face in his hands with a moan of despair.

> On such days, unperused documents would be signed with a furious abandon and with a 'plurality' of epithets at a pen jabbed savagely into paper to make it function. We were working at the time on a touchy subject, and the more vetting of documents the better, so one could feel twinges of unease at contemptuous disposal. However, the system provided for various administrative and legal checks, so no harm was done.[21]

Of course even in an organization as tolerant and accommodating as the Irish Civil Service it couldn't last. To add to the pressures on Garvin, Sean Moynihan, who was Assistant Secretary of the Department of Finance, had now begun to make complaints about matter which appeared in the column. The Department of Finance was the paymaster and Moynihan's section was virtually a Department of Public Service. A pious man, who had been Secretary of the Fianna Fáil party before entering the public service in 1932, he had originally expressed concern about something Myles na Gopaleen had said on the subject of the Holy Year proclaimed by the Pope in 1950. Since then he had appointed himself a scrutineer of the column. He made frequent representations about matter which he believed contravened the regulations and he also felt it his duty to speak about the feud which O'Nolan was conducting with the Guards of Donnybrook as something which it was unseemly for a responsible public servant to be involved in.

The climax came in the first months of 1953 when the Government gave its blessing to a nationwide Festival to be called An Tostal. This was ostensibly an attempt to bring visitors to Ireland during April, or, as Patrick Kavanagh put it in McDaid's, during 'the monsoon season.' For this perhaps laudable end the country was encouraged to whip itself into an orgy of self-congratulation. Local and national politicians spouted high-flown humbug about making the world more aware of Ireland's ancient culture, its missionary role and its heroic traditions of self-sacrifice. The official exposition of what it was all about declared that the Tostal would be, amongst other things, an opportunity to lift the citizens' civic spirit to the level of their spiritual inheritance. Religion was an important feature of the image it was felt desirable to present and the tourist programme for County Clare listed a dozen events of which three were High Masses.

Myles' reaction to An Tostal, and particularly to the Dublin part of it, sponsored by Dublin Corporation, was alas neither particularly witty, nor, in terms of Brian O'Nolan's career, wise. He immediately reverted to the subject of Andy Clerkin's clock, which, a year after the original campaign, was, needless to say, still stopped. He invented a new word, borrowed from the annals of American gangsterism, to describe certain Corporation members – apparently, for there was some obscurity, Clerkin's followers and therefore members of Fianna Fáil. This was the word 'shaymus', plural 'shaymuses', and his thinking seemed – for that too was obscure – to be that the word was needed because these urban persons could not be described in the usual rural terms of abuse.

Some of his later attacks on the Tostal were deservedly admired for their wit and vigour – it was later on that he called the supposedly decorative concrete structure erected on O'Connell Bridge 'the tomb of the unknown gurrier' – but the pieces which he wrote in the fateful February of 1953 were, it must be said, neither very stylish nor even, sometimes, very coherent. He had drawn a strained analogy between the welcome accorded to Marshal Tito in England and the welcome the various tourist authorities were going to accord undesirable visitors, and he had coined a word for the attitude he objected to, whatever it was: Titostalitarianism. Some of his references to foreigners were uncharacteristically racist: the coloured population of Ireland was going to increase as a result of the Tostal; the streets and towns of the country were going to be taken over by 'the scruff and sweepings of Britain and America'.

There were four columns headed 'Titostalitarianism' before the blow fell. Through them all the figure of the Lord Mayor who owned the stopped clock could be dimly discerned as the villain, but on Thursday, 5 February, the column contained a description of an un-named politician whose habitual response to anything requiring intellectual effort was graphically described: 'The great jaw would drop, the ruined graveyard of tombstone teeth would be revealed, the eyes would roll, and the malt-eroded voice would say "Hah?"' '22

Many readers took this to be a portrait of Clerkin, but it was not; and unfortunately everybody in politics and in the Custom House agreed to recognize it as a portrait of O'Nolan's own Minister. During the morning, Smith, who was in Leinster House, telephoned Garvin. 'Have you seen that fellow's column this morning?' he asked. With the finesse that had made him Secretary of a Department, Garvin immediately replied that he had. 'I was just going to talk to you about it, Minister,' he replied. 'Well, you'd better come and talk to me now,' said Smith.

When Garvin presented himself, Smith was blunt. 'I want him out and I want him out immediately,' he said.

Garvin fell back on the usual line of defence. There was no proof that Brian O'Nolan had written the column. There were at least two other people who frequently contributed to 'Cruiskeen Lawn'.

'I don't care,' Smith replied. 'I'm fed up with this three-card trick. I want him out and I want him out now.'

That afternoon Garvin discussed the matter with Barrington, who formed the impression that he was much shaken. Garvin said that Smith had not appeared particularly vindictive but was certainly quite determined. He would have to talk to Brian.

To everybody's relief O'Nolan appeared ready to go. It was a question of negotiation, and negotiations were begun. As Brian had said in his memorandum, there was no provision for voluntary retirement with pension rights. Nor was alcoholism then recognized as a permanent disability of a kind which would qualify him for a pension. There was a further crux when Dr Dixon, the chief medical officer of the Civil Service, refused to accept as evidence of such a disability the medical certificates which O'Nolan was able to procure from doctors he knew. Nor would O'Nolan submit to examination by Dixon.

This was something that had arisen before and, apart from the fact that it was now jeopardizing the possibility of a pension, it also affected the size of it. In August 1951 O'Nolan had been due to be confirmed as a Principal Officer of the Department, having been an

Acting Principal Officer since 1948. His attendance record was by then such as to make a medical examination necessary; but Dixon had offended O'Nolan by speaking to him in a fatherly sort of way about his drinking habits, claiming the right to do so because he had known Michael O'Nolan; and Brian had refused to take the necessary examination. 'I don't want that fellow looking up my arse,' he had said; and he now repeated his refusal.

The deadlock was broken by Dixon, who finally agreed to accept the certificates from private doctors, even though, in his view, none of them substantiated the theory of a permanent disability. On 19 February, O'Nolan wrote, as arranged, to the Secretary of the Department.

> A Chara,
> In connection with medical certificates I submitted recently, I wish to retire from the Civil Service on the grounds of incapacity due to ill-health.
> Mise, le Meas, Brian Ó Nualláin.[23]

It was the last time he would use the locutions 'A Chara', literally O Friend, and 'Mise, le Meas', literally Myself with Respect, so familiar to every civil servant since the foundation of the State. His resignation or retirement was accepted immediately and the following day the Department replied.

> I am directed by the Minister for Local Government to inform you that the Minister for Finance has been pleased to award you (1) an annual allowance of £265 eight shillings and three pence and (2) an additional allowance (lump sum) of £707 fifteen shillings and four pence. The award is payable by the Chief Clerk, Paymaster General's Office, 3 Lower Ormond Quay, with whom you should communicate in writing.
> Mise, le Meas.[24]

Michael Phelan described Brian's final departure from the office. To do so, he fell back on an account he had been given of the going of an errant second lieutenant from the mess during the war. Like that officer, Brian O'Nolan, it would seem, departed from the Civil Service 'in a final fanfare of fucks'.

In the event three days' pay was deducted from the balance due to him and then restored ex gratia. He had told his wife nothing of what was going on up to this point, but when he came home that evening he said, 'I've got the sack.' She was reluctant to believe him, but he told her that if she had any doubts she could telephone Garvin. When she did so Garvin confirmed that Brian had indeed left the Civil Service.

He had been in it for 18 years, seven months and 21 days. He was now a freelance writer and journalist.

The release from the constraints and demands of the Civil Service might have been expected to result in a release of creative energy, but several factors already militated against this. One was the necessity to earn his living. Even in 1953, £265 per annum, or a little over £5 a week, was a miserable sum for a married man, albeit one with no children. This meant that Brian was more closely tied to the *Irish Times* than ever before. It was July of 1953 before he began to increase the number of columns, and there were to be gaps caused by illness or quarrels, but throughout most of the 1950s his aim was to produce six columns a week and for long periods he succeeded.

But he needed to earn more and in 1954 he circularized the editors of a number of provincial papers, offering them a column on a syndicated basis at one guinea per piece used, and declaring his readiness to write in Irish also if there was sufficient demand. He enclosed a sample column in English and promised that he would not write about politics, serious crime or anything that might prove controversial; even so there were few takers. The *Southern Star*, successor to the *Skibbereen Eagle*, famous for having warned the Tsar of Russia that the paper was keeping an eye on him, printed the offered column for a time and it appeared for an even briefer period in the *Longford Leader*. It was entitled 'A Weekly Look Around' and was written under the unimaginative pseudonym John James Doe. But the promise to be uncontroversial was too faithfully kept and the pieces were pedestrian in the extreme.

In the mid-1950s also, he wrote for a short while in the Irish edition of the *Sunday Dispatch*, re-cycling, broadening and largely emasculating 'Cruiskeen Lawn' pieces to suit the presumed taste of a less sophisticated audience; he re-cycled Keats and Chapman stories for *Social and Personal*, a sort of Irish version of *The Tatler*; and contributed to the *Sunday Review*, a tabloid Sunday which the *Irish Times* had launched in a mistaken attempt to improve its financial situation.

In the light of time these Grub Street activities are astonishing. The possible choices open to him were admittedly limited; but even within the limits of those possibilities he made appalling disposition of his talents and resources. It could be argued that the *Irish Times* column was his true *métier* and he was certainly still to do much of his best work there. On the other hand, this was surely the time to buckle down to the writing of books. That he did not do so is evidence of how reactive he was. All his life O'Nolan needed a considerable amount of outside stimulus and encouragement; and in this respect also he differed from the classical model of the avant-garde genius who goes on working whether anybody knows or cares. The other factor impeding the writing of novels was, of course, drink. This was now governing his life to an extraordinary degree.

While latterly he had been disdainful of the restraints imposed on him by his position in the Civil Service, he was now free to drink without any concealment at all and he no longer had to go through the motions of attending the office. From this time on, therefore, he became a more familiar figure in the Grafton Street pubs, particularly in McDaid's, in many ways an alternative place and a bolt hole for refugees from various walks of life.

It would be wrong however to imagine him as a bohemian figure. His garb was still that of the respectable civil servant, indeed of the respectable civil servant of an already vanished era, for whom any apparel other than a dark suit and tie with a clean white shirt and collar would have been unthinkable. Only the slightly wider brim of the hat suggested, in this case, the literary man. And most of the time he was, or imagined himself to be, respectable in demeanour as long as sobriety lasted, any breach of decorum thereafter being the result of drink. Although it now became unusual for him to be sober later than the afternoon, and his bedtime advanced accordingly, he somehow did not give the impression of having set out for a day's drinking but rather that he had come into town for reasons of business and gone to the pub for a drink or two when it was discharged.

Jack White lived not far from him in Blackrock and would often see him at the beginning of his day.

> At this time he was living near me, in Blackrock, and even my children were familiar with the drab little figure in the pork-pie hat who could be seen passing down the road, with the martinet step of the habitual drinker, on the way to get a curative gin at Gleeson's as soon as the doors opened ... The hat seemed to overshadow and almost extinguish his small, rather secretive face.[25]

Except that 'pork-pie' is probably not the correct technical or trade description for the high-crowned, rather wide-brimmed dark hat that he wore, White is correct in emphasizing the importance of his headgear to the persona O'Nolan seems to have wished to present. It was the badge of the literary man but also proof that he was a respectable, responsible citizen with an assured place in the world. Like the black hats of more senior literary men such as Austin Clarke, there was even a touch of the sacerdotal about it, a reminder that the two cloths and the two clerisies, literary and religious, had been in competition in Ireland since ancient times. Its tilt was an important indicator of his mood, being pushed to the back of his head when drink was making him pugnacious and liable to emit a stream of abusive language at those who offended him, or settled foursquare on the brow when he was in better humour. While subject to the accidents of drink, his suits were bespoke tailored and well-pressed, but the hat was ancient.

White quotes one of his pieces for the *Southern Star*, written in 1955: 'My hat is disgracefully aged. Its useful life is long since over. It is stained. It is no exaggeration to say it is frumpy, but its many years of faithful service has [sic] turned it into part of me. To a large extent, I have become myself simply something that fits in under the hat.' And White adds that the well-known portrait head of him by Seán O'Sullivan 'seems strangely naked without this dingy crown'.

All his friends noted his extreme shyness and most concurred in finding him morose, silent and difficult to make conversation with when sober. Once he had been an hour or two in the pub, however, drink would have overcome this. He did not encourage intrusions by unknowns, though he often took part in those long-distance conversations between comparative strangers which, as we have seen, were a common, and perhaps peculiar, feature of Dublin pub life. With those he wished to talk to, he was loquacious, repetitive and somewhat obsessive. His stock in trade as a conversationalist resembled that of his column, a possible topic for which he would often rehearse in the pub, but without the incisiveness or the timing. In the columns which were thus rehearsed, the verbal gaffes, the failures and stupidities of officialdom played a large part.

He also liked small tests and puzzles. At one period, he was fond of asking how Powers and Jameson described their whiskeys on the label of the bottle. The answer was Dublin whiskey, although the person challenged would usually assert it was described as Irish and a bottle sometimes had to be fetched down from the shelf by the barman to decide the question. On an occasion when a bottle was asked for in the Waterloo Lounge, the publican obligingly fetched one and left it behind on the counter while he went to attend to other customers. After the point was established, the bottle was pushed to one side and temporarily forgotten. When the barman came back a few minutes later, it was gone. Then it was noted that Patrick Kavanagh who had been sitting to one side of the company had also vanished. The assumption that he had taken the bottle home was, as the present writer can testify, correct, though who, if anybody, compensated the publican for his loss remains obscure to this day.

At this point also, Brian O'Nolan took to carrying around with him a small machine, which he said was a hydrometer, designed for measuring the proof strength of whiskey and thus capable of indicating whether or not water had been added to it. His insistence on publicly immersing this in the balls of malt he had just been served led to such strained relations with the barmen, however, that it was soon heard of no more.

His accent over the years had become a sort of ersatz Dublin, broadened for purposes of anecdote, and after he had had a few drinks, some people seemed to find it difficult to understand what he was saying. (Kavanagh used to allege that the present writer was one of the few who could.) Almost everybody, including his boon companions, called him Myles, which he did not seem to mind, though most of those who had any acquaintance with him regarded him as a fairly formidable customer with whom liberties could not be lightly taken. He was known for his extreme vituperativeness when roused and, apart from his general or even his literary reputation, there was a somewhat canine aspect to him which kept people on their guard.

He fancied himself to be in most respects a responsible member of society, who paid his rates and taxes, minded his own business and considered it part of his duty to see that other people, particularly those in receipt of public money, minded theirs. This attitude may have strayed into the man from his column, produced perhaps by long years of affectation, originally humorous, later less so, in that forum. After reading one morning's offering around this time, Kavanagh remarked to the present writer, 'That kind of stuff would be all right as material for comedy, but the poor fellow actually takes himself seriously as the ratepayer's friend. And that's bourgeois. Worse, it's phoney,' a comment in which there is a great deal of justice. John Ryan remembers him complaining bitterly that he had to request the Commissioners of Inland Revenue twice for a tax assessment form.

Once, some time in the late 1950s, when he was living in Belmont Avenue, a friend and I had the task of leaving him home. This was not uncommon. Many people found themselves leaving Brian home in those days, sometimes in mid-afternoon when the day's drinking was only just beginning. They were for the most part civilly received by Mrs O'Nolan; and, if Brian had sobered up on the way, they might be asked in for a bottle of stout. On a couple of occasions when John Ryan left him home, he found himself seated at the typewriter, taking dictation for a column, and was amazed at the fluency and lack of hesitation with which it was given. On this day, however, Brian was pretty far gone in drink and had to be helped up the garden path. After he had gone inside, my friend began to turn the car to go back towards

Donnybrook. Another car came up the road at some speed, there was a minor collision, and the driver of this car insisted on telephoning Donnybrook Police Station.

A bit of fuss followed while the road was measured and the condition and positions of the two cars were recorded. Suddenly Brian appeared at his hall door, wearing a coat over blue striped pyjamas and with his hat on the back of his head. He stood for a moment, surveying the scene in front of him. Then he spoke up. 'Would yez get those two motor cars out of there immediately,' he said, swaying slightly on the step. 'There's decent respectable people live here on this road that pay their rates and taxes and have a right of unimpeded passage up and down it. And they don't want any criminals or chancers around here that are an object of interest and concern to the police force.' He had apparently forgotten for the moment his own long-standing feud with the Guards and the frustration he had given them.

As is apparent from the column, his civic sense related mostly to Dublin. It was the peace and good government of his city that principally concerned him and his country origins and experiences were never referred to. Country people generally were a threat to the city, and there were innumerable references in his column to 'bogmen' and 'turnip-snaggers' whose only ambition was to get into the Civil Service in Dublin. Some of them even had artistic or literary pretensions; the Abbey Theatre was largely run by them; and, sad to say, from now on his old mentor and protector, John Garvin, was to be the subject of many thinly disguised references in print to Roscommon peasants who had set themselves up as authorities on 'Jems Jyce'. Some of those who were aware of what Garvin had done for him naturally took a poor view of this. But it should be remembered that it was fate, not choice, that had compelled him to accept Garvin's protection in the first place; and that unless there is an equal relationship between two people, neither party has a right to presume on affection or even, perhaps, gratitude.

In thus adopting Dublin as his own city and forgetting his small-town rural origins, O'Nolan-Myles (for in this, the two were one) was certainly within his rights and even setting a praiseworthy example to others, for Dublin has suffered over the years in its government and polity from the refusal of its rural migrants to transfer their loyalties with a whole heart.

But that he also had a fierce sense of engagement with Ireland as an entity is undeniable; and it amounted almost to a proprietorial claim to be asserted against politicians and other usurpers. In this as in other things he resembled Kavanagh, who often seemed to believe also that he had been unjustly deprived of an inheritance called Ireland which other people were mismanaging, or was at least excluded from the councils of this place by dishonest persons who had a lesser right than his own to be there. No doubt this could be described, in some of its manifestations anyway, as a form of megalomania. It might also be thought to be something both men had derived, in however inchoate a fashion, from their bardic forbears. One manifestation of this feeling in Kavanagh's case was the attempt in the 1950s to found a journal, *Kavanagh's Weekly*, in which he would, in effect, take his case to the people. O'Nolan contributed to this as Myles na Gopaleen, writing a number of attacks on the hated Tostal, which had become an annual event. His own feelings of unjust exclusion resulted, in 1957, in an attempt to run for the Senate.

Most of the seats in this body were filled by politicians, many of them party hacks who had lost their seats in the Dáil, for the cumbersome method of election virtually excluded all who had no party allegiance; but a few seats were reserved for graduates of the National University and Trinity College, the electorate also being composed of graduates of these institutions. He took his chances of election quite seriously, in conversation anyway, and seemed to assume that the readership of his column would vote for him almost en bloc, so that he might even top the poll. One snag was that he was standing as Brian Ó Nualláin and of course not every reader would identify this person with Myles na Gopaleen. Another was that the *Irish Times* forbade him to canvass his candidacy in his column, the result of the ensuing tug of war being that there was no column at all during the vital weeks before the election. And of course, as idealists, visionaries and artists always do when they run for elective office, he neglected to canvass, failing even to circulate the rather unbalanced manifesto he showed to some of his friends, whereas the other candidates procured lists of graduates and canvassed them assiduously by telephone and otherwise.

The result of all this was that he received fewer than 400 votes out of a valid poll of over 9000, which was less than any other candidate. He seemed to bear the disappointment scornfully enough, but it was a serious blow; and one noteworthy result was that attacks on politicians in his column became more frequent than ever in the weeks following the election.

Partly because of the war, which came at a crucial point in both their careers, and partly because of their failure to obtain recognition outside Ireland – this in itself attributable in some degree to the war –

both Kavanagh and O'Nolan found themselves willy-nilly committed to writing in a very intimate way for an Irish audience. The love/hate relationship that in both cases developed out of this kind of shotgun marriage was more intense than that enjoyed by those fairly comfortable literary exiles who had academic standing or a large readership abroad. It led to bitterness but it also led to greater honesty. They had no great commercial temptations to flog the sort of cosy, ersatz Irishness that mars Frank O'Connor's work; and they wanted to 'get their own back' on Ireland, which was pushing in on them from all sides in their daily life. Ireland was in both cases a circumstance as well as a place; and it was a circumstance which could defeat them if they engaged with it in the wrong way while demanding daily engagement nonetheless.

The relationship between the two was mutually admiring and there was even a sense of alliance but it was not that of friends or even drinking companions. If either one came into McDaid's while the other was there he would very seldom join him directly, though he might occasionally engage in one of those length-of-the-counter conversations frequent in Dublin pubs. Kavanagh would sometimes express admiration when the topic of Myles came up – 'The only true sophisticate in the whole bloody country' was how he once described him; but it was an admiration tempered by pity or affected pity: 'Poor Myles' or 'That poor little na Gopaleen' were not infrequent locutions. Perhaps to avoid praising more important works, he professed great admiration for the play *Faustus Kelly* or at least for its first act; but his assertion that Myles had failed to find a myth that would lift the material in his column into art was in its way profound criticism, necessarily suggesting sympathy and understanding. Occasional references to Kavanagh in Myles' column suggest respect as well as a sort of ironic affection, and even when Kavanagh attacked na Gopaleen in a letter protesting against the treatment meted out in the column to W. B. Stanford of Trinity, Myles refused to be drawn.

Yet Brian O'Nolan's general impatience with poetry and his intolerant view of those who set themselves up as 'the artist' or 'the poet' coloured his attitude; and Kavanagh's lack of any visible means of support as well as his disdain for the ethics of buying rounds irked him. 'The Monaghan toucher' he once called him, though not in his hearing. Of course, drink being what it is, there were sometimes incidents and sudden antagonisms of an extra-literary nature. One day in McDaid's when a sneezing fit left snot on Brian's tie and shirt-front, Kavanagh chose to make an audible remark about what he called the 'disgusting' state of the other's apparel; and when Brian left his stool to attack him, something about the nature and character of the two men was revealed, Kavanagh for all his bulk exhibiting nothing but civilized temerity, the much smaller Brian being more terrier-like than ever and following his prey even when the other retreated behind the counter. Of the two, Kavanagh, perhaps because he was functioning as an artist throughout these years, also perhaps because he was quicker to intimacy and declared his joys and sorrows more readily, had far more ability to use drink as a medium through which to dramatize himself and make his burdens public. He was also more adept at bringing about humorous situations and confrontations than Brian, the professional humorist, to whom drinking was a serious and, in a way, sober business. There was more genuine laughter in Kavanagh's company than in Brian's, whose laughter signified a somewhat mechanical apprehension of the funny side of things.

At no time was this more evident than on the Bloomsday pilgrimage which he and John Ryan organized in 1954 on the 50th anniversary of Joyce's fictive occasion. In his book *Remembering How We Stood*, Ryan says:

> We agreed that the company should consist of ourselves, A.J. (Con) Leventhal, Anthony Cronin, Patrick Kavanagh and Tom Joyce. Con Leventhal, being Jewish, was to symbolize Bloom; Cronin, the young poet, his surrogate offspring Stephen; Myles combined Simon Dedalus and Martin Cunningham; I was Myles Crawford (for I had been an editor); Kavanagh – the muse, and Tom Joyce, the Family; for he was a cousin of James – a dentist who had, in fact, never read *Ulysses*![26]

The plan was an ambitious one – the cityscape of the book was to be traversed almost in its entirety in two Dublin 'growlers', beginning with the 'Proteus' section on Sandymount Strand, trundling up to Glasnevin for 'Hades' and back into the city for 'Aeolus', the *Irish Times* being substituted for the vanished *Freeman's Journal*. 'Lestry-gonians' would be commemorated in the happily still-thriving Davy Byrne's and the Bailey, and so on until cab horses and passengers were equally exhausted. It is typical of O'Nolan's ambiguity towards Joyce that he was prepared to organize and take part in this elaborate act of piety although his column that morning contained an attack on Joyce as an 'illiterate' whose 'every foreign language quotation was incorrect.' 'His few sallies at Greek are wrong, and his few attempts at a Gaelic phrase absolutely monstrous.'[27]

We were to start from the architect Michael Scott's house which is beside Stephen's Martello Tower in Sandycove and our host had gallantly set out a tray of drinks. This beneficent early morning hospitality had an unsettling effect straight away. There was a sloping rockface, topped by wire, between Michael Scott's garden and the Tower, and this Kavanagh elected to climb. Not to be outdone, Brian set off after him up the little cliff but, apparently because he was making less progress, he jealously tried to pull Kavanagh down and his hand had to be finally prised loose from Kavanagh's enormous and now panic-stricken foot which was making violent thrashing movements in an effort to shake free.

What was noticeable about the rest of the day, however, was how structured and, in a way, humourless an event Brian wanted it to be. While we were retracing the route of the funeral party he wanted us to preserve a decorum proper to the occasion and to behave at all other times with the outward respectability of the characters in the book. It struck me then that he had a deep imaginative sympathy with them, that he was still part of their world, a world in which the appearances of respectability had to be kept up even as a life collapsed; whereas Kavanagh and the rest of us, even Con Leventhal who was Registrar of Trinity College and an older man than Brian, even the unliterary dentist, belonged to some newer world, not so strictly defined.

Brian objected to our singing songs as we went. He objected to my sitting on the box beside the cabman and to Kavanagh joining me. He thought it was highly improper that I should take the reins. In a way he was right and with one part of me I sympathized with him. If he had had his way the charade would have been more total and the dramatic re-enactment more convincing, but the whole thing would have been, on the whole, less enjoyable. On the other hand, however severe his intentions, he was as responsible as anybody else for the breakdown of the grand scheme and its abandonment after we got to the Bailey. There was a small episode in a pub near Blackrock on the well-traversed funeral route from the city to Deansgrange Cemetery that strikes me as significant. John Ryan has described it as follows.

Perhaps it was the sound of our horses and carriages without, or just the sombre appearance of Myles (for he was wearing one of those black homburg hats he dubbed 'County Manager'), or merely the fact that he usually had funeral parties at about this time, that caused the landlord to approach us. He took Myles' hand to offer condolence.

'Nobody too close, I trust?' he queried hopefully.

'Just a friend,' replied Myles quietly, 'fellow by the name of Joyce – James Joyce . . .' meanwhile ordering another hurler of malt.

'James Joyce . . .' murmured the publican thoughtfully, setting the glass on the counter, 'not the plastering contractor from Wolfe Tone Square?'

'Naaahh . . .' grunted Myles impatiently, 'the writer.'

'Ah! the sign writer,' cried the publican cheerfully, glad and relieved to have got to the bottom of this mystery so quickly, 'little Jimmy Joyce from Newton Park Avenue, the sign writer, sure wasn't he only sitting on that stool there on Wednesday last week – wait, no, I'm a liar, it was on Tuesday.'[28]

Towards the end of 1954 it seemed for a while likely that Brian O'Nolan, Kavanagh and myself would be embarking on another, longer and slightly more hazard-fraught itinerary together. Through the communist novelist Peadar O'Donnell, with whom I was then working on *The Bell*, the task of choosing participants for a trip to the USSR passed into my hands. I asked them both if they would like to come and somewhat to my surprise, they both accepted. As the news leaked out, however, and it became clear that acceptance of the Soviet invitation was likely to be denounced from platform and pulpit, they both changed their minds. Kavanagh feared that the trip would prejudice the success of a libel action that he had embarked on. Brian said that his mother's state of health was such that he would not like to be so far away from Ireland and possibly unable to return in an emergency. It was a bit like the parable of the wedding guests; and I regretted their defection for, apart from anything else, they would have given the Soviets something to think about.

In the event, prognostications about how the trip would be received in Ireland proved all too accurate. Led by the *Catholic Standard*, which almost doubled its circulation during the weeks we were away, there was a furore of denunciation of the 'delegates' who had ventured to go. Several County Councils passed motions condemning them. Myles devoted two columns to the matter and claimed to have stopped the remainder from following suit by pointing out that the passing of such motions was *ultra vires*. The powers of County Councils were 'by statute forever fixed'. Their business was to assess, collect and disburse the rates for certain stated purposes, no more and no less.

In July of 1954, as an editor I published in *The Bell* one of the few pieces of creative writing O'Nolan did in the 1950s, the short story, 'Two In One'. The offer of the story was preceded by a lengthy telephone call in which he described the central idea, one of his most macabre notions, in great detail. It is the story of a taxidermist who murders his hated employer, disposes of the body, retaining only the skin; and then assumes both skin and identity so that the missing person is himself, for the murder of whom he is hanged in the end.

I knew nothing then of *The Third Policeman* but the atmosphere of the story is not unlike the early part of that book. Both murder victims are killed by repeated blows to the head. 'I hit him again. I rained blow after blow on him,' says the narrator of 'Two In One'.[29] 'I do not know how often I struck him after that but I did not stop until I was tired,' the narrator of *The Third Policeman* tells us. The story was published under the name Myles na Gopaleen, the eclipsis in the genitive having by then been dropped. I remember very tentatively and diffidently suggesting that it might be signed Flann O'Brien. 'I don't know that fellow any longer,' was the reply.

Yet he was still certainly ambitious to write novels and he was quite aware that drink was one of his problems. One day around this time, he suggested that he and I adjourn to Sean O'Sullivan's studio during the 'holy hour'. It was possible then to buy poitín from under the counter at McDaid's, as one of the barmen had a friend who was working in the west of Ireland and brought a supply of that beverage up with him every weekend. To my surprise, Brian, whom I would have expected to be more particular about what he drank, bought a bottle of this.

When we got to O'Sullivan's, which was in St Stephen's Green, we found the door locked; so we sat on the stairs while the typists from the offices inhabiting the same building stepped nimbly past us. He spoke rather wistfully of his ambition to go away somewhere, get off the drink and write another novel. He had often talked of going to Mount Melleray, a Cistercian monastery much frequented by Dublin drunks who wanted a place to dry out. Now he spoke of Mount Melleray or Tory Island off the Donegal coast as possible places to effect his design. The latter seemed to me an extraordinary suggestion. There we were, drinking poitín, of which I had no doubt there was plenty on Tory Island; so the likelihood seemed to me that he would drink himself to death if he went there, more especially if, as he suggested, he could prevail on Sean O'Sullivan to go with him, for O'Sullivan's reputation as a drinker rivalled his own.

But he seemed almost desperate and it appeared best to encourage him to try some method of getting off the drink and beginning a book. So I did as writers often do and spoke of the mathematics of it. If he could manage 600 words a day he would have his book written in three months. He was immediately scornful. 'Is it six hundred words a day? Six hundred? Sure them Victorian fuckers wrote six thousand words every day before breakfast,' he declared. Like many who have written a great deal of journalism, he had enormous pride in his capacity and of course he didn't reckon on the day when it could not or would not be done.

Not long before, the government had brought in an Arts Bill which established an Arts Council in Ireland. This innovation was remarked on in a column. 'Certainly Costello was not lacking in courage when, the other day, he introduced in Parliament his Arts Bill: this I take to be a thinly veiled plan to give Paddy Kavanagh a pension for life. I object, of course ... I assert it is contrary to Catholic teaching. Number two, I was not consulted.' He then went on to speak jestingly of great artists who were 'mute'. These, he said, 'do not execute any works of art because they disdain the essential vulgarity of communication ... Such persons treat themselves to the immense luxury of shutting up and go through life quietly and passionately despising the herd. I cannot for the life of me see how that situation is going to be changed by an Act of Parliament ...'[30]

This sort of thing, although not serious, was in keeping with his general individualism and scorn for bureaucratic interference. But he was not above attempting to avail himself of what he thought was on offer and he went to see the Secretary of the new Arts Council, his fellow novelist, Mervyn Wall, who had been a civil servant and worked in Radio Éireann before becoming an arts administrator. In those days, Arts Councils were averse to giving money to unaccountable individuals, preferring to give it instead to organizations and structures. The result was that performance and execution were subsidized but not the individual creator. Wall therefore expressed surprise that O'Nolan should come to him with such a request. As he was to put it later, he 'wasn't in the business of giving out money to people to go away to Tory Island and write novels.'[31] And he told him that. We have, happily, come a long way since then.

Though he felt incapable of sitting down to write a serious book, Brian's quest for paid literary employment led him at this time to offer his services to the editors of the famous Sexton Blake series. Sexton Blake was a sort of poor man's Sherlock Holmes, or, perhaps more accurately, a schoolboy's Sherlock Holmes. Like Holmes he lived in Baker Street in London and was called on to solve mysteries by a wide variety of people, including sometimes the authorities of Scotland Yard. He drove a Rolls-Royce called the Grey Panther and had a boy assistant of indeterminate age called Tinker. Blake's adventures appeared in disposable paperbacks at a rate of one title a month, each title being about 25,000 words in length. Since at various times in his life Brian O'Nolan advanced the claim that he had written or was about to write Sexton Blake stories, it may be as well to summarize the facts.

As far back as 1939, he had gratuitously added to his letter to Ethel

Mannin the information that he was discussing terms with the editors of the series. 'I am negotiating at present for a contract to write 6 Sexton Blake stories (25–30 thousand words for £25 a time, so please do not send me any more sneers at my art.) Sorry, Art.' It seems most unlikely that he had actually been in contact with the then editors of the series at that time for in the new offer of his talents, written on 7 October 1955 to Stephen Ashe, one of the editors of the series, he finds it necessary to introduce himself and begins with an explanation. 'This letter arises from a chat that I had the other day with my friend Martin Cumberland, who gave me leave to quote his name. He told me of the market for Sexton Blake stories and suggested I get in touch with you. I am interested in trying my hand at this sort of work.'

'Martin Cumberland' was the pseudonym of a well-known and highly successful Irish writer of detective stories. O'Nolan proceeds humbly to list his own claims.

My qualifications, briefly, are: M.A. degree; author of novel publ. Longman's, London and in the U.S.; author of many short stories published here and in the U.S., and included in anthologies. I have been writing a sarcastic column for the *Irish Times* here for about sixteen years, have written a lot for the *Sunday Dispatch* and French papers. I regard myself as an accomplished literary handiman.[32]

The claim to have been the author of many short stories and, more particularly, that they had been published widely in the US was simply not true; that he had written a lot for French papers was also a gross exaggeration.

He went on:

I have read the Sexton Blake stories in my day and can, of course, refresh my recollection with the current series. I am sure I could do this job particularly if as Cumberland said, he thought the plot would be supplied. Anyhow I should like to try. I would be willing to supply two chapters as a sample for nothing. If you think we could do business, perhaps you would give me first-hand particulars as to length, time-limit, fee, supply of plot and any other significant details.

Soon after this, when an acquaintance came across him writing in a pub in Blackrock, he declared that he was working on a Sexton Blake story and went into details about its length and rewards. This means little, for references to the writing of Sexton Blake stories were common in his conversation before his letter to Stephen Ashe in 1955. However, in 1963, he repeated the claim in the course of a BBC television interview with Peter Duval Smith, stating at the same time that he had also written 'other books which were not quite pornography and not quite not'. This gave rise to a correspondence in a magazine devoted to Sexton Blake enthusiasts called *The Collector's Digest*, which was published on mimeographed sheets in Tunbridge Wells. Correspondents wished to know which were the titles written by Flann O'Brien, and W. O. G. Lofts, the well-known historian of boys' literature, undertook to investigate the matter.

Lofts wrote to O'Nolan asking for information and received a reply to the effect that yes, he had written some Sexton Blake titles but could not remember what they were called. Nor could he remember what name he had used in his dealings with the publishers. He had often, he continued, found it necessary when dealing with publishers to use a pseudonym quite apart from the pseudonym used for the book.

Lofts also elicited from Howard Baker, then editor of the Sexton Blake series, the information that there had been two Irish writers of the Sexton Blake stories in recent years. One was a well-known peer of the Irish realm; the other called himself Stephen Blakesley but was known in his dealings with the publishers as Francis Bond. On the basis of this information, W. O. G. Lofts concluded that Stephen Blakesley possibly was (or rather Stephen Blakesley and Francis Bond were) Brian O'Nolan but that the stories published under the Blakesley name had been rewritten to a greater or lesser extent. This conclusion was based on the payment made for them, which was only £25, the going rate when stories had to be re-written. (It was otherwise £50.) A perusal of the Stephen Blakesley stories suggests that they could possibly be by Brian O'Nolan. They have a certain stylistic distinction and there are more fat policemen on bicycles in them than is usual even in Sexton Blake stories.

In the catalogue of the British Museum, Stephen Blakesley is also listed as the author of four other books brought out by various publishers, of the sort that are known in the trade as 'bodice-rippers', which O'Nolan, if he was the author, might at a stretch have described as 'not quite pornography and not quite not'. These date from the late 1940s; but apart from the unlikelihood of O'Nolan, who was unable or unwilling to describe a sexual or romantic encounter of any kind in any of his acknowledged books, having been the author of these, one major snag remains. The Stephen Blakesley Sexton Blake stories were written prior to 1955. Thus they pre-date and are impossible to reconcile with the letter to Stephen Ashe of that year. So, the mystery surrounding the claim to have written mystery-thrillers remains; but once again there is a coda.

In 1964, the Sexton Blake Library announced that *The Last Tiger* by Wm. A. Ballinger would be the last of their publications because the great detective, bowing to the years, had just retired and there would be no more adventures to chronicle. Myles na Gopaleen devoted three pieces to this sad news, professing himself shocked by it 'because I have myself belonged to the arch, arcane and areopagetic côterie of authors who have written Sexton Blake stories for Fleetway Publications Ltd. London'.[33]

'With a diffidence quite new to me,' he said, 'I wrote to the publishers a very shy letter asking whether I might attempt this grandiose task of recording an adventure of Blake and his associates in the pitiless battle against crime. The reply was prompt, courteous and encouraging. Certainly, they would consider my work, but it was necessary to send them at the outset the actual first chapters with an outline of the development and conclusion of the plot.' The completed book, he said, had earned him £50. The date was 'ten or twelve years ago'. If his recollection was not at fault, this again means that he (or at least Myles na Gopaleen) claimed to have written a Sexton Blake story prior to the admittedly 'very shy' letter to Stephen Ashe.

As for his reasons for wanting to write one in the first place, Myles na Gopaleen declared: 'No piece of writing can I survey without wondering whether I could not do the same thing better. Usually the conclusion is in the affirmative but too often it is accompanied by a rider that the thing is not worth doing. But not so in the case of Sexton Blake.' Why the idea of doing so, or having done so, appealed so much to him may have been, first, perversity, and secondly because it fitted so well with the idea of the original genius who was also an expert and versatile literary journeyman, prepared, unlike Proust, Kafka and, above all, James Joyce, to turn his hand to anything.

In 1956, Evelyn was ill for some time with lung trouble and was in Rochestown Sanatorium. It was an unusually disorganized period for Brian since he did not like to be alone and he sometimes stayed with other people while she was away. He came to his brother Micheál's studio in Belgrave Square one night and asked if he could stay. Micheál noticed that, rather than arrive with his bag on the doorstep, he left it under some bushes in the Square and retrieved it only when he was sure of his welcome. Micheál was awakened next day by Brian's truly spectacular morning cough and found him at the kitchen table drinking some stout which he had found in a cupboard and already smoking.

Among Brian's closest friends at this time were the barrister,

Tommy Conolly, and his wife Angela. Tommy was like Brian in being short and having a humorous disposition. He was an exceptionally clever and more than ordinarily literate Senior Counsel and Angela was one of the few women Brian seemed to like or would even talk to. He had taken to drinking in the tiny Dawson Lounge in Dawson Street on Saturday mornings because the Conollys went there and when they moved to Tobin's in Duke Street, a well-managed and still somewhat old-fashioned pub, he went there too. During the week, he drank with them in Sinnott's or Neary's.

The O'Nolans had always had a dog, on Brian's insistence, as he was genuinely fond of animals. He often took one particular animal, whose name was Muc, along to the pub with him but when she was at home it was Evelyn who fed it and looked after it. More than once now, when Angela visited her in hospital she expressed anxiety about the dog and whether Brian would neglect to feed it. So Angela began to think it had a somewhat emaciated look. Not quite satisfied with Brian's reassurances about his zeal in feeding the animal, she decided to send her maid, Mary, up to the house with some mince, and told her to put the parcel of meat through the letterbox if there was nobody in. A couple of days later, she received a note from Brian.

> Dear Angela,
> Many thanks for sending stuff for the dog. You might note for future reference that Evelyn has a psychosis about the animal and keeps assuming he is starving to death. In fact he is fed with absolute regularity; in every way I give him far better treatment than I give myself. Many a time he was like Poor Dog Tray – 'I shared my last crust with his pitiful face.' I got talking yesterday in a pub to a man who breeds dogs. I asked was there anything effective to stop Muc destroying the carpets, beds, clothes etc. with his hairs. He said the prime cause of this disorder was overfeeding, and I quite believe it.
> Sincerely,
> Brian O'Nolan[34]

Whether Muc was getting fed or not, Brian's fondness for animals struck a number of people who knew him, and not only his fondness for them but also his way with them. The Conollys had an especially fierce macaw which was liable to take the finger off anybody who attempted to touch or stroke it. When Brian came to the house for the first time he was left alone with the macaw while drink was being fetched and was warned not to make any overtures to it. When Angela returned, she found him talking to the bird which had a Dublin accent and was accustomed to say 'How are you' in the true Dublin manner. He was standing beside its perch and even stroking it at will with his fingers.

On the other hand, like many people with a characteristic or an accomplishment not central to their being, he was inclined to be boastful about it. The Conollys also had a dog called Adam who had become rather wicked. One day when Brian came to the house, Angela told him to go into the drawing-room where Adam was, but not to touch the dog in case he got bitten. 'No dog ever bit me,' was the reply. Moments later he emerged with blood pouring from his head. In spite of the plainly visible wound, he denied he had indeed been bitten. But he allowed Angela to paint the injury with very strong iodine all the same. When they met in Sinnott's the following day, she presented him with a little tuft of Adam's hair, saying, 'Here is a hair of the dog that bit you.' Instead of acknowledging the joke he adopted a pained expression. 'No dog ever bit me,' he insisted, although she could still see what she described as the hole in his head. This may have been the cut referred to in a letter to Gearóid, which, 'dressed by a stupid doctor (for whom I personally did not send) became septic', necessitating a visit to a chemist. He was seeing very little of Gearóid in these years; and when they had some correspondence about a headstone for their parents' grave, could not even remember his address.

While Evelyn was still in the sanatorium, Brian began to press for a change of house. For some reason, he wanted to leave Merrion Avenue and bought a house in Belmont Avenue, Donnybrook, in her name. Belmont Avenue is a road of late Victorian houses with long front gardens and hall door steps, joining Morehampton Road in Donny-brook with Sandford Road in Ranelagh. It was at least closer to town than Merrion Avenue and now that he no longer had a car, this was a matter of some importance. The Conollys had the impression that he had brought pressure on Evelyn to execute this move and that she was taken by surprise. And they disapproved of her leaving hospital to go to a house she had never seen which they found cold and dark and rather depressing. Evelyn found it dark and depressing also, partly because of its brown-painted walls, but as with everything he did, she seemed to acquiesce readily enough. This house now became familiar to those who left him home from whatever pub he was drinking in in mid-afternoon, something that was now becoming increasingly neces-sary. Those who penetrated to his bedroom remarked on the piles of newspapers which covered the floor and also on the electric fire which he seemed to keep burning day and night.

He was now, like some of the characters in his books, spending a good deal of time in bed, partly because of illness, partly because of the disabilities induced by drink and partly from choice. When his mother

and the remaining members of his family had moved from Avoca
Terrace to a new house in 1953, Brian had appropriated the large
double bed which formerly belonged to his parents and this now
moved with him to Belmont Avenue. It was a splendid structure with
mahogany uprights and a basketwork headboard in which he lay in
quasi-regal state. Sadly, he had virtually ceased to read books, though
he still read the newspapers, the English Sundays and weeklies, and
Time magazine, to which, like many of his generation, he had a
life-long addiction. Most of his friends were impressed by the
consideration, even indulgence, with which Evelyn treated him. Each
day, she had a mid-day meal ready for his return from the pub, after
which or even before which, he would usually go to bed. He was a
finicky eater who insisted on soup as a first course and was particular
about what followed, but he often had little appetite for a meal when it
was put in front of him and sometimes rejected it rather abruptly.

He was now seldom sober beyond the early afternoon, when he
would usually decide to go home, perhaps stopping at one or two of
the pubs in Donnybrook on his way. Evelyn feared that the consequences to his health of trying to stop him drinking would be graver
than those resulting from a continuance. She felt that his excitability
was so great that he needed drink to calm him; and his moroseness and
silences when cut off from a 'curer' were such as to discourage her
from the attempt. It had not yet become accepted practice for heavy
drinkers to go into St John of God's or Grangegorman periodically to
be 'dried out'. That was to come later, in the 1960s; meantime only
extreme cases who were suffering from 'the D.T.s' sought refuge or,
more likely, were incarcerated in such places; and probably an attempt
to give up drink without hospitalization would, in his case, have
resulted in a pretty severe trauma.

He was however hospitalized for other reasons towards the end of
1956. Hilton Edwards had written to him about incorporating his
hilarious sketch 'Thirst' in a miscellany he wanted to produce in the
Gaiety. 'Thirst' had been written in the 1940s but Edwards knew it
because the Gate had done it as part of a Christmas show. Edwards
asked about 'Thirst' and also asked for something new 'and, of course,
wildly funny'.[35] O'Nolan replied to Edwards' secretary from the
convalescent home in Lucan. 'I have been very ill and write this from a
nursing-home in Lucan but I am indestructible and hope to go home
on Sunday. I already asked my wife to let Mr Edwards know I was
interested. I don't know did she. [In fact she had.]

'About sketch "Thirst", owing to a recent change of house, all my
books and papers were dumped on the floor like a sack of potatoes. I

think the MS is on the outer fringes. My impression from memory is that at least parts of it would do with rewriting.'[36]

He went on to say that he had recently been 'challenged to write a comic opera. I had begun work when I got sick. Then my mother died, I personally got sicker and there was never a dull moment. The title of the opera is *The Palatine's Daughter* and the sketch "Thirst" would be the guts of the first act. It would be uproarious farce, with songs which will bring down any house and it is a show that could not fail. It would be a three-act full night's entertainment.'

The death of his mother, which took place in 1956, upset him very greatly. It was one of two deaths in the 1950s to do so, the other being that of his boyhood friend, Dickie McManus. McManus, a bachelor, lived nearby in Blackrock and Brian had continued to see him fairly frequently. He once accompanied Brian and Evelyn on a holiday in the south and west of Ireland.

Dickie McManus' death meant the loss of one of his few real human contacts. And the death of his mother was an even greater loss. She had been to some extent his confidante and also Evelyn's. Although a biographer might be tempted to trace some of his psychological difficulties to his relationship with his mother, there is no evidence to support any such view. Agnes O'Nolan seems to have been a cheerful, capable and courageous woman, free from the conflicts and tender sensitivity from which some of the talented Gormleys suffered. She was not over-possessive; she did not oppress her children with mothering; and it is difficult to lay any of his psycho-pathology at her door. His brother Kevin records that he remembered Brian after her death 'asking helplessly how we deserved or came to have the mother we had'. One biographical commentator finds this 'surely an extra-ordinary reaction in a man of 45 to his mother's death.'[37] The record of human experience would seem to be against this assertion. On the night she died, Brian came into McDaid's where Kavanagh comforted him by recalling his own grief on his mother's death. 'You only have one mother,' he said. It was trite perhaps, but Brian was much moved.

Negotiations over *The Palatine's Daughter* came to nothing. O'Nolan was hospitalized again in January 1957 and by this time Edwards' secretary had written to say that he was interested and would like to see the completed script. This peeved O'Nolan who wrote back:

I am a bit mystified by the intent of the second paragraph. To quote from the work of Mr Joyce's youngster, Mr Edwards thinks I should put my comic opera where Jacko put the nuts. This I don't agree with but accept. He wants a re-write of the comic piece known as 'Thirst'.

That he shall have next week. For what purpose though? I mean, what medium? You mention the 'Irish Hills' as if it were the Gas Company or I.C.I. or something dreadfully familiar. I never heard the phrase before. Is it straight stage stuff in Dublin or in Britain, television or sound radio? Be a good girl and let me know more explicitly what is wanted.

Your servant, Brian O'Nolan.[38]

He had begun at this point to see a good deal of Brendan Behan, the scale of whose international success had been one of Dublin's major sensations in 1956. Behan was to turn out to be another victim of the self-consciousness that Dublin encouraged in its better known figures, particularly those who lived out much of their lives in the pubs and felt it necessary to dramatize themselves for the benefit of pub audiences. In Behan's case the burden of such self-dramatization was compounded by the fact that his international fame was largely due to the image he chose to project. Owing so much to the image of the drunken genius, he felt he had to live up to it; and so, before long, he was dancing to the image-makers' tune on a path which was to end with his death.

Brendan was actually a more considerable and more sensitive person than his public image or even his writings suggest. He was also more capable than Brian O'Nolan was of the self-revelations and intimacies that are a necessary part of friendship; but the fame which came to meet him on such a staggering scale, and finally destroyed him, had already begun its work when he and Brian O'Nolan began to consort with each other. In a 'Cruiskeen Lawn' written in 1959 Myles na Gopaleen describes a day they spent together.

A few mornings ago I was visiting in Donnybrook and about 11 A.M. I was waiting for a bus back. A large car came to a screaming halt and from the interior there was directed at me a torrent of what I must describe as ebullience, loud vulgar shouting and – let me be honest for once – plain bad language. This bus stop is just outside the police station and I did not want what the newspapers call an altercation. I advanced in genteel gait to this raucous taxi and said in a courteous undertone: 'Good morning, Brendan.' In reply to this greeting Mr Behan used words I cannot print because, as our beloved late editor Bertie Smyllie had to point out to me more than once, this is a family newspaper. 'Come on into this dangerous rattle-trap,' Mr Behan said. 'Will ya come with me to the Brazen Head?'[39]

Myles agrees, on condition that they go by Meredith's pawn shop where he wants to redeem a watch he had pawned. The pawning of a watch was rather untypical behaviour for Brian O'Nolan; and in the event its redemption is accompanied by much roaring and blathering to the passers-by during which the narrator's innate sense of respectability is contrasted, probably quite accurately, with Behan's general exhibitionism.

In 1962 Brian O'Nolan was to write to his then publisher Tim O'Keeffe, who had had some unfortunate dealings with Behan when he worked for Hutchinson's, 'Behan is a friend of mine but that does not blind me to the fact that he is a lout and sometimes something worse.'[40] But there was generosity in the column he wrote on Behan's rise to fame in 1956, a piece which began their relationship, and both generosity and affection in the obituary he wrote in the *Sunday Telegraph* in March 1964 at the end of it. In this he said with truth that Behan's playwriting 'which I personally found crude and offensive as well as entertaining, was only a fraction of a peculiarly complicated personality. He was in fact much more of a player than a playwright or, to use a Dublin saying, "he was as good as a play".'[41]

However, the limits of the one's knowledge of the other are illustrated by his surprising acceptance of Brendan's assertion that he 'could not be bothered with Joyce "or any of that jazz" and in fact had not read the work of the supercilious unDublinly émigré.' When the present writer first knew Brendan Behan he used to quote lavishly from *Ulysses*, often without acknowledgement, as if some of its best phrases were part of his own inherited knowledge of Dublin speech. It was only later, when he felt himself disdained by Kavanagh and others in McDaid's, that, in reaction against their admiration for *Ulysses*, he affected indifference and finally even ignorance of Joyce's works, declaring that the greatest Dublin writer was Sean O'Casey.

Francis Stuart remembers going around to Behan's house during a visit to Ireland in 1958. Behan's wife, Beatrice, was a daughter of Francis's old friend, Cecil French-Salkeld, the original of Byrne in *At Swim-Two-Birds*, and he wanted to enquire about her sister, Celia. He found a party in progress at which Brian O'Nolan was present. Behan was in a white shirt considerably stout-stained and open to the waist. Brian O'Nolan was wearing his hat. When they adjourned to Mooney's of Baggot Street Bridge, O'Nolan fell on the hard terrazzo floor of the pub. A by-stander who attempted to pick him up was rewarded with an angry 'How dare you.'

O'Nolan was now in the position of having a considerable reputation in Ireland – even if one of which the stereotype of the brilliant failure was an inextricable part – and none at all beyond its shores; and this at a time when a new generation of Irish writers, Behan among them, was beginning to find fame abroad. He was also afflicted by money problems; indeed, considering the amount he spent on drink, it was inevitable that there should be little left over for anything else. He entertained the idea that a collection of Keats and Chapman stories, illustrated by his friend Sean O'Sullivan, might attract an English publisher and prove a profitable Christmas book and he asked me to scout this idea in London where, he probably thought, I had more contacts with publishers than I possessed. When I tried to do so, I found that very few people had ever heard of him. Around this time also he tried unsuccessfully to re-enter the jobs world, asking the *Irish Times* if they could give him employment as a proof-reader. He offered a play *The Boy From Ballytearim* to the BBC in Belfast as a preliminary to an application to become a scriptwriter. In his letter he said he had an 'important project' in hand which was impeded by hack-writing which he found 'difficult' and 'distasteful'.[42] He also wrote to Bryan Guinness, Lord Moyne, for a reference which he proposed to use when applying to Trinity College for the post of Assistant Lecturer in English. This last possibility had been suggested to him by Niall Montgomery, but, like the others, it came to nothing.

That a degree of pathos attaches to these efforts is not his fault, but it is noteworthy that he should have sought salvation, first in an extension of hack-writing and then in a search for a job, though all the while the manuscript of *The Third Policeman* lay among his papers. Evelyn more than once called his attention to the fact that they had a possibly saleable novel in the house, but his reply was that it would have to be recast in the third person, which would be a lot of trouble, and would probably turn out not to have been worthwhile. It is of course probable that if it had been offered to an English publisher at this stage it would have met with no better fate than it had in 1939. In any event in 1958 even his ability or his willingness to write the six columns a week that had latterly been his target seems to have vanished. Whole weeks, sometimes whole months, passed without 'Cruiskeen Lawn' appearing in the *Irish Times*. Then, early in 1959, he received a letter from a young man called Timothy O'Keeffe who worked for the London publishers MacGibbon and Kee, a comparatively new firm with a sophisticated list. O'Keeffe proposed to re-issue *At Swim-Two-Birds*, if the rights were available and if O'Nolan was willing. It was the turn of the tide.

4

The Close

Tim O'Keeffe had been an enthusiast for *At Swim-Two-Birds* since he had been an undergraduate at Oxford. In the 1950s he had worked for Hutchinson, who were then successfully improving their image and were shortly to publish Irish authors such as Brendan Behan and James Plunkett. He had urged Hutchinson to consider a re-issue of *At Swim-Two-Birds* but the proposal had eventually been vetoed by the dynamic head of the firm, Robert Lusty, who did not like the book and did not understand it. It is part of Brian O'Nolan's tragedy that O'Keeffe did not succeed in getting to him then. Even three or four years might have made a difference. However, in May 1959, after discussions with his colleagues in MacGibbon and Kee, O'Keeffe was able to write to O'Nolan to suggest a re-issue.

'Along with a number of other people,' he wrote, 'I've been a great admirer of *At Swim-Two-Birds* and some time ago began making the preliminary moves to try to get the book re-issued. I am now glad to tell you that, provided the rights are available and that you wish to have the book in print again on this side of the Atlantic, we would publish it.'[1]

As it turned out, Longman's still had the rights; but they were due to expire in five months unless they wished to produce a new edition in that time. So they were willing to surrender them to MacGibbon and Kee.

O'Nolan's own attitude to *At Swim-Two-Birds* was now such that the mere mention of it appeared to cause him great annoyance. When people sought to praise it he would dismiss it as 'mere juvenilia' and he seemed, for the most part, intolerant of any mention of it whatever. This may even have been because he was much more of a traditionalist at heart than his authorship of it would lead one to believe; and now in retrospect distrusted the methods by which it had been composed and the part chance had played in the sort of collage he had made. Such an attitude could well have been part of his general puritanism, even his philistinism. But in any case his first novel seemed now in his mind to be associated with the image of the brilliant failure which Dublin had imposed on him. To praise the work of his youth, was, he felt, to write off the living man.

After it had been safely re-issued in 1960 he reluctantly conceded to O'Keeffe that the book must have something but when he inscribed

the new edition to Angela Conolly, he begged her to remember that
it was 'written by a schoolboy', and in 1964 when he was interviewed
by John Bowman on Irish radio he said, 'I cannot express my
detestation for that damn book.' To account for the critical attitude
towards it he said that 'there must be some diabolical code, some
anagram buried in it' that he had not intended, and he called it 'a
painfully bad book'.[2]

However, over the years it had been acquiring that best of all
literary reputations, one conveyed from reader to reader by word of
mouth. The Hibernophiles of English criticism had been aware of it
for some time and so had the sedulous avant-gardeistes. All this was
reflected in the chorus of praise which now greeted its re-issue. It got
lead reviews from Philip Toynbee in the *Observer* and V. S. Pritchett
in the *New Statesman* and was praised almost everywhere. Toynbee
was inclined to emphasize the Joycean aspect of things, but Pritchett
was, as usual, right on the mark.

> Mr O'Brien's gifts are startling and heartless. He has the astounding
> Irish genius for describing the human animal, its shameless and dilapi-
> dated body, its touching and proliferating fancy, its terrible interest in
> useless conundrums. On top of this he has an extraordinary freedom of
> the English language ... His people are either seedy Dubliners or
> ludicrous giants, but their wits are alight; they live in language, in comic
> image, rather than in life. It looks as though his idea was to knock the
> regionalism out of Irish literature by magnifying it.[3]

The biographical note on the jacket now disclosed the author's real
name and identity but the copyright was taken out in the name of
Brian Nolan. When O'Keeffe spotted this it was too late for correc-
tion, but, to his surprise, O'Nolan seemed unperturbed and said it did
not matter.

The best immediate result of the re-issue was that O'Nolan immediately set to work to write another book. That he needed this sort of
encouragement is again evidence of how far he was from Joyce in
certain attitudes. He was always in great need of reassurance about
anything he had written and sometimes almost pathetically grateful
for praise, even of an *Irish Times* column. The critical reception of the
new edition of *At Swim-Two-Birds* had given him back some of the
creative self-esteem which the rejection of *The Third Policeman* had so
long ago destroyed.

He began work almost immediately and against all the odds – the
long disused talent, the inveterate drinking, the profound self-distrust

– the result was a small masterpiece, *The Hard Life*. Most things were long in gestation with him but when he worked at all he worked quickly. 'Considerable works of art,' he had said in his column, 'are produced very fast. What takes an awful lot of time is usually a bad piece of work.'[4]

By 27 January 1961 he was able to send a draft to Mark Hamilton of A. M. Heath, who, after all these years, were still his agents. As usual, he needed reassurance: 'Needless to say, I begin to have enormous doubts about this material. I would be obliged if you would read the MS and let me know your opinion. I would be enormously interested in it.'[5]

Hamilton, in fact, had his doubts and O'Nolan immediately began to defend his book against the charges that were made:

> I feel that the doubts you personally had will turn out to be mistaken. Everything was done with deliberation, the characters illuminating themselves and each other by their outlandish behaviour and preposterous conversations. The plot, episodically evolved, is sternly consecutive and conclusive and makes the book compact and short. Digression and expatiation would be easy but I feel would injure the book's spontaneity. You are right in saying that I deliberately avoided direct narrative on description. The 'I' narrator, or interlocutor, is himself a complete ass. A few people here whose opinion I value have seen the MS and all are really impressed, particularly by the Collopy–Father Fahrt dialogues, which are set down in absolutely accurate Dublinese.[6]

One of the people who had seen the book was Brendan Behan, who told him that it was 'a gem' but suggested that Father Fahrt was not objectionable enough and that he should have some disease. O'Nolan rejected TB, which he thought was never funny, but decided that there was a lot to be said for some scaly skin disease which need not be named but could be conveyed by itching and scratching. In the end it was named as psoriasis.

He now began to nourish the hope that this new book would be banned in Ireland. The Censorship of Publications Act which prohibited the sale of literature that was 'in its general tendency obscene' or which advocated contraception was still being applied with some rigour; and many quite reputable works of literature had, over the years, been banned under it. There were, indeed, so many that to be censored was considered something of a mark of distinction; and since in the 1950s and 1960s banned books could be fairly easily obtained 'under the counter' it was not, as it once had been, a severe financial blow. Nearly every professional Irish author had had a book banned and O'Nolan's gleeful anticipation of the prospect makes it clear that he was anxious to join the club. This anxiety may be partly attributable to his uneasy sense that although he had written millions of words he had not yet established himself as an author of books. But it might equally be because of the noticeable absence of sex in the books themselves. He knew, he told O'Keeffe, that the book did not offend under the heads named in the Act 'but the mere name of Father Kurt Fahrt S.J., will justify the thunder clap'. He returned to the theme two months later. 'The name will cause holy bloody ructions here. It will lead to wirepulling behind the scenes here to have the book banned as obscene (for there is no other statutory ground for a ban than advocating birth control).'[7] If that happened he would challenge the ban in the High Court and seek damages from those who imposed it. 'The upper judiciary here are quite intelligent and in fact I know most of them but the fact that it would be a jury case would be the complication.'[8] Besides the wish to establish himself as one of those professionals whose books were deemed worthy of the attentions of the Censorship Board, his hopes reveal that tendency, evident in his character since student days, to want to outrage and annoy without suffering any real personal damage as a result.

In order not to afford ammunition gratuitously to the 'Reverend Spivs' who controlled the banning process, he had told O'Keeffe that he thought 'the book in appearance should be utterly colourless, anonymous (pseudonymous), neutral. All biographical matter should be cut right out. Our bread and butter depends on being one jump ahead of the other crowd.'[9]

In the event the appearance of the book pleased him, particularly the portrait of Mr Collopy on the cover, which he said was an excellent portrait of Sean T. O'Kelly to whom he had once been Private Secretary. 'This sort of thing helps enormously.' And he added that he had lent the book to two people deliberately chosen for their incongruity of temperament.

> The first found it very, very funny – uproarious. The second (a lady) handed it back to me sadly. She said she did not understand me and now doubted whether she ever had. But of one thing I could be sure. Not one night would pass but she would say a Hail Mary for me. And wasn't it a good job that my poor mother wasn't still alive?
>
> I gather that she had been shocked, not so much by Mr Collopy's words but by the name of the good Jesuit Father.[10]

He had doubts, though, as he told Gerald Gross of Pantheon Books in New York, about the British reaction. 'Those people are very hard to amuse – they look for overtones, undertones, subtones, grunts and "philosophy", they assume something very serious is afoot. It's disquieting for a writer who is only, for the moment, clowning.'[11] This modest view of his new work was not, however, a consistent one. A year later he was telling O'Keeffe that '*The Hard Life* is a very important book and very funny. Its apparently pedestrian-style is delusive.'[12]

In spite of this latter assessment, however, to grow too solemn about *The Hard Life* or to make over-large claims for it would be to affront the essentially modest nature of the work itself. Within its limits it is, as Behan said, 'a gem', but the limits are there. The book is basically a sequence of jokes, often dependent for their effect on a mild feeling of outrage, akin to that which he hoped would be provoked by the name of the Jesuit who is Mr Collopy's interlocutor, rather than a true comedy, even though the central joke, the bodily necessities of existence and the ills that flesh is heir to, is a grimly important one. Still, that said, it is a total success. The conversation pieces are classics of pointless dialectic; the seediness of a run-down middle-class life largely confined to kitchen and basement is superbly conveyed; the futile, obsessional nature of Collopy's Irish outlook on things is memorably contrasted with the brother's get-up-and-go cosmopolitanism. A basic improbability is that the brother would have sufficient filial feeling for Mr Collopy to pay for the pilgrimage to Rome, but since this is essential to the plot it is blithely and properly ignored by the author. A more important weakness concerns the narrator. We do not know enough about his ambitions, his sense of destiny or his values to get the full effect of the revulsion he feels at the kind of life described in the book. And this certainly invalidates it as any sort of a portrait of the artist as a young man or even as the parody of Joyce's book which some critics have held it to be.

One doubts, however, that any sort of commentary on Joyce was part of O'Nolan's intention and he was certainly annoyed that the reviewers, though enthusiastic, insisted on invoking Joyce's shade once again. To some extent this was because of the subject matter. He had chosen to set his book in Dublin at the turn of the century, just as he had chosen to make the life of a student at Dublin's Catholic University part of the subject matter of *At Swim-Two-Birds*. Since these were the territories of his imagination and experience he had every right to do so. Yet they made comparison with Joyce inevitable. To some extent also, these comparisons were the result of what Anthony Burgess, reviewing *The Hard Life*, called his 'word-loving logomachic' outlook.[13] This was, however, something he shared with many Irish writers, most of whom are markedly more logomachic than their English counterparts, rather than just with Joyce. The repeated comparisons with Joyce annoyed him intensely. 'If I hear that word "Joyce" again I will surely froth at the gob,' he wrote to O'Keeffe.[14]

The insistence on bodily ailments and bodily unpleasantnesses in the book also provoked one or two references to Swift. O'Nolan's zestful descriptions of physical horrors had been referred to as early as Thomas Hogan's piece in *The Bell* in 1947. Hogan had instanced the case of a lecturer who at the end of a high-flown exordium 'pours used shaving water into exquisite vase on mantelpiece and starts removing bandage from sore neck.'[15] In *The Hard Life* the perils and debilities of bodily existence are unremittingly emphasized. There is a lengthy disquisition on the symptomatology of venereal disease (lifted, incidentally, almost straight out of the *Encyclopaedia Britannica*, one of O'Nolan's great stand-bys all his writing life) which is only very tenuously justified by its place in the narrative.

To describe this side of him as Swiftian is, however, inaccurate. O'Nolan finds the sordidities of bodily existence positively funny and he describes them with a zest which contains little hint of Swiftian disgust. And although Hogan had also quoted H. G. Wells' famous remark about Joyce as exemplifying 'the cloacal obsession of the Irish', it is perhaps noteworthy from a psychological standpoint that there is little that is specifically cloacal either in the novels or in 'Cruiskeen Lawn'. It is the 'wide variety of physical scourges, torments, and piteous bloodsweats' which the Pooka McPhellimy threatens to inflict on Dermot Trellis that he finds funny. His brother Kevin remembered an occasion when some Strabane relatives were describing the death of a local doctor who had stumbled down a flight of stairs with such exactitude of trajectory as to have his skull pierced by a solitary nail which projected from the lintel of a door at the end of it. Brian found this so amusing that his mother and his aunt had severely reproved him, but he continued to find the grotesqueries and macabre accidents of human existence funny all his life. Like all humour, it was of course a defence against shock; but on the other hand it probably enabled him to bear his own ever-present physical misfortunes and his extraordinary proneness to accident better than he might have done otherwise.

Two other characteristics of *The Hard Life* ought to be noted. One is its Catholicism. The jokes are to a large extent irreverent, but they presuppose something to be reverent about. They are funnier if you are mildly shocked or shockable by scandalous talk about the Jesuits or by the idea of Mr Collopy trying to enlist the Pope's support for the provision of public lavatories for women. There is an assumption that the Catholic Church is a very important institution, that it occupies a place of primary importance in the world, and that its existence affects life and one's outlook on life in enormously important ways.

The second feature of the book is in a way related to the first. It poses a conflict between a sort of secular humanism – or rather two sorts of secular humanism: one, represented by the brother, being the heartless, commercial one of the contemporary world; the other, represented by Mr Collopy, being the liberal, mildly progressivist one of the late Victorian era – and the transcendentalism of Father Fahrt. Around this central conflict, there are many orbital ones: the relationship of violence to reformism as an instrument of change and of nationalist fervour to practical reform, for example, being most noteworthy. The immediate reform Mr Collopy is working for is the provision of public lavatories for women. In opposition to it the transcendentalist view is seen as male, hierarchical and dismissive. A victory for Mr Collopy in the book's terms would mean an acceptance of women as equal human beings and of their bodily needs as something of great importance. The Pope, supreme patriarch of a patriarchal world, draws back from such an acceptance. 'Bona mulier fons gratiae,' he says. 'Attamen ipsae in parvularum rerum suarum occupationibus verrentur. Nos de tantulis rebus consulere non decet. A good woman is a fountain of grace. But it is themselves whom they should busy about their private little affairs. It is not seemly to consult us on such matters.'

What makes the book an oddity in the O'Nolan canon is that the author seems to be on Mr Collopy's side. He, more than the brother or the narrator, is the book's informing spirit, the comic creation which makes us remember it with affection. Mr Collopy accepts the bodily necessities of women as a proper subject for social concern. Through Mr Collopy the book's author had made an act of acceptance too. To the emancipated liberal it will doubtless not seem a great deal; but in terms of Brian O'Nolan's general outlook it is both significant and important.

'I did the job, in addition to other jobs, in two months dead and found I was nearly dead myself,' he was to say a year later.[16] But he had written a good funny book, it had been published and it had been praised, at home and abroad. Graham Greene, who had been the recipient of a somewhat overpolitic and calculated dedication, wrote to say he was gratified and declared, '*At Swim-Two-Birds* has remained to my mind ever since it first appeared as one of the best books of our century. But my God, what a long time it has been waiting for the next one.'[17]

But the publication of a new novel did not solve O'Nolan's economic problems and they were increasingly severe. Quarrels with the *Irish Times* were now endemic. Many columns were being rejected and he was also writing less than he had been. In the last three months of 1959 only 18 columns appeared. Some of the rejected columns he gave to a new friend, Patricia Murphy, the former wife of the poet Richard Murphy who had once published poetry herself under her maiden name Patricia Avis and now founded a periodical called *Nonplus*. *Disjecta membra* from the column both new and old appeared frequently there in 1959 and Brian O'Nolan was a regular visitor to her flat in Wilton Place, though not even Dublin gossip alleged that there was any romantic attachment on his part. Patricia was a medical doctor, a capable woman who knew her own mind and she was hospitable enough to supply both Kavanagh and Brian with whiskey in exchange for what she hoped would be conversation. She also gave Brian a gold watch, probably the one he redeemed from pawn in company with Brendan Behan. Her journal was to be short-lived enough, only three issues appearing, and publication there, however useful as a way of showing the *Irish Times* that he had an outlet for rejected pieces, was of course not sufficient to provide him with an income.

An old *Irish Times* hand, Brian Inglis, whose 'Irishman's Diary' column had once appeared on the same page as 'Cruiskeen Lawn', was now editing the *Spectator* and Brian wrote to thank him for a favourable review of the re-issue of *At Swim-Two-Birds*. After describing the book as 'juvenile nonsense' he approached the main topic of his letter.

I am most anxious to leave the dirty *Irish Times*. It was an odd enough paper in Smyllie's day but it has now become really quite intolerable. I need not discourse to you on their shocking notions of pay but in addition much of the material I send in is suppressed and for that work they pay nothing whatever. Other articles are mutilated and cut, often through sheer ignorance. The paper has in recent years bred a whole new herd of sacred cows and, cute as I claim to be, I have never been certain of their identity. In any case they are always being added to. I wrote stuff about the Irish Army's Imperial exploit in the Congo but this was all utterly killed. Alec Newman is a perfect gentleman but a complete weakling ... accepting instructions on petty matters from certain directors who make prams and who should properly be in them (and who don't like me, think I'm dangerous) ... NOW HEAR THIS—

is there any possibility of finding space in the *Spectator* for a piece by me, preferably regular. Such a piece, which need not be long or expensive, would naturally be primarily addressed to English readers, though no doubt often based on the queer things that happen over here. Naturally I would be happy to send you a sample or two to give some indication of climate, temperature, obsessions, etc.[18]

Through the early months of 1961 O'Nolan was busy in the continuing quest for a job, even attempting to get back into the Civil Service by way of application for a job as Dáil translator. The acuteness of his anxiety about means of subsistence may be measured by his willingness to spend his days turning the hated Dáil oratory into Irish, and by the fact that he could contemplate returning to an ambience which, in retrospect anyway, he hated. When, two years later, his youngest brother Micheál became an inspector of art in secondary schools and thus a civil servant, he wrote:

CONGRATULATIONS

Nuala called to-day and told me you'd got that job. I kinda knew you would though I could not absolutely exclude dirty work. (You must remember that —— has been married for many years now and HE may have brats coming up who require to be planted, like obscene puppies on a dunghill.)

You are in the civil service now and in due course shd. contact me for cute, informed advice, with my background of field work. Always remember the rat is very smart too.

See you soon. B.[19]

Once when I met him about this time he was on his way to see Allen Figgis, a director of the Dublin bookselling firm, Hodges Figgis, which also did some book publishing. 'I am skating on very thin ice,' he told me. 'The only security I have is the pension and that's not much.' He asked me did I know Figgis and I said I knew of him only by repute. He was going to ask for a job, he said. I believe he did get some reading to do but it was not a happy association for either party. Two years later Figgis had the misfortune to be interviewed on the same programme when Brian made his only Irish television appearance. About halfway through Brian seemed suddenly to realize who this other person was and, though not very sober, laid a classical trap for him. Ignoring the interviewer, he asked, 'Is your name Figgis?' On receiving the only answer possible he supplemented the question. 'Are you the so-called publisher?' he asked. There was no possible answer to this.

At the same time he was contributing an article every week to a provincial paper, the *Nationalist and Leinster Times*, published in Co. Carlow. The column was called 'Bones of Contention' and the pseudonym he had adopted was 'George Knowall'. It was discursive and pedestrian rather than funny or astringent and he made shameless use of the *Encyclopaedia Britannica* in writing it. It seemed crazy that he should be doing it at all for he now had an international reputation.

He had ended the conversation about the possibility of a job with Hodges Figgis by saying somewhat boastfully, 'Between the two sides of the Atlantic I can get a thousand pounds sight unseen for a book,' but of course he had to write the books first. It was almost inconceivable that he should turn into what Patrick Kavanagh called a novel-a-year-man but it might have been better to try to do so rather than turn himself into 'George Knowall'. He had discovered that his manuscripts were saleable and discussed with me the possibility of retrieving the manuscript of *At Swim-Two-Birds* from the daughter of a distinguished civil servant and former colleague to whom he had presented it long ago as a christening gift. I said I saw no reason why he should not ask for it back, but I did not tell him that the person concerned, now a married woman and fallen on hard times, had also consulted me about the possibility of raising money by selling it.

Besides everything else he was in and out of hospital, first with a cracked coccyx and then with an eye injury, both of them awkward and painful ailments which he bore bravely, as he always did pain. He was drinking so much that his day was virtually over by 3.00 P.M. and he was usually at home in bed by the late afternoon. To meet him in the evening was a great rarity, though once, for some reason or other, he came into McDaid's towards closing time. We were seated at a table in the little half compartment at the back, a rather cramped space sometimes known as 'the intensive care unit' which one had to share with other people. He took exception to something said by a stranger who was sitting there and grew quite obstreperous about it. When, at closing time, we all emerged into the lane he continued to abuse this unoffending person violently and, though he had his hat and coat on, to offer to fight. It was impossible to pull him away and since at one point his terrier-like abusiveness seemed likely to provoke the other chap to strike him I feared for the outcome.

Because his day usually ended so early, when there was a change in the licensing laws around this time, which allowed the pubs to remain open later, he was for a while the only drinker in Dublin who knew nothing about it, though he knew full well what time they opened in the morning. Like many heavy drinkers in Dublin he was no stranger to the pubs which have special early or 'market' licences, where there is a certain freemasonry among those who are driven from their beds by sleeplessness or morning thoughts. He rarely went as far as the cattle markets; but the White Horse, which owed its special licence to its position on the quays near the *Irish Press*, was one of his ports of call.

In 1960 the O'Nolans moved again, this time to a new house in the extensive suburbia growing up on either side of the Stillorgan Road. Evelyn had always been unhappy in the house on Belmont Avenue which she thought oppressively dark. They had discussed moving many times and had thought it would be nice to find a house along the coast, in Dalkey or Killiney, but although they studied the advertisements nothing became available. The house in Waltersland Road was a single-storey modern bungalow and Evelyn, who conducted the transaction while Brian was much of the time in bed, felt it was a little incongruous for a writer, but she nevertheless thought it had certain advantages, one of which was that there were no stairs for him to climb or fall down. It was such a long way from town that eventually Brian would spend a fortune on taxis. The only pub in the locality was a vast place, with huge spaces in its various lounges. As he told John Ryan, it was like 'Croke Park roofed over'. He also patronized Byrne's of Galloping Green, whose proprietor would later have the distinction of being the only publican ever to bar him, or perhaps anybody, by letter.

With another pub somewhat further afield which he had known since Blackrock days, Baker's of Kill O' the Grange, he also had a difference of opinion. This concerned a slate which the publican said had not been cleared and a further amount allegedly owing for a bottle of whiskey and a half dozen of stout. In a letter marked 'Dictated' and typed by Evelyn, Brian wrote:

Me dear man,
Since last seeing you I went down with a ferocious dose of flu (or that's what they call it) and am still out of action.
I have however managed to do some quarrying in bed in the matter of cheques. You said that prior to the recent call of self and younger brother, I owed you money which I had not paid. I said I was certain I had paid. I enclose the paid cheque, which please return.
I know nothing about the bottle of whiskey and half doz. stouts connected with our visit. It is quite true that I am capable of drinking the contents of a bottle of whiskey, but not the bottle itself. There is no empty bottle in my house ...
It would be no harm for you to realize that you, too, can make

mistakes. You owe me an apology in connection with the cheque
enclosed.

With regards
Brian O'Nolan[20]

In Waltersland Road he had appropriated the best room in the
house, one which was bright and sunny and had French doors into the
garden. Into this he moved the double bed which had belonged to his
mother and father and here he spent a great deal of time, sometimes
writing in bed, always, except in the warmest weather, with the
electric fire on.

He had now turned his attention to what was in Ireland the new
medium of television and in 1962 he wrote some plays for it. One,
'The Boy from Ballytearim', was an adaptation of what had been a
stage play; another, 'The Dead Spit of Kelly', was a dramatized
version of the story which had appeared in *The Bell*, 'Two in One';
but 'Flight' and 'The Time Freddy Retired' were written for television. It was, once again, a rather extraordinary use to make of his
talents. Like the original short story, 'Two in One', these are extended
anecdotes rather than plays in any real sense. They are certainly not
explorations of the medium (he did not even possess a television set)
and they were not very rewarding financially either. In part the
writing of them was another assertion of his belief in himself as a
hard-bitten literary journeyman who could turn his hand to anything
and was now turning it to television in a coolly exploitative way.

Even more strangely still perhaps, he now suggested to Guinness,
the great Dublin brewing firm, that he would write some television
advertisements for them and went so far as to supply them with a
sample. The scene was to be a group of men sitting round a table in a
Dublin pub drinking Guinness. Over this, before any word was
spoken, was to be superimposed the slogan GET TOGETHER WITH
A GUINNESS. Then one of them was to tell a stage Irish story about
a friend who was driving in New York and bumped into another car.
The policeman who comes up says, 'It's to prison you're going for
this,' to which the friend replies, 'It wasn't my fault at all.' The
policeman recognizes his accent: 'Is it from Dublin you are? Then wait
a while till I go and arrest those cheating rogues for bumping into you
like that.' They all laugh and agree that that calls for another stout. The
barman comes up with a tray of glasses of Guinness and places it on
the table. It is noteworthy that the author of this lamentable stuff
knew his technical terms, for the script goes on 'Super title; There's
Nothing Like A Guinness! In sync. *with voice over*; THERE'S
NOTHING LIKE A GUINNESS!'[21]

Sadly enough, Guinness did not employ the author of 'A Pint Of Plain Is Your Only Man' as an advertisement scriptwriter and neither did the newly organized Irish Distillers Group warm to the proposal the same author made in 1964. This was that he should write a history of the Irish Whiskey Distilling Industry. To entice them he wrote a 3,500-word synopsis of the proposal, a very strange document which begins with some information about himself.

A preliminary personal note about myself is called for. After considerable University studies, which included experience abroad, I joined the Irish Civil Service in 1935. I resigned in 1953, with a rank of Principal Officer, having found the milieu increasingly distasteful. It was bad enough that nearly all Ministers were either peasants or uneducated shopboys (to some of whom I acted as Private Secretary) but there was undisguised graft, jobbery, and corrupt practices large and small. This is not the place to detail such matters though it will be recalled that some cases – e.g., the Locke's Distillery and the Monaghan Bacon Factory – came to public notice, and then only because certain of the shady operators had quarrelled among themselves. I had meantime been engaged in writing of various kinds and felt I could make an honest living that way. I have written 7 books, published in London and New York with 3 of them translated internationally, as well as plays, short stories, radio and T.V. material, and over the years an immense amount of work that might be ranked as better class journalism. I have discontinued the last mentioned activity so far as Ireland is concerned owing to the deplorable conditions of publishing here; there is parochial and sectarian prejudice, there is something approaching illiteracy to be met on all sides, and some of the ideas of financial reward are ludicrous. I now write for the (Manchester) *Guardian* and various reviews, some in the U.S. Last year I wrote a book which will be published in London next October and by Macmillan of New York early in 1965. This book should create a stir. I have never published anything under my own name.[22]

He went on to give a rather lurid historical account of the drinking habits of the Irish as described in the memoirs of such 18th-century writers as Jonah Barrington, a summary of the career of the temperance reformer Fr Matthew, a history of the introduction of a state excise duty on the manufacture of alcoholic drink and some statistics about the number of licensed premises in Ireland at various times since the 1830s. After this he went on to describe the advantages he believed might accrue to the Irish whiskey distilling industry by the publication of a book which would be the fruit of 'exhaustive research' into the history of Irish whiskey and its economic, fiscal and social context.

The drink business is intrinsically a considerable social issue, with an impact far beyond its immediate self. The Fr Matthew campaign here, the horrifying Prohibition interlude in the U.S. and Scandinavian regulation by State monopoly are examples of the interaction of alcohol with political, religious and social concepts. Ignorant and exaggerated attitudes to drink present it in a uniformly pejorative light, and it is in the interest of the industry to explain itself. So far as we are concerned, the immediate objective should be to make genuine Irish potstill whiskey from Ireland a familiar and prized drink in the United States.[23]

He wound up by stating his terms. He would 'expect an honorarium of £600 a year for a possible maximum of 2 years, this to include all travel and similar expenses outside Dublin.' Such an honorarium, he said, would be in no sense payment for writing the book, which he 'would conceive as a genuine work of literature, subject to world-wide review and notice on its own merits. The sponsor would not be faced with any publication or other imponderable technical problems, as I am already under contract to a large publisher in London and another in New York, the subject matter of a book being a matter of my own choice.' The nature of his own hope is conveyed by the statement: 'The arrangement would largely free me from other work to concentrate on this specialized task.'

Irish Distillers seem not to have read more than the first few pages of his synopsis, which included an extended description of a typical 18th-century debauch by Jonah Barrington, for they replied that they did not think that to call attention to the history of drinking in Ireland was a good idea and that the industry was in process of projecting a new and more dignified image, which of course was more or less what he had suggested it should set about doing.

In his prospectus he had described himself as the author of seven books. In fact the best count at the time it was written reveals only six and that would include *The Dalkey Archive*, which had not yet appeared, and the play *Faustus Kelly* as well as the extracts from 'Cruiskeen Lawn' which had been published by the *Irish Times* in 1943.

In an autobiographical piece which had appeared some weeks before in a Belfast student magazine the total had been raised to ten. This piece, entitled 'De Me', had begun life as an autobiographical memorandum, written for his sister Nuala when he stayed in her house during the time of Evelyn's illness in 1956. He had subsequently adapted it to furnish the material for a talk to the New Ireland Society of Queen's University in Belfast and as a contribution to their magazine, *New Ireland*, in March 1964.

It is notable as one of the few times when he adverted to his Northern Irish origins. In doing so he invited his audience to come with him:

... to a neat smiling town near several tumbling rivers, once a great rail junction. The name is Strabane, happiest town in Tyrone, and that is where I was born. And I can prove it. My late mother's people, the Gormleys, are still to be found at Main Street, and if you call there introducing yourself as a friend of mine, my uncle Eugene or Joe, or my aunt Teresa, will instantly take the hint and offer you a glass of malt. The actual address of the birth-bed is 17 The Bowling Green.[24]

It was in fact 15; but this rare essay in autobiography went on to say:

... in 25 years I have written ten books (that is, substantial opera) under four quite irreconcilable pen-names and on subjects absolutely unrelated. Five of those books could be described as works of imagination, one of world social comment, two on scientific subjects, one of literary exploration and conjecture, one in Irish and one a play (which was produced by the Abbey Theatre).[25]

The tone of this must of course give the biographer pause. There is an air of painstaking accuracy about it, underlined by the mention of the play. And at this time there were five 'works of imagination' if *The Third Policeman* and the not yet published *Dalkey Archive* are included. But the po-faced claim to have written one book of 'world social comment', two books on 'scientific subjects' and 'one of literary exploration and conjecture' is probably to be viewed in the light of his general mendacity and love of puzzle-making, more particularly since only seven books were to be claimed a few weeks later.

The autobiographical discourse went on to claim that on top of all that he had 'produced an enormous mass of miscellaneous material consisting of short stories, scripts for radio and TV, contributions to newspapers and magazines and even book reviews.' This sort of activity, it declared somewhat defensively, 'is work and can be very rewarding financially, often surprisingly and unpredictably so. But is it insufferably hard work? Not necessarily.' Then came the most revealing passage:

Apart from a thorough education of the widest kind, a contender in this field must have an equable yet versatile temperament, and the compartmentation of his personality for the purpose of literary utterance ensures that the fundamental individual will not be credited with a certain way of thinking, fixed attitudes, irreversible techniques of expression. No author should write under his own name nor under one permanent pen-name; a male writer should include in his impostures a female pen-name, and possibly vice versa.

There is no evidence that O'Nolan ever used a female pen-name, though Niall Montgomery was then writing a would-be humorous

column in the *Irish Times* under the pseudonym 'Rosemary Lane' to
which he may have contributed a piece or two. The compartmentation
of personality for the purpose of literary utterance is a shrewd piece of
advice which applies to all writing, though he practised it more
sedulously, and perhaps in the end more damagingly, than most. What
is more startling is the fear of 'being credited with a certain way of
thinking' or 'fixed attitudes'. Not all writers are as fond of disappear-
ing tricks of one sort or another as Brian O'Nolan was since many of
them are to a greater or lesser degree messianic. They bring their own
revelations, even if only psychological, with them into this world and
they want people to see things in the way they do. Brian O'Nolan had
his own fixed attitudes; and, as often happens, he delivered his
injunctions to others at a time when he may have felt he could be
accused of transgressing against them himself.

The fifth of his 'works of the imagination', *The Dalkey Archive*, had
first been mentioned in a letter to Tim O'Keeffe in late 1962 and he
was beginning to talk of it in Dublin at about the same time. Generally
these conversations would begin with his demanding of the favoured
interlocutor whether it had ever occurred to him that St Augustine
might have been 'a black man'. An interlocutor with no interest at all
in St Augustine then had to listen to a disquisition which concluded
that he probably was, but that nobody had seen fit to mention it at the
time since the Romans did not advert to people's colour. Brian
appeared to find something very funny and perhaps shocking in the
notion of the saint's negritude. Later on he would pretend that he had
done exhaustive research on St Augustine, reading everything
published about him in English, French and German, and even going
so far as to spend a fortnight in the British Museum reading him in the
original Latin, thus becoming 'the only person who has ever done so,
not excluding Augustine himself'. The truth is however that his
knowledge of St Augustine was quite sketchy and could easily have
been derived from the *Catholic Encyclopaedia* and the Everyman
edition of the *Confessions*; nor did he spend any time whatever in
the British Museum.

But the topic of the novel bulked increasingly large in his conversation and it became obvious to anyone with experience of such
matters that there was even a danger that he might talk it away. He had
adopted a method of composition which is sometimes a sign of
desperation. This was to complete a draft at all costs without worrying
overmuch about subtleties of expression or overall shape and structure, attending to them afterwards with the cooler judgement and the

increased confidence the completion of a draft had hopefully created. Eventually the day came when one was given a typescript copy of the first hundred pages or so. In my own case the disappointment was immense. He had been speaking of a new work, experimental in nature, with a time shift of a bold order and a plot that was full of surprises. What he now handed over for inspection and comment was, in essence, a traditional novel, rather flatulently composed. The writing was far below the standard its acerbic author had for the most part set himself, and sometimes embarrassingly so, as passages like the following still sadly show:

> Without swallowing whole all the warnings one could readily hear and read about the spiritual dangers of intellectual arrogance and literary free-booting, there *was* menace in the overpoise that high education and a rich way of living could confer on a young girl. Unknowingly, she could exceed her own strength. Did she find his own company a stabilizing pull? Mick had to doubt that, for the truth was that he was not too steady himself. Confession once a month was all very well but he was drinking too much. He would give up drink. Also, he would make Mary more of his own quiet kind, and down to earth.[26]

In the 'De Me' piece he had spoken of the 'compartmentation of his personality for the purpose of literary utterance' as a desirable aim for the writer. In this book, for the first time, aspects of the author's own personality seemed to have escaped from their compartments and to be hanging out all over the place. Of course the central character, Mick, some of whose reflections have just been quoted, was not intended to be a self-portrait; indeed O'Nolan was to say in a letter to Cecil Scott that 'all the characters are intended to be obnoxious, particularly the narrator', but the general tone of the book was his and it is impossible to escape the feeling that Mick and the author are very much the same person. For the first time in a long career the mask appeared to have slipped or to have been mislaid. I was reminded of a time about 10 years before when we both had been to see Charlie Chaplin's *Limelight* and he asked me what I thought of it. I praised it, for although I had been made uncomfortable by its naivety at times I had been moved as well. Brian said in reply that he could not stand seeing Chaplin's face. He thought it was 'horrible'. Now here was his own face without the mask, and the effect was sometimes embarrassing.

Furthermore, although he had spoken with pride of the speed of composition, it began to be obvious as one read that this was old stuff re-hashed. I knew nothing of De Selby or *The Third Policeman* then but, if this was a new work, there were disturbing anachronisms.

Women were not served in the Metropole Lounge; the side roads of
Dalkey were empty and silent; trams still ran in the streets of Dublin.
When, years later, I read *The Third Policeman*, I discovered that a long
passage of description had been lifted from one book to the other
along with the comic policemen and the molecular theory. He was
mining a masterwork to produce the dull dross of a tired and inferior
one.

But the anachronisms were not the only disturbing thing. By the
1960s one expected an Irish writer, particularly someone like O'Nolan
who had read *A Portrait of the Artist as a Young Man* practically in
his cradle, to have acquired a more sophisticated attitude towards
Catholicism. The author of *The Hard Life* had, right enough,
expected one to be amused and perhaps mildly shocked by certain
kinds of jokes about it. But the author of *The Dalkey Archive* clearly
expected his audience to gasp with shock before being overcome with
mirth at such schoolboy jokes as the questions De Selby puts to St
Augustine in the cave and the saint's answers. As one read on it
became, to say the least, remarkable that De Selby, who could have
called up anybody he liked from the past, should confine himself to St
Augustine, the Greek Fathers and gossip about Heaven in the fashion
of an inquisitive nun trying to find out what the Pope had for
breakfast. Nor, in spite of the author's pretensions, was the theology
on a much higher level than the rather sketchy physics. De Selby's
reasons for wanting to bring life on this planet to an end are confused
and contradictory; but the most interesting thing about them is their
strongly Manichaean tone. There is a clear impression that the author
was trying to have it both ways, to affirm his orthodoxy while at the
same time making an uneasy suggestion that a different view of things
might be nearer the truth of existence as he sees it.

> – I feel, he announced, that you are entitled to some personal expla-
> nation concerning myself. It would be quite wrong to regard me as a
> christophobe.
> – Me too, Hackett chirped impudently.
> – The early books of the Bible I accepted as myth, but durable myth
> contrived genuinely for man's guidance. I also accepted as fact the story
> of the awesome encounter between God and the rebel Lucifer. But I was
> undecided for many years as to the outcome of that encounter. I had
> little to corroborate the revelation that God had triumphed and ban-
> ished Lucifer to Hell forever. For if – I repeat *if* – the decision had gone
> the other way and God had been vanquished, who but Lucifer would be
> certain to put about the other and opposite story?

And as with religion, so with certain personal dilemmas – the conflict
between the leanings of the natural anchorite and the merits of the

married state, for example, or between alcohol as an anodyne and
alcohol as a destructive addiction. The book leaves the impression that
there is a tentative and very half-hearted attempt to tackle them, but
that after a skirmish or two the author hurriedly withdraws. One
should not perhaps lean too heavily on a work that is after all meant to
be funny. But there is a feeling that he is tackling, or trying to tackle,
matters that were of fundamental importance in terms of his whole
being but has neither the determination nor the invention to bring
them within the scope of such a work. Even the idea of having James
Joyce turn up as a barman in Skerries reads, as with much else, like 'a
fair notion, fatally spoiled'.

It was some time in the summer of 1963 that I was shown the first
half or so in what he said was draft form. I kept it, I am afraid, longer
than I should, partly because my own circumstances of the time made
it difficult for me to read it or to think about it, partly because I was in
a quandary as to what to say. Then I got a note saying, 'If this reaches
you, and not otherwise, please meet me in the Bailey at 1 o'clock on
Thursday.'[27]

It would, I thought, be necessary to praise it, for he must be kept
going at all costs; yet one had to say something about one's reservations too. In the end I erred on the side of praise, but at least I told him
he should distance himself from the narrator, perhaps by turning the
book into the third person, and I tried to impress on him that it should
have an altogether more pungent tone; but I am afraid I also offended
him by pointing out the anachronisms, thereby more or less calling
him a liar, for he had been keeping up the pretence that this was an
altogether new work.

Looking back now, and assessing all the evidence, the conclusion
must be that the ransacking of *The Third Policeman* to create a new
work was begun some time in the late 1940s, when the war was over
but the trams were still running; James Joyce would have been, were
he still living, in his mid-60s and women were not yet being served in
certain lounge bars. If this is the case it suggests that the personal
conflicts which I believe are touched on but ultimately shirked in the
book – the hero's alcoholism and his relationship with the opposite sex
– must be read in the light of Brian O'Nolan's situation and psychology at that time, when it was beginning to be obvious to him that he
had a drink problem of a major kind and was wondering whether he
could or should ever embark on a serious relationship with a woman,
perhaps even marry.

As the months of composition wore on and he asked his question
about St Augustine of many other people his attitude to the book
revealed a certain duality. Both O'Keeffe and Cecil Scott had serious

reservations and he accepted these readily. By 15 November 1963 he was writing to O'Keeffe that 'the book is not meant to be a novel or anything of the kind but a study in derision, various writers with their styles, and sundry modes, attitudes and cults being the rats in the cage. The MS is all bleary for want of definition and emphasis but I regard the MS as something worthwhile to chew on after I have shown it for comment to a few know-all bastards hereabouts.'[28] This was also the line he took with Mark Hamilton of A. M. Heath a couple of weeks later:

> *The Dalkey Archive* is not a novel, though on the surface there is a perfectly coherent story suitable for a girl of 14, provided she could overlook certain theological discourse and a threatened denouement worse than the nuclear bomb. The book is really an essay in extreme derision of literary attitudes and people and its pervasive fault is absence of emphasis in certain places, to help the reader.[29]

The gap between these descriptions and the finished work, which reveals little derision either of literary attitudes, other writers or contemporary modes and cults, will be fairly obvious. To O'Keeffe he wrote:

> My ultimate plan is to excoriate the MS ruthlessly, cutting short here and rebuilding there, giving the book precision and occasionally the beauty of jewelled ulcers. It must above all be bitterly funny. The first person sing. must be made into a more awful toad than now. I know some of the writing is deplorable for a man of my pretences, and I am not happy at all about the treatment of Joyce; a very greater mess must be made of him. Would one of his secret crosses be that he is an incurable bedwetter? After I am through I'll hire a girl to produce a new, bright, clean, stifling typescript. All that could be done within 6 weeks.[30]

He had somewhat gratuitously agreed a deadline of 30 November 1963 with Macmillan of New York to give himself something to aim at, and by taking what he called 'steps so extreme as to be almost supernatural'[31] he did despatch a copy to Cecil Scott at that publishing house before that date. But even after despatching it he wrote to O'Keeffe that 'it would be a pity to release material that is ruinously flawed, particularly where the repair job might be comparatively easy and in parts very obvious.'[32] Shortly after the New Year he was agreeing with Cecil Scott that 'James Joyce has been dragged in by the scruff of the neck' and that 'Mary is also unsatisfactory, though she had not been intended as very much more than a "fringe benefit".'[33]

Towards the end of January he was apologizing to O'Keeffe for the closing sections of the book: 'I just can't believe that the last third of the MS – a farrago of mis-writing, slop, mistypes, repetition, with many passages quite meaningless – ever issued from here. The stuff about Joyce is withering in its ineptitude.'[34] But he also declared that what he called 'The Authorized Version' was now finished. O'Keeffe was not satisfied, however, and when Brian delivered what he called 'The Authorized Version, Mark II' towards the end of February, he said: 'This book has been pitilessly excoriated for verbal weeds, bad sloppy writing, and the entire last quarter has been completely rewritten.'[35]

Nevertheless he was insistent throughout that the basic idea was an excellent one and that the book would be what he had called in an earlier letter to Mark Hamilton 'a scalding success'.[36] To those who had not seen it, he was, perhaps understandably, somewhat more emphatic about its excellence than he could be to those who had. My own reaction had, I think, led to a certain coolness, but when we appeared on television together shortly afterwards on a books programme he sang its praises unblushingly. It was Brian's only personal appearance on the medium and it was also noticeable for the appearance of a fellow author, Aidan Higgins, who is perhaps the only person ever to have been a member of a discussion panel who did not utter a single word of any kind. The reason was that from the start Brian took control of the proceedings. He refused to talk about *At Swim-Two-Birds*, which he dismissed according to his custom, as 'mere juvenilia'. Then he asked the startled interviewer if he knew anything about the colour of St Augustine's skin. Finally he discoursed at length about the merits of a work in progress which would reveal some startling facts about this and other matters. He was not sober, but this might not have mattered except that he had a half bottle of whiskey carelessly stuffed into the pocket of his jacket and at a certain point the neck of this began to protrude, so we were cut off rather hurriedly. Yet the failure of *The Dalkey Archive* cannot, I think, be attributed to drink, or if it can it was perhaps the efforts he was making at this time to control and abate his drinking that were taking their toll. Nor, probably, can his failure to make the reality match the conception more closely be attributed to a lack of technical resource or ingenuity. Perhaps one could say that it was sheer strength that was lacking rather than technical resource or, to put it another way, that he would have found the technical resources if he had had the human. But he was plagued with illnesses and mishaps, major and minor.

*

One night towards the end of September Brian was in bed reading *Time* magazine and remembered leaning out of bed to stub out a cigarette in an ashtray. About midnight, Evelyn came into the room to find him unconscious on the bedroom floor. He came to in hospital and, typically enough, immediately began to demand of a person he thought was a doctor why he was not wearing a white coat. In fact this was a priest who had come to give him the last rites. At a rough count he was to receive this sacrament at least a dozen times before his death. When white-coated figures did appear he heard mention of 'a massive coronary'. A few days later he was transferred to St Michael's Hospital in Dún Laoghaire, where tests disclosed that he was suffering from severe uraemia, a condition caused by the kidneys' failure to eliminate urinary matter from the blood. Characteristically he made a joke of this, alleging that after vast quantities of blood had been taken from him for analysis a consultant who was called in to make a minute examination and scrutiny of the records and X-rays told him that his heart was perfectly sound. 'But,' he said, 'there is one thing I must tell you and it is important. You are suffering from anaemia.' After transfer to a third hospital, St Vincent's, for certain surgical probes, he decided he was all right and went home.

About a week later, according to his own story, he went out to buy a stamp for an urgent letter, but found the local Post Office 'closed for lunch'. This naturally necessitated a bus into town and a few drinks. It was his custom on boarding the bus for home to ask loudly for 'one ticket to John of God's'. St John of God's was a hospital which was a well-known curing station for alcoholics and his nearest bus stop was beside the entrance on the Stillorgan Road. On this occasion, he said, he stepped off the bus with his usual care and remembered no more until he woke up once again in St Michael's. A passing motorist had found him unconscious at the bus stop and in the hospital his right leg was found to be broken above the ankle in exactly the same place where it had been broken in the 1947 car accident. The surgeon said that it would require a bone-graft. Then, he was to write later, the following dialogue took place.

- How much of a hospital stay would that mean?
- Only two months or so.
- And wouldn't living bone be required for a graft?
- Certainly. You have any amount of bone about you going to waste.
- Where, for instance?
- All around your arse.
- Thanks. I couldn't face two months of hospital food. We will chance the usual setting.[37]

Three weeks later he insisted on discharging himself and went home, where, on top of everything else, he found he had developed an attack of sycosis or barber's rash. His leg remained in plaster for quite a long time, much of which he spent in bed, though he would occasionally venture into town.

These indispositions and mishaps occurred during the closing stages of the composition of *The Dalkey Archive* and they cannot have done the book much good. For most of 1963 he had anyway been imposing on himself a very heavy burden of other work which must have impeded its progress. Towards the beginning of that year Radio Telefís Éireann had asked Jimmy O'Dea to do a series and, after some discussion, the great comedian had suggested that he would like Brian to script it. The producer appointed to the programme was James Plunkett, the author of *Strumpet City*, a novel which had recently been a great success, and the first meeting about the projected series took place in the stalls of the Gaiety after a Saturday matinee. It was decided that it should be called 'O'Dea's Yer Man' and would present Jimmy as a railway signal man of a humorously philosophical and anecdotal bent, the whole thing being supposed to take place in his signal box.

To begin with O'Nolan was asked to supply monologues for Jimmy, but after a trial run in the studio it was found that this format had certain disadvantages. Jimmy needed a straight man and in order to get through a programme he needed cues as a mnemonic. Otherwise he tended to ad lib and depart from the script. So it was decided to introduce a second character, Ignatius, who was to be a sort of comic helper; and O'Nolan was asked to write dialogue instead.

Rather to his surprise, Plunkett found that O'Nolan's attempts to do this were failures. Ignatius' interjections had no dramatic quality of their own and tended to be merely token stuff with no flavour of a real exchange. As the scripts came in he arrived at the conclusion that O'Nolan had no real gift for dialogue at all and that his forte was for monologue with interjection. This conclusion was inclined to baffle him until he looked at *The Hard Life* again and found that in truth it contained no dialogue. The same he found to be true of *At Swim-Two-Birds*, though here the exchanges were brisker and the characters more differentiated. But in any case the scripts were not long enough and so, with some misgivings, he set to work himself, to give Ignatius more to say and to introduce a little more drama into the proceedings.

O'Nolan never mentioned these additions and alterations to his scripts. He did not attend rehearsals and Plunkett never knew whether he was watching the programmes or not. In fact he was, going down in

the evenings to his sister Nuala's house and watching them with her
and her husband, Paddy O'Leary, a chemist who had a shop in
Thomas Street, and a Dubliner whom he had always liked.
Throughout the scripting of the programme he was very cordial to
Plunkett and mostly fairly sober in his dealings with him, though their
meetings sometimes took place quite late in the evening in the Green
Room at the Gaiety. Plunkett felt that O'Nolan's affection and respect
for Jimmy O'Dea somehow encompassed him too and procured him
absolution for the alterations in the scripts, though he often felt too
'from the set of his jaw' that O'Nolan was near enough to being
truculent on occasion. Often after a meeting he would drive Brian
home to Waltersland Road and would occasionally go in. There were
always a few bottles of stout in the house which Evelyn would bring
out while O'Nolan produced a couple of 'baby Powers' from an inside
pocket and they would sit by the fire.

There were 24 scripts in all and they were intended to be done one
by one. But neither the state of Jimmy's health nor his theatre
commitments would permit this and eventually they were written and
produced three at a time. The subjects were varied, but there was a sort
of principle of topicality. Jimmy would discourse in rather rambling
fashion on such matters as the budget, supermarkets, the Irish
language question, TV itself, St Patrick's Day or the Dublin Horse
Show. The programmes were certainly not a laugh a minute and the
jokes were sometimes rather strained. Funny or otherwise, though,
Brian wrote them and his 'George Knowall' pieces and even occasional columns for the *Irish Times* in a year that was attended by
accident and largely given over to the composition of *The Dalkey
Archive*. His pride in his capacity was still driving him on.

As we have seen, he watched most of the 'O'Dea's Yer Man' series
at the O'Learys', for the O'Nolans still had no television. He came
there also to watch the week-long coverage of John F. Kennedy's visit
to Ireland in the early part of 1963. Though a professional cynic he
admired Kennedy enormously, the young and handsome President
seeming to bring out in him a latent idealism and even a suspension of
disbelief in the sincerity of politicians, as he did in so many others.
One night during the visit I sat with him and Kavanagh in McDaid's.
The talk turned to Kennedy and to the garden party which the President of Ireland was giving for the American President later in the
week. Brian asked Kavanagh if he knew anybody who had been
invited. Kavanagh replied that he didn't, but Brian pursued the matter.
Had Frank O'Connor, 'The Dean of the Celtic faculty' been invited?
It became obvious that he would have liked to be invited. He wanted
to meet Kennedy.

Later in the week we all read reports of the garden party, the attendance list of which included the names of no literary figures whatever. It seemed that those who had been invited, the presumed elite of Irish society, had behaved like pultogues or perhaps gawsh-kogues. When Kennedy appeared on the steps into the garden they rushed forward, excitedly pulling at him and at his clothes so that they would have it to say that they had shaken the great man's hand; and Kennedy, considerably mauled, was forced to retreat indoors while they were calmed down.

O'Nolan was a fairly frequent visitor to the O'Learys at this time, for part of the strategy of cutting down on drink was for him and Evelyn to go to the cinema in Cornelscourt three times a week, after which they would walk on to the O'Learys'. Sometimes he would walk as far as the O'Learys' house on his own, or accompanied by the large bewhiskered airedale he had named Hackett after a character in the *The Dalkey Archive* and which had succeeded Muc. Once seated in their living room he would demand a glass and immediately produce a naggin or a quarter bottle of whiskey to put in it. It was on the O'Learys' television too that he watched the many hours of coverage of the aftermath of Kennedy's assassination, an event which affected him, as it did others, quite deeply.

All his life Brian O'Nolan, avant-garde author, disciple of Joyce, industrious bureaucrat and underpaid journalist, had dreamed of getting rich quick. In all his books except *The Dalkey Archive*, there is a discussion of the ways and means of doing this, though a passage relating to this had been among those excised from *At Swim-Two-Birds*. Even the hero of *An Béal Bocht* dreams of getting his hands on 'all the plundered fortune which O'Poenassa took away with him in the time of the deluge'. Now, at 53 and enjoying a measure of international as well as a considerable amount of local fame, he was in search of adequate means of subsistence. In May of the previous year Niall Montgomery had written to Trinity College to suggest that he could adequately fill an advertised post for a Junior Lecturer in English. In 1964, less than ten years before that institution was to start giving courses and examining students in his work, he applied for the job of student records and calendar officer. Nothing came of either of these applications. His income from the *Irish Times* had sunk very low in 1963, due to illness, his other writing activities and, of course, quarrels about copy; but he needed the money, little though it was, and through the closing months of 1963 and the early ones of 1964 a fair average was maintained, sometimes with the help of Niall Montgomery. In his prime, he had seldom had any difficulty with composition and, once started, would type away at machine-gun speed.

Usually columns were got through without any groaning, head-
scratching or pacing up and down. He would complain about the
difficulty of finding subjects, not about the labour of writing. Now he
found subjects more difficult than ever to come by, perhaps in truth
because he cared about fewer things or was moved less often to
protest or reproof. It is possible also that the more liberal and
sophisticated Ireland which was beginning to emerge in the 1960s had
less fundamental appeal for him as a humorist than the one which had
preceded it. Subjects for satire still abounded, but he had been more at
home among the earlier varieties of 'thooleramawn' or 'gawshkogue'
than he was now among the later. To most readers he appeared even
angrier than he had been, but the new Ireland did not move him to the
curious mixture of anger and a sort of affection which is the primary
emotion of the satirist.

The attempt to control his drinking in these years had meant a
change in his habits of composition and the writing of a column was
now often postponed until quite late in the evening, when he would
turn up at Paddy O'Leary's with his copy and a request to be driven
into town to deliver it. Columns began to dry up again in February
1964, and after a single contribution in April there were none at all
until December. Illness continued to afflict him. On a visit to hospital
to have the plaster cast on his leg removed and replaced, the surgeon
noticed his peculiar breathing and diagnosed pleurisy, which necessitated a stay in the hospital for three weeks. He had a persistent pain in
the left side of his face which he thought of as some form of neuralgia.
For some time after the removal of the plaster he used a stick and when
I met him one day in the street without it I asked him, as a matter of
courtesy, how was the leg. 'Did you ever hear of the dominant theme
in the symphony?' was the reply. 'Well, the leg is no longer the
dominant theme.'

His drinking, which he had been making a brave effort to control, had
begun to creep up again, but he was still determined to conquer it in
one way or another and now, after consultation with Evelyn and with
one or two of his friends, he decided to seek medical help. Dr John
Dunne, whom he had known since they both drank in the Dolphin,
was in charge of Grangegorman, the large mental hospital in North
County Dublin, and some of his friends, including Sean O'Sullivan,
whose death in April had shocked and distressed him, had made
occasional sojourns there. Dr Dunne was surprised that he should
apply for admission to Grangegorman, or St Brendan's as it is more
commonly known nowadays, rather than to one of the private

hospitals with more comfortable provision for paying patients which were now becoming acceptable, even fashionable, places for middle-class alcoholics to resort to. He did not know how poor the O'Nolans were.

In Grangegorman there were no private facilities, so he had to sleep in a public ward, eat at a communal table and spend his leisure time in rooms of public resort. Dr Dunne found him co-operative, anxious to lead a normal life undistorted by drink and consequently willing to face the truth about himself in therapeutic sessions. The doctor was a believer in what he called 'conversion'. A patient converted one sort of problem into another, substituting drink and the problems it caused for others which he was unwilling to face. He thought Brian suffered from a lack of creative and sexual fulfilment and when he discussed this with him found him prepared to admit that it could be so. The therapy was the basic one of helping a patient over the hump of withdrawal by medication, then seeking to elicit the psychological cause of the alcoholism, impressing on him the danger of continuance and the importance of support groups after discharge.

Dr Dunne was also convinced that most alcoholism was hereditary in the psychological rather than the genetic sense, the victim following a pattern of behaviour which had become the role model through the parents. He believed too that an inability to form a loving relationship with another had the same origin, there being no model of love and its expression for the sufferer to follow, although of course he was prepared to believe that in the case of a loveless or sexless marriage the difficulty might be the other party's inability to enter into a full relationship. In Brian O'Nolan's case there was certainly plenty of alcoholism among his immediate forbears but a pattern of dependence on drink can scarcely be said to have been, to use the Freudian term, 'introjected' since neither of his parents drank. Michael O'Nolan was uncommunicative with his children and unexpressive of such love as he may have felt for them; he was no more or no less expressive of love for his wife than other Irish parents of the time. Like most Irish children of his generation Brian would have been expected to deduce his father's love of his children from his efforts as a breadwinner and of his wife from the size of his family.

Conflicts in Brian's sexual nature can only be guessed at. Whatever they were, the Irish pattern of heavy drinking bachelorhood, common enough in his day, might have concealed them from himself and others; whereas marriage probably brought them to the fore. If the creative frustrations which Dr Dunne identified existed, they are evidence that, however highly some readers may rate 'Cruiskeen

Lawn' or however we may delight in it, it did not satisfy him; and that the 20 years of creative silence he suffered – 17 if we date them from *Faustus Kelly* – between the rejection of *The Third Policeman* and his rediscovery by O'Keeffe must have been bitter ones. Why the rejection cost him so dear, and why he did not turn his natural competitiveness and unwillingness to be 'bested' to use by going on writing novels even after rejection, is another matter. His self-doubt was extraordinarily deep, as all who knew him can testify.

Perhaps he was combative only in areas where no real hurt, to the spirit anyway, could accrue from defeat. Almost up to his death he was conducting quarrels with the Royal Hibernian Academy, an insurance company, the Electricity Supply Board and his father's old firm the Revenue Commissioners. The quarrel with the Revenue Commissioners was about the taxing of money accruing from translation rights and the sum involved was very small. He requested the inspector dealing with his returns to send him a form on which he could apply for a rebate on tax withheld by his German publisher in accordance with German regulations; and in the course of correspondence he discovered that although a Double Tax agreement was about to be signed with Germany, there were none with France and Italy where *At Swim-Two-Birds* was also about to be published.

He wrote several rather abusive and acrimonious letters to the Commissioners about this and he also wrote an article, 'A Writer's Writhings', evidently designed for publication abroad, but not, it would seem, actually published. 'I live in Dublin and occasionally write a book, which is marketed through an excellent literary agency with head office in London,' it began, and there followed an account of how he had applied for the relevant tax form and made his discovery. Then he warmed to the attack:

> The great majority of Irish civil servants as well as parliamentary deputies, including Ministers, is in origin of the peasant or shopboy class. And it should be stated that Ireland has neither a Chancellor of the Exchequer nor a Treasury; a member of the reigning party is styled Minister for Finance and, since politics is not regarded as a respectable activity, it follows that persons of standing and intellectual accomplishment are not available for any of the ministerial appointments. No Minister of Finance *ab urbe condita* has had the slightest training in public finance or the fiscal labyrinth ... the Minister is body and soul in the hands of three public clerks who are designated the Revenue Commissioners – two members and a chairman.[38]

As was often the case in other contexts, there is more than a touch of shopkeeping Strabane in the reference to peasants and shopboys, and it would seem that there is a strange note of father-slaying about the references to the Revenue Commissioners:

> The Revenue Commissioners since 1922 (whoever they may have been) are answerable for this disgraceful and humiliating mess: the present trio should be subjected to severe disciplinary action, the chairman's grossly excessive salary of £4,492 should be permanently abated, and the Minister should resign.

He also wrote to A. M. Heath telling them of his battle with the Revenue Commissioners and referring to the fact that his father had been one. 'The present set of bastards,' he said, 'are quite afraid of me, for I have got quite a name here for damaging public vituperation in print.'[39] In reality most of the targets singled out in his column had been uncaring or oblivious of his attacks, which had been shot peppered in vain against institutional juggernauts of their nature immune from damage, or against individuals who looked to other commentators for their self-image and other constituencies for their power. Such is the fate of the licensed humorist, more especially one whose humour does not incorporate a basic critique of the society in which he lives. Even Brian O'Nolan's affectation of being an insider who knew the ropes was against him here.

But combative he certainly was. Before going into Grangegorman he had been at odds with the Electricity Supply Board, on the grounds that the meter in his house was registering a consumption of electricity far in excess of what was actually the case. He had been refusing to pay his bills until they admitted this was the case and from the hospital he wrote to Tommy Conolly. Since his presence in the hospital was supposed to be a secret he gave no address on the letter which was dated 10 March.

> Dear Tommy,
> Thanks for your letter of Sunday about the E.S.B. Chieftains. I await your final diktat with interest, as I know it will be final.
> I should tell you that I first raised this matter with the E.S.B. about two years ago, demanding that they state their authority for having unchecked meters. At the time I consulted the special E.S.B. statutes in the Nat. Library to find if there was special provision and found there was not, though an amateur's legal researches must be suspect. At the time their tone was most conciliatory and smooth. I did not pursue the matter at the time because something very important distracted me. (So very important was that thing that I cannot now recollect what it was!)
> Though not a peasant I have a nose, e.g. I can tell that a plate of food is not right merely by looking at it. In this case I am convinced that this shower of bastards is relying on the general impression that their outrageous behaviour MUST have a legal sanction simply because it is

thus carried on. It is possible as you say that they are covered by
umbrella regulations long pre-dating them. But I think it is unlikely.
They are very shy in themselves and would before now have cited their
authority in a dry faceless note if in fact they had any to cite. I share your
own horror of litigation but they also think every citizen is too terrified
to challenge them. Both of us could be on to something here, with the
State doing the paying.

I am glad to hear you are looking after yourself, and not too
Flahoolock so far as drink is concerned. I wd like to see you some of
these nights prior to my re-entry to the Big World.

Yours,
Brian[40]

There was no set period for Dr Dunne's patients to stay in hospital;
and since he had his typewriter there and had found a place to work in,
there was no urgency about leaving. So he stayed as long as Dr Dunne
thought was necessary. That he was not in fact 'cured' was probably as
much due to his general physical condition as to weakness of will. In
his heart he must have known that the time for taking cures was now
past.

But the remainder of 1964 went by without any more ominous
warning signals than the intermittent neuralgia. Though not very
productive either of columns or anything else, he seemed well and
optimistic and during the course of one long session which took us
from Neary's to Kehoe's in South Anne Street and then to Sinnott's I
remember being surprised at his capacity for drink, which, on this
occasion at least, seemed far to exceed my own.

He was in correspondence with Tim O'Keeffe about a collection of
Keats and Chapman stories, an old project, now revived, which he was
insistent would make money for all concerned. Once the English got
the craze, he said, there would be no holding them. I remember
thinking that the build-up of the stories is, more often than not,
English-Edwardian, with a strong dash of *The Boy's Own Paper* or the
Rider Haggard sort of adventure story. To O'Keeffe he wrote, 'there
is more involved than a mere pun; there is a canon, after the manner of
the Sherlock Holmes-Watson concept. If the publication of even a
small collection in cheap format established that the disease is infec-
tious, as I suspect it to be, then there is easy money to be made all
round.'[41]

Towards the end of the year he began to develop an idea for a novel,
soon to be entitled *Slattery's Sago Saga*. Like all his books, even *At
Swim-Two-Birds*, it depends on one primary situational joke. An
American millionaire who hates the Irish and wants to stop them

emigrating to the United States is to buy Ireland and turn it into one vast sago forest. The inhabitants will live on sago, distil sago whiskey, manufacture sago tables and chairs and so on. The basic joke was suggested by the enthusiastic schemes of a character in a novel of my own, *The Life of Riley*, who envisages the extraction of electricity from potatoes, the paving of the streets of Dublin with sods of turf and the 'possible utilization of the various parts of the herring's anatomy, down to the tail and the fin, in portable, pre-fabricated factories, themselves made of herring-bone cement, along the west coast.' But since the Kennedy visit he had become imaginatively obsessed with the subject of Irish America and a large part of the book was to be set in the United States and to culminate in the election of an Irish/American President. This idea gave Cecil Scott of Macmillan in New York pause; and he wrote to say that in thus stepping outside his Irish patch O'Nolan was taking a risk. The reply, dated 19 March 1965, is a typical piece of O'Nolan braggadocio and also reveals something of the quality of the book he had in mind:

> Far from being a hopeless gamble, this book would be no gamble at all; its U.S. rights would be eagerly sought and it almost certainly [will] be made into a film, very likely by my pal John Huston, who now lives in these parts. After it, works like *Babbit*, the *Great Gatsby* and *G.W.T.W.* can be shoved into the attic with Oxford bags, warped tennis rackets, Model T. starting handles, and porcelain jars of blue-stone prohibition liquor.
>
> Four chapters have been written since mid-January and this is an American book to the extent that 2/3rds of the action will be sited there. What do you think of an Irish well-to-do agricultural scientist who, fed up with the stick-in-the mud peasants here, emigrates to Texas to grow corn, has his beautiful crops ruined by an eruption of dirty black stuff, has 205 derricks in action within two years, and discovers an ancient covenant which enables him lawfully to invade the ranch of L.B.J.? What do you know of Dr the Hon. Eustace Baggeley, who lives on a combined diet of morphine, cocaine and mescaline? How many hoodlums, political crooks and girlies do you know? Harry Poland? Cactus Mike Broadfeet? Senator Hovis Oxter? Katie ('the Dote') Bombstairs? George (The Girder) Shagge, Steelman? Congressman Theodore Hedge? Pogueen O'Rahelly? Nothing, I suppose. Shows how much you know yourself about the U.S.[42]

G.W.T.W. is *Gone with the Wind*, the archetypal best seller of O'Nolan's youth, frequently referred to then in correspondence with Saroyan and others. However unserious the letter, it is rather odd that the success of such a book should have made such a lasting impression

on him and even odder too that he should mention it in company with
The Great Gatsby; though he may not have known that Fitzgerald's
book was a comparative failure in terms of sales on its first appearance.

Progress on *Slattery's Sago Saga* was slow by his standards and by
November only three more chapters had been added to the four he had
mentioned. In November he wrote to Scott to say that the scene was
now set and the characters established

> ... ready for the paroxysms of bedlam, which is planned to take place in
> the U.S. and culminates in the election of a President. Though never
> stated, the analogy with the Kennedy reign will not escape any reader
> over the age of 8. No censure whatever of the late J.F.K. will be implied
> but I do consider old Joe a crook and the two Senator Bostoons as
> lickspittle time-servers, eternally dining out on the late President's
> corpse. They are no better than Sorenson and the rest of the crowd of
> vultures who are out to make fortunes on producing books full of near
> scandal.[43]

There were reasons for this unspectacular rate of composition. The
first was his return to the *Irish Times* after a ten-month absence.
Douglas Gageby, who as a newly appointed Joint Managing Director
had negotiated with Niall Montgomery the end of an earlier quarrel,
was now Editor and he agreed to a pact. Myles would deliver his copy
direct to him; he would read it and sub it and unless there were serious
objections on the grounds of libel every word would go in. The pact
almost broke down straight away because the first three pieces that
Myles – as Gageby, in common with everyone else, called him –
delivered were about his old teacher John Charles McQuaid, still
presiding over the archdiocese of Dublin, and they contained, according to Gageby, gross errors of fact which Myles refused to acknowledge. In the end he took away the pieces peaceably enough and the
agreement lasted. Though columns were to become scarce again after
May 1965 relations with Gageby remained cordial; and when he
became seriously ill in the following year, the *Irish Times* took an
unheard-of step, continuing to pay him on a weekly basis even though
he was unable to produce copy. That his own perception of the
agreement was different from Gageby's, however, is shown by a letter
to O'Keeffe, written some weeks after the event, in March 1965.

> Some short time ago the *Irish Times* invited me on their bended knees to
> go back and write for them. I agreed to do so, subject to some tyrannical
> stipulations by me. (How could you get down on your knees without
> them being bended?) This relieves all finance worry and enables me to
> indulge my sago enthusiasm.[44]

Relieved or not, at midsummer he began negotiations with R.T.E. for a new television series to be called 'Th'oul Lad of Kilsalaher'. This was to be a weekly series of 15-minute programmes with, again, two principal characters, Uncle Andy and his niece Marie-Thérèse, known to her uncle as Puddiner. Uncle Andy was a Collopy-like figure who was seldom to leave his kitchen armchair but was repeatedly to show 'that he not only knows everything that is going on but more than appears on the surface and the proper remedy for big snags when they arrive.' Puddiner was to be 'young, witty, flighty, and in dress and manner could be called a tart. There is a never-ending private war between her and Uncle Andy, but usually Puddiner manages to give as good as she gets.' Remarkably, Puddiner was given more lines to say than any other female character in the O'Nolan canon, but she failed to save the series. Less funny even than 'O'Dea's Yer Man', it ran for an unlucky 13 episodes between September and December 1965 with the Dublin comedian Danny Cummins as Uncle Andy and Máire Hastings as Puddiner and was suddenly taken off after the Controller of Programmes had decided that it was not worth continuing. O'Nolan agreed with the Producer, Jim Fitzgerald, that 'the show never really got going'.

The most important reason for the flagging composition of *Slattery's Sago Saga*, however, was the deterioration of O'Nolan's health. The progression of events as he saw it is described in one of his letters to Scott:

My adventure has been briefly as follows: a diversified pain about the left side of the face, present and increasing for about a year, made me seek medical advice about the end of July. A 'specialist' diagnosed neuralgia, a quasi-fictional disease meaning 'nerve pain'. Later, when I drew attention to a slight 'knottiness' in the neck region, my man said this was a matter for a commoner sort of surgeon. I saw the latter, who operated and immediately afterwards told me to enter a certain hospital for 'ray treatment'. In my innocence I thought this meant ultra-violet rays or some such harmless cosmetic radiation. Too late I realized I was getting what is called deep X-ray therapy, and under a reckless lout of a doctor who exercised no supervision or control. Briefly, I was fried alive and, on a tide of vomit, had to enter another hospital to be decarbonized, or 'decoked'. I'm still under drug treatment and have to go back at the end of this month for blood transfusions. In other words – never a dull moment but total stasis of that literary project that has come to be called S.S.S. – *Slattery's Sago Saga*.[45]

A somewhat different account of his ghastly tribulations was given in a piece written for the *Guardian* in January 1966 called 'Can a Saint Hit

Back' and built around the idea that they were attributable to St Augustine.

> About that time (i.e. in the Spring of the previous year) I began to suffer from what seemed to be an abscess in the middle ear. Then this pain became more defined and was diagnosed as neuralgia, very severe, cause unknown. Later, tiny 'knottiness' in the side of the neck made me consult a surgeon. He decided to operate in this glandular region and examined the situation by way of biopsy. The Pathologist who examined the tissue found evidence of secondary cancer. So far a primary cancer has not come to light elsewhere in the body but deep X-ray radiation of the area has caused a painful swelling, and there is evidence of generalized anaemia.[46]

From the hospital where the biopsy was done he had rung up his brother-in-law, Paddy O'Leary, and said, 'Paddy, for the first time cancer has been mentioned.' O'Leary tried to cheer him up, saying that a mere mention of the possibility was not conclusive, but soon there could be no doubt. At least from the beginning of September 1965 he knew he had cancer and possibly knew he was dying. He was suffering from cancer of the cavity at the back of the nose and mouth. A primary cause was probably his lifelong consumption of cigarettes; but it could certainly also have been drink related.

That September he attended a first performance of a dramatization of *The Dalkey Archive* by the popular playwright Hugh Leonard as *When the Saints Go Marching In* at the Gate. This had been under discussion since the autumn of the previous year, when he had offered the adaptor some advice:

> It would be presumptuous on my part to tell you anything about playwriting but I think you will agree with me that the main changes from book to stage will be by way of deletion. I would leave the Anti-Jesuit stuff more or less intact (everybody cheers when your men are attacked, even obliquely) but the biblical material, which is funny but not invented by me – just taken straight out of the Bible – and the Holy Ghost theory, also authentic and documented, seems unsuitable for overt public presentation. We wouldn't want a *Playboy* sort of row.
>
> I take great care with dialogue and would like the style of the book preserved.[47]

He had been intensely annoyed when Leonard's agent sent him a bill for typing the scripts but was pleased with the adaptation when he saw it and particularly admired the final curtain. In the play, as in the book, Mick and the Sergeant steal the cask of D.M.P. but instead of depositing it in the Bank of Ireland, they throw it into Dublin Bay. Then they go to the Colza Hotel where they find De Selby. He knows nothing about the theft but in the course of conversation incidentally reveals that the detonation agency for D.M.P. is seawater.

O'Nolan asked Douglas Gageby to join him for the opening night and he and his wife had dinner beforehand in the Moira Hotel with the Gagebys. Mrs Gageby was struck by the gentleness and good manners of someone she had expected to be fearsome. 'Like an old Parish Priest,' she remarked to Douglas. Throughout the first act O'Nolan laughed hugely and appeared to be enjoying himself. According to Gageby at the end of the first act they adjourned to Groom's Hotel, a famous haunt of theatre people and politicos, across the road for a drink. There Patrick Kavanagh came by the table and said something derogatory about the play after which O'Nolan slumped down in his chair and said, 'You go back. I'll stay here and have another drink.' He returned to the theatre, somewhat the worse for wear, just before the final curtain fell to great applause. Next day however the newspapers reported that he had been taken ill and had had to leave after the first act.

He was, nevertheless, delighted with the success of the play and he wrote rather boastfully to Uncle Eugene in Strabane, who had expressed a hope of coming to Dublin to see it, that it would be necessary to book seats in advance. 'If you try to book by post you will have to give a wide choice of nights as the theatre is completely booked out. It will probably go on for a 4th week and even longer if the theatre can be got.' He added the information that he hadn't properly seen it himself yet. 'I saw most of the first act on opening night but could not go back except for the extreme end because I had suddenly become very ill following a fortnight's course of deep X-ray therapy (THERAPY!) in a Dublin hospital after I had had a small operation on my neck at the Mater. It is only now beginning to feel a bit better.'[48] He then sent his regards to Aunt Teresa and added the address of the Gate Theatre to which Eugene might write for tickets.

He had been in Strabane in the summer of the previous year when he and Ciarán and the O'Learys had impulsively decided to travel one weekend in the O'Learys' car. It had been an enjoyable trip.

The shop in the Main Street had been sold and Eugene and Aunt Teresa had moved to a new house in the Melmount Road. The errant Tom had died in the County Hospital, having been at last committed there by his long-suffering elder brother; but Joe was still alive and still organizing musical events. Another death later in the year was that of Jenny, an elderly spinster who had been a 'maid' or, perhaps more accurately, a cook, nursemaid and housekeeper of sorts, in the

Gormley household for as long as Brian could remember. When she died he wrote to Eugene:

> I would like to write this line of sympathy to yourself, Teresa and Joe on the death of Jenny. She was a great old scout and I remember her over the years with great affection. Even when her health went against her in later years, she never lost her poise and good humour. I remember that she had a great regard for your own mother. May they both rest in peace, with George.
>
> Delay in sending this little message is due to my own dashing in and out of the Mater Hospital, mostly for blood transfusions, though nobody seems very clear as to what's wrong with me. Just now I feel all right again.[49]

The character of Sergeant Fottrell in the play proved very popular with Dublin audiences and with his usual quickness to exploit such an opportunity – he was, alas, slower to exploit more important ones – Brian conceived the idea that he might make him a central character in yet another television series. This was to be called 'The Detectional Fastidiosities of Sergeant Fottrell'. When R.T.E. proved responsive he entered into a correspondence with Gunnar Rugheimer, the Director of Television, about it in which he expressed his belief that 'the Sergeant's personality and tongue' would ultimately 'form a country-wide treasure', at which point 'the Sergeant may well take a hand in interfering with other people's programmes and ultimately could become the unofficial voice of T.E. He would make his remarkable views known on Nelson, the Budget, Decimals ... anything of current import; he transcends all his situations.'[50]

There were recurrent visits to hospital now for what he called 'blood transfusions and other boons'. Visitors found him cheerful and, for the most part, talkative. He nearly always had a supply of drink in his bedside cabinet and most people who came to see him brought some with them, but he complained that it appeared to be a Dublin custom that people drank more than they brought. At home he was in bed most of the time and was troubled by fits of vomiting, though he might get up and sit by the fire when a visitor came.

One such caller was an English journalist, Michael Wale, who wrote a description of his visit for *Town Magazine*. Discussing Brendan Behan, they talked of drink. Brian argued that in life one had to choose between drinking and being bored to death. 'You're in danger all the time not only from death but boredom. Behan made the choice,' O'Nolan said. He talked of *Slattery's Sago Saga* enthusiastically, as he usually talked about his books. 'The thing I have in my head is so compelling I'll go like an express train to get it down on paper.' He declared that he had no politics but when questioned about his philosophic beliefs affirmed that he was what Wale called 'a Roman Catholic', though it is unlikely that O'Nolan would have used the term Roman. Discussing his work he declared that *At Swim-Two-Birds* was 'juvenilia, public nose-picking' and said that he found it 'quite unreadable' while *The Hard Life* was 'simply a study in the Dublin way of speaking'. He had 'made a bit of a fetish of the natural way of speaking in Dublin' which was usually 'botched' by people who 'don't know how to listen'.

Inevitably the topic of Joyce came up. He said Joyce was a 'toucher' who used to 'bum off people' and had 'got Sylvia Beach and that other woman to give him money in Paris.' He was 'certainly not a shrine at which to kneel, though a man to be praised'. *Finnegans Wake* was the result of the dubious influence of Americans on Joyce. But, he conceded, 'I suppose I was influenced by Joyce,' subconsciously at least, as Joyce himself had been by Proust and Henry James. Joyce also, he said, 'must have read a lot of Sexton Blake.'

Then he made an extraordinary statement: 'I met him in Paris several times. He was a morose, completely self-contained little man. I was curious about him. I admired certain aspects of his work. There had been a lot of rubbish written about him, especially by Americans. I have met some of them, ignorant swine . . .'[51] He went on, as he often had in conversation with others, to instance the scene in Glasnevin Cemetery in *Ulysses* in which the caretaker tells the mourners at Paddy Dignam's funeral about the two drunks who arrive at the graveyard one foggy evening to look for a friend's grave. They ask for Mulcahy from Dublin's famous Coombe and are told where he is buried. After blundering around in the fog they find the grave, on the headstone of which they are able to spell out the name Terence Mulcahy. Then one of them looks up at the statue of the Saviour which is part of the memorial. After gazing at the sacred figure for a while he says, 'Not a bloody bit like the man. That's not Mulcahy, whoever done it.' Brian knew this passage by heart and he repeated it now for Wale, as he had often done for others over the years, as an instance of Joyce's genius. Then, returning to the attack, he asked, 'Do you know Joyce and his little bit of a wife, both of them from Dublin, ended up taking a house in Italy and speaking Italian to each other?'

Wale noted that he had few books; that among the few were some Latin classics in school editions and books in the Irish language; but that there were none of his own works on the shelves in the study at least. Before they parted O'Nolan, or Nolan as Wale calls him throughout, asserted his lack of interest in literary fame. 'I'm not a bit bothered about recognition,' he said. 'It's the money end of it I'm interested in. If Sago made £50,000 I would not write another line again, except a very very few lines on cheques.' This joke about cheques was one he often made in many forms.

Another visitor was Douglas Gageby, who on one occasion brought a bottle of Middleton which of late had become Brian's drink. Gageby was amazed by his vitality. He remembered Brian sitting up in bed, denouncing this, denouncing that. Suddenly he began to vomit. Evelyn came in and cleaned him up while Gageby looked out of the window; then he resumed what he had been saying almost as if there had not been any interruption.

He was continuing to write his column but there were many repeats. On 2 March he wrote that anybody who 'has the courage to raise his eyes and look sanely at the awful human condition ... must realize finally that tiny periods of temporary release from intolerable suffering is the most that any individual has the right to expect.' Towards the end of the month he was hospitalized again. He died peacefully and rather unexpectedly on 1 April 1966, April Fools' Day.

Sources

ORIGINS

1. Ciarán Ó Nualláin. *Óige An Dearthár*. Foilseachain Naisiunta. Dublin, 1973, p. 32. Translation by A.C.
2. Ibid. p. 33.
3. Gearóid Ó Nualláin. Unpublished memoir. Copy in possession of present writer.
4. Ciarán Ó Nualláin. Op. cit. p. 62.
5. Flann O'Brien. *The Hard Life: An Exegesis of Squalor*. London, 1961.
6. Myles na Gopaleen. 'Cruiskeen Lawn', 20 December 1965.
7. Ciarán Ó Nualláin. Op. cit. p. 62.
8. Ibid. p. 57.
9. Ibid. p. 78.

THE BRILLIANT BEGINNING

1. Brian O'Nolan in *The Centenary History of the Literary and Historical Society, 1855–1955*, edited by James Meenan, Tralee, 1956.
2. Niall Montgomery. 'An Aristophanic Sorcerer', *Irish Times*, 2 April 1966.
3. Brian O'Nolan. *The Centenary History*.
4. Donagh MacDonagh. *Creation*, October 1967.
5. Desmond Roche in conversation with A.C.
6. Niall Sheridan in conversation with A.C. See also Richard Ellman, *James Joyce*, London, 1982.
7. Myles na gCopaleen. 'Cruiskeen Lawn', 13 August 1959.
8. Niall Sheridan. 'Brian, Flann and Myles' in *Myles: Portraits of Brian O'Nolan*, edited by Timothy O'Keeffe. London, 1973. p. 34.
9. Niall Montgomery. Op. cit. April 1966.
10. Sheridan. *Myles* p. 37.
11. Brian Ó Nualláin. Letter to Ned Sheehy, 16 January 1938. National Library Dublin.
12. Sheridan. *Myles* p. 36.
13. Brother Barnabas. 'Should Pin-Money Girls Be Sacked? Mein Kampf'. *Comhthrom Féinne*, December 1933.
14. Brother Barnabas. 'Scenes in a Novel'. *Comhthrom Féinne*, May 1934.
15. Sheridan. *Myles* p. 40.
16. Sheridan. Op Cit. p. 38.
17. Brian O'Nolan. *Centenary History*.
18. Niall Sheridan in conversation with A.C.
19. *Comhthrom Féinne*, May 1932.
20. *Comhthrom Féinne*, March 1932.
21. *Comhthrom Féinne*, Summer 1931.
22. *Comhthrom Féinne*, January 1932.
23. Brian O'Nolan. *Centenary History* p. 246.
24. R. N. Cooke. *Centenary History* p. 249.
25. Brian O'Nolan *Centenary History* p. 245.
26. Patrick Purcell. Quoted in *Centenary History* p. 262.
27. R. N. Cooke. *Centenary History* p. 250.
28. Kevin O'Nolan. Contribution to BBC Broadcast, 'Discords of Good Humour', 12 November 1978.
29. Kevin O'Nolan in conversation with A.C.

30. Myles na Gopaleen. 'Cruiskeen Lawn' (C. L.) 16 May 1951.

31. 'Eire's Columnist'. *Time* magazine, 23 August 1943.

32. Brian O'Nolan. Contribution to *Twentieth Century Authors*. Quoted in Anne Clissmann. *Flann O'Brien: A Critical Introduction to His Writings*, Dublin, 1975.

33. Peter Costello and Peter Van De Kamp. *Flann O'Brien*, London, 1987, pp. 47–8.

34. Myles na Gopaleen. C. L. 13 April 1960.

35. Niall Sheridan in conversation with A.C.

36. Brian Ó Nualláin. *Comhthrom Féinne*, March 1935.

37. *Comhthrom Féinne*, April 1935.

38. Brian O'Nolan. *Comhthrom Féinne*, May 1935.

39. Myles na Gopaleen. C. L. 28 July 1958.

40. Ibid. 2 March 1966.

41. *Blather*. Vol 1. No 1. August 1934.

42. Ibid.

43. Ibid. December 1934.

44. John Garvin. 'Sweetscented Manuscripts'. *Myles* p. 54.

45. Ryszard Kapuscinski. *The Emperor*. Translated by William R. Brand and Katarzyna Mroczkowska-Brand. London, 1983, p. 49.

46. Records of the Department of Local Government and Public Health.

47. Ibid.

48. Ibid.

49. Ibid.

50. Micheál Ó Nualláin. *Irish Times*, 1 April 1986.

51. Ciarán Ó Nualláin. Op cit.

52. Niall Sheridan. *Comhthrom Féinne*, June 1935.

53. James Branch Cabell. *The Cream of the Jest*, London, 1972, p. 39.

54. Aldous Huxley. *Point Counter Point*, London, 1953, p. 72.

55. Brian O'Nolan. Letter to C. H. Brooks, 31 January 1938.

56. B. O'N. Letter to A. M. Heath & Co. 3 October 1938.

57. Typescript material in the Morris Library, University of Carbondale, Carbondale, Illinois.

58. B. O'N. Letter to Longman's Green & Co. Ltd. 10 November 1938.

59. B. O'N. Letter to Longman's, 12 March 1939.

60. Graham Greene. Reader's report to Longman's, quoted on dust jacket of first edition.

61. John Garvin. Op cit. p. 56 et seq.

62. Ibid. pp. 57–8.

63. *TLS*. 18 March 1939.

64. Frank Swinnerton. *Observer*, 19 March 1939.

65. Anthony West. *New Statesman and Nation*, 17 June 1939.

66. B.O'N. Letter to Longman's, 1 May 1939.

67. Niall Sheridan to Timothy O'Keeffe, 4 March 1960.

68. B.O'N. Letter to Ethel Mannin, 12 July 1939.

69. B.O'N. Letter to Ethel Mannin, 14 July 1939.

70. B.O'N. Letter to Longman's, 1 May 1939.

71. B.O'N. Letter to William Saroyan, 10 July 1939.

72. B.O'N. Letter to William Saroyan, 25 September 1939.

73. B.O'N. Letter to William Saroyan, 14 February 1940.

74. Ibid.

75. Ibid.

76. Ibid.

77. John Garvin. Op Cit.

78. Myles na gCopaleen. C. L. 17 December 1941.

79. Graham Greene in conversation with Elias Canetti and the present writer, 1952. Canetti concurred that he was of the same persuasion.

80. Patrick Kavanagh. Book Review. *Irish Times* 20 July 1940.

81. Jude the Obscure. *The Honest Ulsterman*. Jan/Feb 1972.

82. Patrick Kavanagh. Letter to the Editor. *Irish Times*, 7 August 1940.
83. Niall Sheridan. *Myles*.
84. Benedict Kiely in conversation with A.C.
85. Myles na Gopaleen. C. L. 10 October 1940.
86. Myles na Gopaleen. C. L. 5 October 1955.
87. Gerald Griffin. *The Collegians*, Dublin, 1963, p. 82.
88. 'West Briton Nationalist'. Letter to the Editor, *Irish Times*. 17 October 1940.
89. Niall Sheridan. *Ireland Today*, July 1938.
90. Quoted in *Myles na Gaeilge: Lámhleabhar ar shaothar Gaeilge Bhrian Ó Nualláin* by Breandán Ó Conaire, Dublin, 1986.
91. Myles na Gopaleen. C. L. 3 January 1957, p. 81.
92. Myles na gCopaleen. C. L. 15 March 1943.
93. Michael Collins. *The Path To Freedom*, Dublin, 1923.
94. Myles na Gopaleen. C. L. 3 January 1957.
95. Ibid. 9 December 1965.
96. Ibid. 25 October 1950.
97. Browne and Nolan. Reader's report. Quoted in Ó Conaire. Op. cit. p. 104.
98. Letter from Brian Ó Nualláin to Browne and Nolan, 16 April 1941.
99. Letter from Pádraig Ó Canainn to Brian Ó Nualláin, 17 June 1941.
100. Letter from Brian Ó Nualláin to Pádraig Ó Canainn, 28 November 1941.
101. Myles na gCopaleen. C. L. 12 December 1941.
102. P.O'S. in *The Bell*, February 1942.
103. Frank O'Connor. Letter to the Editor, *Irish Times* 3 March 1942.
104. Letter from Sean O'Casey to Brian Ó Nualláin, 2 April 1942.
105. Patrick C. Power. Preface to *The Poor Mouth*. London, 1973, pp. 5–6.
106. Letter from Brian Ó Nualláin to Sean O'Casey, 13 April 1942.
107. Letter from Brian O'Nolan to Hilton Edwards, 20 June 1942.
108. Ibid.
109. Myles na Gopaleen. 'The Fausticity of Kelly'. *Radio TV Guide*, 25 January 1963.
110. *Joseph Holloway's Irish Theatre*. Edited by R. Hogan and M. J. O'Neil. Vol. 111. pp. 83 and 86.
111. Letter from Brian O'Nolan to Ernest Blythe. 21 June 1942.
112. Myles na Gopaleen. C. L. 3 April, 1954.
113. *Dublin Evening Mail*. 23 March 1943.
114. Records of Department of Local Government and Public Health.
115. Report of the Tribunal Appointed to Enquire into the Cavan Orphanage Fire, Dublin, 1943.
116. Records of Dept of Local Government and Public Health.
117. Myles na gCopaleen. C. L. 27 August 1945.
118. Ibid. 4 March 1964.
119. Flann O'Brien. 'The trade in Dublin', *The Bell*. November 1940.
120. Myles na Gopaleen. C. L. 12 April 1958.
121. Bruce Williamson in conversation with A.C.
122. Patrick Kavanagh. *I Had A Future: Collected Poems*. London, 1964.
123. Terry Eagleton. *Literary Theory*. Oxford, 1983.
124. Frederic Jameson. 'Post Modernism'. *New Left Review*. October 1982.

THE DUBLINER

1. Myles na gCopaleen. 'Cruiskeen Lawn'. 1949.
2. Ibid. 2 March 1966.
3. Ibid. 10 May 1944.
4. Ibid. 25 September 1944.
5. Heads of Superannuation Bill. National Library of Ireland.
6. Thomas Hogan. 'Myles na gCopaleen'. *The Bell*. November 1947.
7. Evelyn O'Nolan in conversation with A.C.
8. Ibid.
9. Quoted in Clissmann p. 310.
10. Samuel Beckett. Quoted by Aidan Higgins. 'Discords of Good Humour'. BBC Radio 3, 12 November 1980.
11. Myles na Gopaleen. C. L. 9 February 1956.
12. Brian O'Nolan. 'A Bash in the Tunnel'. *Envoy*. May 1951.
13. Letter from Brian O'Nolan to Ewan Phillips. 24 May 1950. Patricia Hutchins' papers. Ms Department Trinity College, Dublin.
14. Niall Sheridan in conversation with A.C. Also unpublished notes by Richard Ellmann.
15. Jack White. 'Myles, Flann and Brian'. *Myles*. p. 70.
16. Myles na Gopaleen. 'Cruiskeen Lawn'. Various dates, May 1951.
17. Jack White. Op. Cit. pp. 74–5.
18. Civil Service Circular No 21/32. Civil Servants and Politics.
19. Ibid.
20. Michael Phelan. 'Watcher In The Wings'. *Administration*, Spring 1976.
21. Ibid.
22. Myles na Gopaleen. C. L. 5 February 1953.
23. Records of Department of Local Government and Public Health.
24. Ibid.
25. Jack White. Op. cit. p. 74.
26. John Ryan. *Remembering How We Stood*. Dublin, 1975, p. 138.
27. Myles na Gopaleen. C. L. 16 June 1954.
28. John Ryan. Op. cit. p. 141.
29. Myles na Gopaleen. 'Two In One'. *The Bell*. July 1954.
30. Myles na Gopaleen. *Further Cuttings from Cruiskeen Lawn*. London, 1976, pp. 130–3.
31. Mervyn Wall. RTE Television. April 1976.
32. Brian O'Nolan to Stephen Ashe, 7 October 1955.
33. Myles na Gopaleen. C. L. 27, 28, 29 February 1964.
34. Brian O'Nolan to Angela Connolly, 29 October 1956. In possession of recipient.
35. Hilton Edwards to B.O'N. November 1956.
36. B. O'N. to Miss Pyer 30 November 1956.
37. Jude the Obscure. *The Honest Ulsterman*. Jan/Feb. 1972.
38. B. O'N. to Miss Pyer. 5 December 1956.
39. Myles na Gopaleen. C. L. 3 September 1959.
40. Brian O'Nolan to Timothy O'Keeffe. 21 September 1962.
41. Flann O'Brien. 'Behan: Master of Language'. *Sunday Telegraph*. 22 March 1964.
42. Letter from Brian O'Nolan to BBC Belfast. Quoted in Clissmann, Op. cit. p. 27.

THE CLOSE

1. Timothy O'Keeffe to Brian O'Nolan, 7 May 1959.
2. Brian O'Nolan. Interview with John Bowman, RTE Radio, 1964.
3. V. S. Pritchett. 'The Death of Finn'. *New Statesman*, 20 August 1960.

4. Myles na Gopaleen. *Further Cuttings from Cruiskeen Lawn.* p. 132.

5. Brian O'Nolan to Mark Hamilton, 27 January 1961.

6. B.O'N. to Mark Hamilton, 20 February 1961.

7. B.O'N. to Timothy O'Keeffe, 1 September 1961.

8. B.O'N. to Timothy O'Keeffe, 5 November 1961.

9. B.O'N. to Timothy O'Keeffe, 1 September 1961.

10. B.O'N. to Timothy O'Keeffe, 25 November 1961.

11. B.O'N. to Gerald Gross, 16 January 1962.

12. B.O'N. to Timothy O'Keeffe, 5 November 1962.

13. Anthony Burgess. *The Novel Now.* London, 1971, pp. 78–80.

14. B.O'N. to Timothy O'Keeffe, 25 November 1961.

15. Thomas Hogan. 'Myles na gCopaleen'. *The Bell.* November 1947.

16. B.O'N. to Cecil Scott, 13 October 1962.

17. Graham Greene to Brian O'Nolan, 25 October 1961.

18. B.O'N. to Brian Inglis, 17 August 1960.

19. B.O'N. to Micheál Ó Nualláin. 1963. In posseession of recipient.

20. B.O'N. to M. Baker, 25 November 1961. Copy in possession of M. Ó Nualláin.

21. Draft of proposed Guinness advertisement by B.O'N. Copy in possession of present writer.

22. Memorandum from Brian O'Nolan to Irish Whiskey Distillers, May 1964.

23. Ibid.

24. Myles na Gopaleen. 'De Me', *New Ireland*, March 1964.

25. Ibid.

26. *The Dalkey Archive*, London, 1964. pp. 55–6.

27. B.O'N. to the present writer, 23 May 1963.

28. B.O'N. to Timothy O'Keeffe, 15 November 1963.

29. B.O'N. to Mark Hamilton, 28 November 1963.

30. B.O'N. to Timothy O'Keeffe, 27 November 1963.

31. B.O'N. to Timothy O'Keeffe, 15 November 1963.

32. B.O'N. to Timothy O'Keeffe, 27 November 1963.

33. B.O'N. to Cecil Scott, 6 January 1964.

34. B.O'N. to Timothy O'Keeffe, 22 January 1964.

35. B.O'N. to Timothy O'Keeffe, 26 February 1964.

36. B.O'N. to Mark Hamilton, 28 November 1963.

37. Flann O'Brien. 'Can a Saint Hit Back?' *Guardian*, January 1966.

38. Flann O'Brien. 'A Writer's Writings'. Morris Library typescript.

39. B.O'N. to Mark Hamilton, 27 February 1964.

40. B.O'N. to Tommie Connolly, 10 March 1964. In possession of recipient.

41. B.O'N. to Timothy O'Keeffe, 16 May 1964.

42. B.O'N. to Cecil Scott, 19 March 1965.

43. B.O'N. to Cecil Scott, 22 November 1965.

44. B.O'N. to Timothy O'Keeffe, 9 March 1965.

45. B.O'N. to Cecil Scott, 22 November 1965.

46. Flann O'Brien. *Guardian*, 19 January 1966.

47. B.O'N. to Hugh Leonard, 27 October 1964.

48. Brian Ó Nualláin to Eugene Gormley. In possession of Micheál Ó Nualláin.

49. B.O'N. to Eugene Gormley, 5 December 1965. In possession of Micheál Ó Nualláin.

50. B.O'N. to Gunnar Rugheimer, 15 March 1966.

51. Michael Wale. *Town Magazine*, Vol. 6, No. 7, September 1965.

Bibliographical Note

At the time of writing all of Brian O'Nolan's novels as Flann O'Brien are in print, as is *An Béal Bocht* as *The Poor Mouth* by Myles na Gopaleen, translated from the Irish by Patrick C. Power and *Stories and Plays by Flann O'Brien*, which includes his unpublished novel, *Slattery's Sago Saga* and the text of the play, *Faustus Kelly*.

There are three collections of Myles na Gopaleen's 'Cruiskeen Lawn' columns available: *The Best of Myles, The Hair of the Dogma* and *Further Cuttings from Cruiskeen Lawn*. Two further collections of miscellaneous writings are *Myles Away From Dublin* edited by Martin Green and *Myles Before Myles* edited by John Wyse Jackson.

Of books about him may be mentioned:

Óige An Dearthár: i. Myles na Gopaleen by Ciarán Ó Nualláin, Dublin, 1973.

Flann O'Brien: A Critical Introduction to His Writings by Anne Clissmann, Dublin and New York, 1975.

Myles: Portraits of Brian O'Nolan edited by Timothy O'Keeffe, London, 1973.

Alive Alive O!: Flann O'Brien's At Swim-Two-Birds edited by Rudiger Imhof, Dublin and New Jersey, 1985.

Myles na Gaeilge: Lamhleabhar ar Shaothar Gaelige Bhrian Ó Nualláin by Breandán Ó Conaire, Dublin, 1986.

Four Irish Legendary Figures in At Swim-Two-Birds: A Study of Flann O'Brien's Use of Finn, Suibhne, the Pooka and the Good Fairy by Eva Wappling, Upsala, 1984.

Index

Note: Flann O'Brien/Brian O'Nolan/Ó Nualláin
appears in the index under the name O'Brien, Flann,
abbreviated to FOB in subheadings. His works
appear directly under title, while works by others
appear under authors' names. There is an entry for
Myles na Gopaleen to cover instances when Myles
appears as a separate persona.

Abbey Theatre, Dublin, 58, 131–4, 178
AE Memorial Fund, 94; see also Russell, George
  William
Alexander, Mr (Strabane neighbour), 12, 14, 16
Allen, Walter, 145
Anglo-Irish Treaty, 1922, 15, 21, 46
Aquinas, St Thomas, 104, 106
Arts Council (Ireland), 198
Ashe, Stephen, 199–201
At Swim-Two-Birds (FOB): on Dublin choral
  society, 27; writing of, 31, 54, 56, 73, 85; on
  University College Dublin, 43–4; revolt of
  characters in, 58; construction, 82–5, 89, 165;
  characters in, 84; modified and published, 85–8;
  title, 87, 88, 90; reception, 91–2; Joyce reads,
  93–4, 97, 172; wins prize, 94; unpublished in
  USA, 98; sales, 99; prose style, 106; suggested as
  play, 131; Grogan's pub in, 143; post-modernist
  mode, 145–9; Hogan on, 162, 164; nihilism of,
  165; 1950 New York reissue, 170; republished by
  MacGibbon and Kee, 208, 211; FOB
  denigrates, 211, 247; success, 220; foreign
  editions, 238
Augustine, St, 226, 228–9, 231, 244
Avis, Patricia see Murphy, Patricia
Auxiliary Police, 20

Baker, Howard, 200
Baker's of Kill O'the Grange (pub), 221
Ballinger, William A.: The Last Tiger, 201
Barrington, Jonah, 223–4
Barrington, T. J., 182, 185
'Bash in the Tunnel, A' (FOB article), 173
'Beachcomber' see Morton, J. B.
Béal Bocht, An (by Myles na Gopaleen, i.e. FOB):
  parodies O'Grianna, 37, 125–30; nature in, 65;
  modified, 127; publication, 127–8; reception,
  128–31; English translation (as The Poor Mouth),
  130; comic effect, 130–1; FOB's regard for, 131;
  Hogan on, 162, 164
Beckett, Samuel, 93, 130–1, 172; Exagmination
  Round His Factification of Work in Progress
  (with others), 55
Behan, Beatrice (née French-Salkeld), 207
Behan, Brendan: friendship with FOB, 144,
  206–7, 211; on The Hard Life, 213, 215; and
  drink, 246
Belfast, 4–5
Bell, The (journal), 142, 162, 196, 216
Belloc, Hilaire, 34
Bergin, Osborn, 66
Betjeman, John, 144
Birmingham, George A.: Spanish Gold, 18
'Black and Tans', 20
Blackrock, 30–1, 169–70
Blackrock College, 31–6

Blake, Sexton (fictional character), 198–201
Blakesley, Stephen: identity, 200
Blasket Islands, 125
Blather (journal), 68, 72–4, 80, 162–3
Bloomsday (1954), 194–6
Blythe, Ernest, 15, 134–5
Board of Revenue Commissioners, 23: FOB
  quarrels with, 238–9
Boucicault, Dion: The Colleen Bawn, 116
Bowman, John, 212
Boy from Ballytearim, The (FOB, play), 208, 222
Boyle, Miss (teacher), 12
Brick, Brother, 26
British Broadcasting Corporation (BBC), 199
Brooks, C. H., 85
'Brother Barnabas' (pseud. for FOB), 56–8, 63, 68,
  74, 116
Browne and Nolan (publishers), 126–7
Browne, Noel, 178
Broy, Colonel, 73
Burgess, Anthony, 215
Bürke, Edmund, 27

Cabell, James Branch, 58, 83; The Cream of the
  Jest, 82; Jurgen, 82
'Can a Saint Hit Back' (FOB; article), 243–4
Čapek, Karel: Insect Play: FOB adapts, 135–6,
  162
Carney, Jack, 129
Catholic Standard (weekly), 35, 108, 178, 196
Catholicism: dominance in Ireland, 46–9; Joyce
  and, 48–50; FOB's belief in, 52, 104–6, 157–8,
  174, 228; in The Hard Life, 216–17; in The
  Dalkey Archive, 228
Catullus, 85
Cavan: orphanage fire tribunal, 137–8
celibacy: in Ireland, 61–2
Censorship of Publications Act (Ireland), 49,
  213
Centenary History of the Literary and Historical
  Society, University College, Dublin, 43–4, 53,
  63–4, 67
Chamberlain, Neville, 113, 118
Chaplin, Charlie, 227
Chekhov, Anton: The Three Sisters, 108
Chesterton, G. K., 34
Christian Brothers School, Synge Street, Dublin,
  24–6
Churchill, Winston, 118
Civil Service (Irish): FOB's career in, 74–8, 81, 95,
  120–1, 136–9, 167, 179–80, 185–6; FOB's memo
  on pension proposals, 159–62; FOB offends in,
  181–3; FOB leaves, 184–6
Civil War, 1922, 22, 46, 48
Clarke, Austin, 90–1, 111, 188
Clerkin, Andy, 181, 184
Cleverdon, Douglas, 153
Coffey, Brian, 51
Coffey, Denis, 54
Collins, Mr (or Ó Coileáin; teacher), 12–13
Collins, Michael, 125
Collins, William (publisher), 86
Cologne university, 67–8
Combthrom Féinne (student magazine): FOB

Comhthrom Féinne cont.
  writes for, 54–6, 58, 61, 63, 67; on FOB, 62;
  FOB edits, 64; attacks Literary and Historical
  Society, 70; humour, 73
Connolly, Cyril, 144
Conolly, Angela, 201–3, 212
Conolly, Tommy, 166, 201–3, 239
Cooke, R. N., 64–5, 67
Cooper, Stanford Lee, 67, 70
Coyle, Rosemary, 60–1
Craig, J. P., 13
Cronin, Anthony, 194; *The Life of Riley*, 241
Crowe, Eileen, 133
'Cruiskeen Lawn' (newspaper column, *Irish
  Times*): on school brutality, 24–5; on Cabell, 83;
  first appears, 112–14; in Irish, 115; writing of,
  115; on railway engines, 140; on The Scotch
  House, 143; social-political pessimism, 158;
  Hogan on, 163; achievement of, 165; references
  to Joyce, 172–3; extracts published, 224; *see also*
  Myles na Gopaleen
Cumann na mBan (organization), 15
Cumann na nGaedhael party, 73
Cumberland, Martin, 199
Cummins, Danny, 243
Cusack, Cyril, 133
Custom House, Dublin, 74–5

Dáil Éireann: formed, 21; de Valera in, 46; FOB
  attends, 121, 133
Dalkey Archive, The (FOB): mawkishness, 87;
  origins in *The Third Policeman*, 105, 227–9;
  Manichaeism in, 106; writing of, 226–7, 229–31,
  233; autobiographical element in, 227; qualities,
  227–30; dramatization (as *When the Saints Go
  Marching In*), 244–5
'Dead Spit of Kelly, The' (FOB; TV play), 222
'De Me' (FOB; autobiographical article), 224, 227
Denhoff, Maurice, 93–4
'Detectional Fastidiosities of Sergeant Fottrell, The'
  (TV series), 246
de Valera, Eamon: at Blackrock College, 31; draws
  up 1937 Irish Constitution, 34, 53; leads Fianna
  Fáil, 37; radicalism, 46, 48; wins 1932 election,
  64, 72; dismisses O'Duffy, 73; as 'Sean the Post'
  in *Finnegans Wake*, 75; finances *Irish Press*, 112;
  in World War II, 118; and Gaeltachts, 125; 1948
  defeat, 157; founds Institute of Advanced
  Studies, 177
de Valera, Vivion, 37, 64–5
Devlin, Denis, 51, 103
Dillon, James, 116
Dineen, Father Patrick Stephen, 114
Dixon, Dr (Civil Service Chief Medical Officer),
  185–6
Dolan, Hugo, 143
Dolan, Michael J., 133
Dolphin Hotel, Dublin, 154
Donnelly, Charles, 51
Donnybrook: FOB buys house in, 203–4
'Drink and Time in Dublin' (FOB), 173
Dublin: Michael O'Nolan in, 10, 23–4, 27–8; in
  Easter Rising, 11–12; FOB in, 23–4; cultural life,
  27; social conditions, 47–8, 141; Civil Servants
  in, 76; trams in, 140–1; amusements and pubs,
  142–4, 153–5, 171; and FOB's civic sense, 191;
  and 1954 Bloomsday, 194; *see also* individual
  buildings and institutions
Dublin Opinion (journal), 76
Dún Laoghaire, 35–6
Dunne, J. W.: *An Experiment With Time*, 103; *The
  Serial Universe*, 103
Dunne, Dr John, 236–7, 240

Eagleton, Terry, 147
Easter Rising, 1916, 11
Edwards, Hilton, 132–3, 135–6, 204–5
Einstein, Albert, 103
Electricity Supply Board, 238–9
Eliot, T. S., 58, 82
Ellmann, Richard, 176
Envoy (journal), 170–5
Euripides: *Hercules Furens*, 85
Evening Telegraph (newspaper), 63

Fáinne An Lae (journal), 29
Farren, Robert: *The Course of Irish Verse*, 169
Faustus Kelly (FOB), 69, 131–5, 162, 193
Ferguson, Samuel, 17
Fianna Fáil (Irish Republican party): de Valera
  leads, 37; as Republican party, 47; 1932 victory,
  64, 72; and Civil Service, 77; in office, 96;
  encourages Irish language, 125; housing drives,
  141; 1948 defeat, 157; populism, 180; 1951
  victory, 181
Figgis, Allen, 219
Fitzgerald, Jim, 243
'Flight' (FOB; TV play), 222
Flower, Robin, 126
Foley, Richard, 127, 129
French-Salkeld, Cecil, 84–5, 207

Gaelic League, 121
Gaeltacht, 37–9, 124–5; satirized in *An Béal Bocht*,
  125–30
Gageby, Douglas, 154, 242, 245, 248
Gandon, James, 74
Garvin, John ('Andrew Cass'): and FOB in Civil
  Service, 75–6, 78, 85, 95; and FOB's *At
  Swim-Two-Birds*, 90; and FOB's 'lost
  manuscript' of *Third Policeman*, 102; and FOB
  in Scotch House, 153; and FOB's driving, 156; as
  Secretary of Department, 167, 179, 183; and
  FOB as Myles na Gopaleen, 181; and official
  complaints against FOB in Civil Service, 181–2;
  and FOB's resignation from Civil Service, 185–6;
  FOB lampoons, 191; *James Joyce's Disunited
  Kingdom*, 75
Gate Theatre, Dublin, 108, 132, 244
Germany: FOB visits, 67–9
Gibbon, Edward, 103
Glasgow, 10
Glasgow Orpheus Choir, 27
Gorman, Herbert, 87
Gormley, Eugene (FOB's uncle), 6–7, 15, 21, 131,
  245–6
Gormley, George (FOB's uncle), 8–9, 30, 60
Gormley, Joe (FOB's uncle), 7–8, 29, 245
Gormley, John (FOB's maternal grandfather), 6
Gormley, Teresa (FOB's aunt), 12–13, 15, 245
Gormley, Tom (FOB's uncle), 7–8; death, 245
Grangegorman (or St Brendan's) hospital, 236–7, 239
Greene, Graham, 86, 89, 104, 145–6, 217; *England
  Made Me*, 145
Gregory, Augusta, Lady, 106, 125, 132
Griffin, Gerald: *The Collegians*, 116
Gross, Gerald, 214
Guinness (brewers), 222–3
Guinness, Sir Arthur E., 53
Guinness, Bryan, 2nd Baron Moyne, 208
'Gúm' publishing house, 123

Haile Selassie, Emperor of Ethiopia, 75
Hamilton, Mark, 213, 230–1
Hard Life, The (FOB): 24, 213–16, 228, 233, 247
Hardy, Thomas, 171
Hastings, Máire, 243

Hayes, Michael, 73
Heath, A. M. & Co. (literary agents), 85–6, 98, 101, 111, 213, 230, 239
Heffernan (Dublin teacher), 145–6, 164
Hemingway, Ernest, 58, 107
Henry, O., 172
Hergesheimer, Joseph, 58
Higgins, Aidan, 105, 172, 231
Hiroshima: atomic bomb dropped on, 158
Hitler, Adolf, 67–8
Hodges Figgis (publishers), 219–20
Hogan, P. J., 70, 74
Hogan, Thomas (*pseud., i.e.* Thomas Woods), 162–4, 216
Holloway, Joseph, 133–4
Holy Ghost Fathers, 31–2
Horizon (journal), 171
Huston, John, 241
Hutchinson's (publishers), 211
Huxley, Aldous, 58, 83; *Point Counter Point*, 83–4
Huysmans, Joris Karl: *A Rebours*, 103
Hyde, Douglas: teaches at University College Dublin, 53, 65, 67; imperfect Irish, 53–4; as President of Republic, 97; as Gaelic League president, 121; *A Literary History of Ireland*, 17

Inchicore (Dublin), 10–11
Inglis, Brian, 218
Institute of Advanced Studies, Dublin, 177
Institute of Contemporary Arts, London, 175
Ireland Today (journal), 55–6, 122
Irish Distillers Group, 223–4
Irish Free State, 21–2, 47–9
Irish Independent (newspaper), 72, 112
Irish Press (newspaper), 63, 112
Irish Republic: proclaimed (1916), 11, 22
Irish Republican Army, 15, 21, 119–20
Irish Rugby Football Union, 155
Irish Statesman, The (journal), 29, 108
Irish Times (newspaper): Sheridan writes for (as 'Birdcatcher'), 51; controversy over Frank O'Connor play, 107–8; Patrick Kavanagh writes for, 108–9; FOB writes 'Cruiskeen Lawn' column in, 110–15, 118; character, 111–12; pro-British stance, 119; publishes selection of Myles na Gopaleen, 139; Hogan on, 163; and sub-editing of FOB's copy, 176–9, 218; settles libel case, 177–8; and FOB's senatorial candidacy, 192; FOB quarrels with, 218; FOB returns to, 242; *see also* 'Cruiskeen Lawn'; Myles na Gopaleen
'Irish Volunteers' (*later* Irish Republican Army), 15

James Joyce Yearbook, 53, 175–6
Jameson, Frederic, 148
Jenny (Gormleys' servant), 245–6
John O'London's Weekly, 29, 92
Johnston, Denis, 135; *The Old Lady Says No*, 22, 132
Jolas, Maria, 175
Joyce, James: addresses UCD Literary and Historical Society, 46; and Catholicism, 48; influence, 49–52, 57–8, 83, 102, 135, 247; loses Auditorship of Literary and Historical Society, 65; literary devices, 82; intransigence over publication of work, 87; on *At Swim-Two-Birds*, 92; receives and reads *At Swim-Two-Birds*, 97, 172; and FOB's self-doubts, 101; Hogan on, as influence on FOB, 162–4; *Envoy* special edition on, 172–4; FOB's view of, 172–4, 247; references to in 'Cruiskeen Lawn', 172–3, 194; casts shadow on FOB's life, 176; and 1954 Bloomsday, 194; Behan on, 207; FOB compared

with, 215–16; in *The Dalkey Archive*, 229–31; FOB denigrates, 247; *Dubliners*, 102; *Finnegans Wake*, 55, 75; *Portrait of the Artist as a Young Man*, 46, 228; *Ulysses*, 49, 135, 149, 247
Joyce, John Stanislaus (father of James), 52–3, 153, 175
Joyce, Tom, 194

Kafka, Franz, 58
Kapuscinski, Ryszard, 76
Kavanagh, Patrick: on discussions in Palace Bar, 90, 144; wins AE Memorial prize, 94; writes for *Irish Times*, 108–9; mocked by FOB, 109–10; reviews *Faustus Kelly*, 134; on 1944 Normandy invasion, 145; behaviour, 153, 193–4; on FOB's creativity, 165; contributes to *Envoy*, 171–2; on An Tostal, 184; removes bottle of whiskey, 189; on FOB's accent, 190; commitment to Ireland, 191–2; writes for Irish audience, 193; relations with FOB, 193–4; and 1954 Bloomsday, 194–5; declines trip to USSR, 196; on death of mother, 205; Patricia Murphy entertains, 218; and J. F. Kennedy's visit, 234; criticizes *When the Saints Go Marching In*, 245; *The Green Fool*, 109
Kavanagh's Weekly, 192
Kelleher, John V., 175
Kempis, Thomas à: *Imitatio Christi*, 34
Kennedy, Hugh, 65
Kennedy, John F., 234–5, 241–2
Kenny family, 32
Kenny, Desmond, 37
Kenny, Joseph, 37
Kenny, Tom, 37
Kiely, Benedict, 112
Kierkegaard, Søren, 58
'Knowall, George' (FOB pseudonym), 220, 234
Kraus, Karl, 117

Lehmann, John, 145
Leonard, Hugh: *When the Saints Go Marching In* (dramatization of FOB's *The Dalkey Archive*), 244
Leventhal, A. J. (Con), 194–5
Limelight (Chaplin film), 227
Locke's of Kilbeggan (distillery), 17, 75
Lofts, W. O. G., 200
Longford Leader (newspaper), 187
Longford, Edward Arthur Henry Pakenham, 6th Earl of, 108
Longman's (publishers), 86–9, 93, 99, 101–2, 211
Lusty, (Sir) Robert, 211
Lyons (Civil Servant), 182–3

McCabe, Alec, 91
McCormack, John, 14, 27
McCormick, F. J., 133
McDaid's (Dublin pub), 171, 188, 193, 197, 220
MacDonagh, Donagh, 49–51, 84, 102–3, 144
MacDonagh, Thomas, 50
MacDonogh, Patrick 111
MacEntee, Seán, 120–1, 180–1
McGibbon & Kee (publishers), 93, 208, 211
MacLiammóir, Micheál, 132, 135
McManus, Richard, 33, 37, 43–4, 169–70; death, 205
Macmillan of New York (publishers), 230, 241
MacNamara, Brinsley, 85, 111
MacNeice, Louis, 144
McQuaid, John Charles, Archbishop of Dublin, 33–4, 178, 242
Mangan, James Clarence, 17
Manichaeism, 104–6, 157–8, 228
Mannin, Ethel, 94–5, 199

Marie Antoinette, Queen of France, 27
Markievicz, Constance, Countess, 10
'Martyr's Crown, The' (FOB, short story; *formerly*
  'For Ireland, Home and Beauty'), 172
Matson, Harold, 98, 101
Matthew, Father (temperance reformer), 223
Mitchell, Margaret, 95
Montgomery, Jimmy, 50, 58
Montgomery, Niall: on FOB at University College
  Dublin, 43, 54; talents and reputation, 50–1;
  friendship with FOB, 52; represented in *At
  Swim-Two-Birds*, 84; letters in *Irish Times*, 108;
  suggests dramatizing *At Swim-Two-Birds*, 131;
  Beckett and, 172; view of Joyce, 173; writes
  'Cruiskeen Lawn', 182; suggests academic post
  for FOB, 208, 235; writes as 'Rosemary Lane',
  225–6; helps FOB, 235
Mooney, Ria, 133
Morton, H. V., 117
Morton, J. B. ('Beachcomber'), 117
Moyne, 2nd Baron *see* Guinness, Bryan, 2nd Baron
  Moyne
Moynihan, Sean, 183
Murphy, Patricia (*née* Avis), 218
Murphy, Richard, 218
Myles na Gopaleen (na gCopaleen) (pseud. for
  FOB): claims to knowledge and acquaintances,
  103, 139; FOB adopts name, 115–16; character
  and background, 116–17; and Irish language,
  117–18; on effect of foreign influences, 123–4;
  appears as author of *Faustus Kelly*, 134; selection
  of writings published, 139–40; Dublin
  reputation, 144–5; social pessimism, 157–8; on
  Sexton Blake stories, 201; *see also* O'Brien, Flann

Nagasaki: atom bomb dropped on, 158
National Press, The, 127–8
National Student (journal), 54
Nationalist and Leinster Times (newspaper), 220
Neary's (Dublin pub), 155
Nevin, Jack, 45, 47
New Ireland (journal), 224
New Ireland Society, Queen's University Belfast,
  224
Newman, Alec, 90–1, 218
Newman, John Henry, Cardinal, 43
New Statesman (weekly), 92
Nolan, Brian *see* O'Brien, Flann
Nolan, Donal (FOB's grandfather), 4–5
Nolan, Jane (*née* Mellon; FOB's paternal
  grandmother), 4
Nolan, Michael *see* O'Nolan, Michael Victor
Nonplus (journal), 218
Nugent, Jack, 153

O'Brien, Conor Cruise, 162
O'Brien, Flann (Brian O'Nolan; Brian Ó Nualláin;
  Myles na Gopaleen): birthplace, 3; family
  background, 8–9; born, 9; speaks Irish, 9;
  childhood in Inchicore, 10–11; no schooling,
  10–14; shyness, 11, 189; card tricks, 11; speaks
  English, 13–14, 18, 33; boyhood in Strabane,
  14–16; reading, 16–18; in Tullamore, 17–19;
  makes films, 20; drawing and sketching, 20;
  moves to Dublin, 23–4; at school in Dublin,
  24–7; at Blackrock College, 31–2, 34–6; violin
  playing, 29; in Avoca Terrace, 30; appearance
  and dress, 36, 188–9; at
  University College Dublin, 36, 43–7, 52–4,
  59–60, 63–4, 71–2; cycling, 37–9; blood
  poisoning, 39; speaks at College Literary and
  Historical Society, 44–7, 63; reads Joyce, 49;
  circle of friends, 50–2; Catholic beliefs and

Manichaeism, 52, 104–6, 157–8, 228; attitude to
  Ireland, 52; visits John Joyce,, 52–3; writes in
  Irish for student magazine, 54–6; Joycean
  influence on, 56, 83, 102, 136, 247; indifference
  to poetry, 58; literary influences on, 58–9;
  billiards, poker and chess playing, 59; as
  dog-track scrutineer, 60; drinking, 60, 153, 164,
  168–9, 186, 188, 197, 204, 207–8, 220, 229, 236,
  240; few girl friends, 60–3; university degree,
  63; short stories for newspapers, 63–4; edits
  Comhthrom Féinne, 64; loses Auditorship
  election for Literary and Historical Society,
  64–5; MA thesis, 65–7; trip to Germany and
  supposed marriage, 67–70; knowledge of German
  language, 68–9; political neutrality, 69; defends
  Literary and Historical Society, 70–1; founds
  Blather, 72; Civil Service career, 74–8, 95–7; on
  name, 79, 88–9; family responsibilities on death
  of father, 80–2, 136; vanity, 91; wish for popular
  success, 95; and Saroyan, 97–100; self-doubts,
  98–102, 212–13, 238; lacks intellectual curiosity,
  104–5; prose style, 106–7; pseudonymous letters
  to *Irish Times*, 107–8; wears black hat, 111,
  188–9, 195; writes 'Cruiskeen Lawn' for *Irish
  Times*, 110–16; on Irish language, 113–14, 121–4;
  as Private Secretary to MacEntee, 120–1; play
  writing, 131–5; conflict with Civil Service
  appointment, 134; adapts Čapek's *Insect Play*,
  135–6; promoted to Assistant Principal Officer,
  136–7; fails in application for Wireless
  Broadcasting Section post, 139; in Dublin pubs,
  142–5, 188, 220–1; reputation in Dublin, 145;
  and rugby, 154–5; driving, 156, 166–7; memo on
  Civil Service pensions proposal, 159–62; Hogan's
  1947 article on, 162–4; creative difficulties,
  164–6; first breaks leg, 166; feud with
  Donnybrook Guards, 166–7, 183, 191; promoted
  Acting Principal Officer, 167; marriage, 167–9;
  buys house, 169; contributes to *Envoy*, 171–3;
  view of Joyce, 172–6, 247; copy edited, 176–9;
  libel actions against, 177; heads Planning Section,
  179–80; and Civil Service constraints, 180–3;
  attacks An Tostal, 184; forced retirement from
  Civil Service, 185–7; pension and earnings,
  186–7; journalism, 187–8, 220; manner and
  behaviour, 189–91; accent, 190; civic sense,
  190–1; runs for Senate, 192; writes for Irish
  audience, 193; relations with Kavanagh, 193; in
  1954 Bloomsday, 194–6; declines trip to USSR,
  196; claims to Sexton Blake stories, 198–201; and
  dogs, 202–3, 235; moves to Belmont Avenue,
  Donnybrook, 203–4; spends time in bed, 203–4,
  222; and mother's death, 205; relations with
  Behan, 206–7; money problems, 208, 218–19,
  235; relish for physical misfortune, 216; health
  and accidents, 220, 232–4, 236, 242–4; truculence,
  220, 234; moves to Waltersland Road, 221–2; TV
  plays, 222; proposes history of Irish Distilling,
  223–4; autobiographical summaries, 223–5; TV
  appearance, 231; writes scripts for Jimmy O'Dea,
  233–4; increasing writing difficulties, 235–6;
  takes drinking cure, 236–7, 239–40; sexual
  nature, 237–8; quarrels and feuds, 238–9; returns
  to *Irish Times*, 242; negotiates TV series, 243,
  246; cancer, 244; interviewed by Wale, 246–8;
  death, 248; *see also* Myles na Gopaleen; and
  titles of individual works
Observer (newspaper), 92
Ó Canainn, Pádraig, 127
O'Casey, Sean, 129, 131, 207; *I Knock at the Door*,
  131; *The Plough and the Stars*, 22
O'Connor, Frank: poetry, 58; FOB attacks in *Irish
  Times*, 89; play criticized, 107–8, 112; on *An Béal*

Bocht, 129; Irishness, 193; and J. F. Kennedy's visit, 234
O'Connor, Paddy, 155
Ó Criomhthain, Tomás: *An t-Oileánach*, 126, 129–30
O'Dea, Denis, 133
O'Dea, Jimmy, 155, 233–4, 243
Odlum family, 17–18
O'Donnell, Peader, 196
O'Duffy, General Eoin, 73
O'Faoláin, Sean: FOB criticizes, 58, 89; reviews *At Swim-Two-Birds*, 92; defends Frank O'Connor's play, 107–8, 112; exile in England, 129; FOB reads, 169
O'Farrelly, Agnes, 54, 65–7
O'Flaherty, Liam, 31
Ó Grianna, Séamas, 37, 126
O'Higgins, Brian, 133
O'Higgins, T. F., 138
O'Keeffe, Timothy, 99, 207–8, 211–12, 214–16, 226, 229–31, 238, 240
O'Kelly, Sean T., 96–7, 120, 181, 214
O'Leary, Nuala (*née* O'Nolan; FOB's sister), 224, 234–5, 245
O'Leary, Paddy, 234–6, 244–5
O'Mahoney, Pussy, 91
O'Nolan family, 3
O'Nolan, Agnes (*née* Gormley; FOB's mother), 6, 8–9, 12, 27; death, 205
O'Nolan, Brian *see* O'Brien, Flann
O'Nolan, Ciarán (FOB's brother): born, 9; childhood, 10, 14; education, 13; storytelling, 16; makes films, 20; school fight, 26; on relations with father, 27–8; at Blackrock College, 32, 34; and Irish language, 33, 39; at University College Dublin, 36; cycling trips to Gaeltacht, 37–9; on FOB at Literary and Historical Society, 45; poker-playing, 59; founds *Blather*, 72; unemployed, 80; writes novel, 80; uses pseudonyms, 108; works as Irish language journalist, 136; revisits Strabane, 245; *Oiche i nGleann na nGealt*, 80; *Óige An Dearthár*, 26
O'Nolan, Evelyn (*née* McDonnell; FOB's wife); marriage, 167–9; background and career, 168; and FOB's resignation from Civil Service, 186; and FOB's drinking, 190, 235–6; lung trouble, 201, 203; and move to Belmont Avenue, 203; devotion to FOB, 204; and *The Third Policeman*, 208; moves to Waterslang Road, 221, 234; and FOB's final illness, 248
O'Nolan, Fergus (FOB's uncle), 4–5, 131
O'Nolan, Fergus (FOB's brother), 9, 136
O'Nolan, Gearóid (Gerald; FOB's uncle), 4–5, 9, 11, 16
O'Nolan, Gearóid (FOB's brother), 9, 20, 24–7, 32, 80, 136, 203
O'Nolan, Kathleen (FOB's aunt), 10
O'Nolan, Kevin (FOB's brother), 66, 69, 205, 216
O'Nolan, Micheál (FOB's brother), 80, 82, 85, 201, 219
O'Nolan, (or Nolan), Michael Victor (FOB's father): name, 3–4; education, 4–5; commitment to Irish language and culture, 5–6, 11, 18, 23, 33, 53, 122, 125; writing, 5; career, 6, 9–10, 12, 16–17, 23; marriage, 6, 8; character, 8–9; in Glasgow, 10; in Dublin, 10, 23–4, 27–30; and children's education, 10–11, 13, 24, 27; Strabane house, 12; walking, 16, 27; in Tullamore, 16–18; books and reading, 17–18; croquet, 18; motoring, 18; attitude to British soldiers, 18; nationalism, 21; employed by Irish Board of Revenue Commissioners, 23; home life, 27, 30, 33; relations with children, 27–8, 237; and Dublin

cultural life, 28–9; chess playing, 29; and FOB's Civil Service work, 78; death, 80–1; and *At Swim-Two-Birds*, 84; and FOB's drink problem, 237
O'Nolan, Nuala *see* O'Leary, Nuala
O'Nolan, Peter (FOB's uncle), 4–5, 9, 11
O'Nolan, Roisín (FOB's sister), 9, 80, 136
Ó Nualláin *see* O'Nolan
O'Rahilly, Alfred, 66, 178–9
O'Rahilly, T. F., 177–8
O'Rourke's (Blackrock pub), 155
Ó Súileabháin, Muiris, 126
O'Sullivan, Sean, 155, 169–70, 197, 208; death, 236
'Oul lad of Kilsalaher, Th'' (TV series), 243

Palace Bar, The (Dublin), 90, 143–4, 153
Palatine's Daughter, The (FOB; unfinished), 205
Pantheon Books, New York, 170, 214
Parnell, Charles Stewart, 10, 53
Pascal, Blaise, 157
Pearl, The (Dublin pub), 153, 171
Pearse, Patrick, 4, 10–11, 122, 125
Penguin New Writing (journal), 145
Phelan, Michael, 182–3, 186
Phillips, Ewan, 175
Pinget, Robert, 149
Plunkett, James, 211, 233–4
Poor Mouth, The see *Béal Bocht, An*
Pound, Ezra, 82
Power, Patrick C., 130
Pritchett, V. S., 212
Proust, Marcel, 58
Provisional IRA, 3
Purcell, Patrick, 65

Quidnunc (*Irish Times* columnist), 118, 123, 176
Quigley family, 33
Quigley, Oscar, 35, 43–4

Rawlins, David, 102
Razzle (English journal), 72
Redmond, Liam, 102, 133, 144
Reeve, Alan, 144
Revenue Commissioners *see* Board of Revenue Commissioners
Robbe-Grillet, Alain, 149
Rodgers, W. R., 153
Ross, Patience, 101
Royal Hibernian Academy, 238
Rugheimer, Gunnar, 246
Russell, George William (AE), 29, 94
Ryan, John, 170, 172, 190, 221; *Remembering How We Stood*, 194–5

Saroyan, William, 97–101, 241; *Sweeney in the Trees*, 99, 132
Sarraute, Nathalie, 149
Sayers, Peig, 126
Schroedinger, Erwin, 177
Scotch House, The (Dublin pub), 143, 153–4, 182
Scott, Cecil, 227, 229–30, 241–3
Scott, Michael, 194–5
Senate (Irish): FOB runs for, 192
Sexton Blake series, 198–201
Shaw, George Bernard, 34
Sheehy, Ned, 55–6
Sheridan, Niall: friendship with FOB at University College Dublin, 50–1, 54, 59; career, 51; writes as 'Birdcatcher', 51; admonished by Denis Coffey, 54–5; chess playing, 55, 59–60; and FOB's student writings, 56; on literary influences, 58; on FOB's German trip, 70; founds *Blather*, 72; on *At Swim-Two-Birds*, 82;

Sheridan, Niall *cont.*
  represented in *At Swim-Two-Birds*,84–5, cuts *At Swim-Two-Birds*, 85; marriage, 92; takes *At Swim-Two-Birds* to James Joyce, 93–4; entertains Saroyan, 98; and FOB's 'lost manuscript' of *Third Policeman*, 102; lends Huysmans to FOB, 103; letters to *Irish Times*, 107–8; on Irish language revival, 122; and V. Wright letter, 147; correspondence with Joyce, 175; meets Joyce, 176; writes 'Cruiskeen Lawn', 182
Sinn Féin (party), 15, 21
Sinnott's (Dublin pub), 155, 202–3
Slattery's Sago Saga (FOB), 240–3, 246
Smith, Patrick, 181, 185
Smith, Peter Duval, 199
Smyllie, R. M. (Bertie): as editor of *Irish Times*, 90–1, 110–12, 153, 206; appoints FOB, 112, 114; in Palace Bar, 144; as literary patron, 171; decline, 177; and FOB's controversies, 179
Social and Personal (journal), 187
Southern Star (newspaper), 187, 189
Spectator (weekly), 218–19
Stack, Austin, 15
Stanford, W. B., 193
Stein, Gertrude, 107
Stephens, James, 11, 17
Sterne, Laurence: *Tristram Shandy*, 84
Strabane: FOB's family home in, 3–4, 6–7, 9, 225; FOB's father takes house in, 12–16; and Irish language, 13; O'Nolan brothers cycle to, 37–8; FOB revisits, 245
Stuart, Francis, 207; *Pillar of Cloud*, 169
Sunday Dispatch (newspaper), 187
Sunday Press (newspaper), 154–5
Sunday Review (newspaper), 187
Sunday Telegraph (newspaper), 207
Sweeney, James Johnson, 170
Swift, Jonathan, 216
Swinnerton, Frank, 92
Synge, John Millington, 58, 106, 125

Third Policeman, The (FOB; known as *Hell Goes Round and Round* in USA): Tullamore background, 17, 105; nature in, 65; writing of, 97–100; rejected, 101–2, 165, 212; FOB claims manuscript lost, 102; literary influences on, 103; character of De Selby in, 103–5; philosophical content, 104; evil in, 105; and *The Dalkey Archive*, 105, 227–9; syntax and style, 106–7;

proposed stage adaptation, 132; murder plot, 196–7; unpublished, 208
'Thirst' (FOB, sketch), 204–5
Time magazine, 67, 70, 132
'Time Freddy Retired, The' (FOB, TV play), 222
Times Literary Supplement, 91
Tito, Marshal Josip Broz, 184
Toller, Ernst, 135
Tostal, An, 1953, 184, 192
Town Magazine, 246
Toynbee, Philip, 212
Trinity College Dublin: FOB applies for posts at, 208, 236
'troubles, the' (Irish), 15–16, 20
Tullamore, 17–18, 20, 105
Tuohy, Patrick, 93
Twentieth Century Authors, 68
'Two In One' (FOB, short story), 196–7; adapted for TV (as 'The Dead Spit of Kelly'), 222

Ungerland, Clara, 67, 69
Union of Soviet Socialist Republics (USSR), 196
University College Dublin: FOB attends, 36, 43–7, 52–4, 59–60, 63–4, 71–2; Literary and Historical Society, 43–6, 63–4, 70–1; and Irish politics; 48; FOB gains degree, 63; FOB loses Auditorship of Literary and Historical Society, 64–5; FOB's MA thesis, 65–7

Wale, Michael, 246–7
Wall, Mervyn, 198
Walsh, Maurice: *The Hill is Mine*, 109–10
Ward, Dr, 75–6
Wells, H. G., 34, 216
West, Anthony, 92
White House (Dublin pub), 221
White, Jack, 176–7, 179, 188–9
Wilkes, Dick, 154
Williams, D. E. (distillery), 17
Williamson, Bruce, 144
World War II, 118–20
Wright, V., 147
'Writer's Writhings, A' (FOB), 238
Woods, Thomas *see* Hogan, Thomas
Wyer, Molly, 63

Yeats, Jack, 23
Yeats, William Butler, 23, 58, 125, 129; *The Tower*, 58